**Systems of Care for
Children's Mental Health**
Series Editors:
Beth A. Stroul, M.Ed.
Robert M. Friedman, Ph.D.

Transition to Adulthood

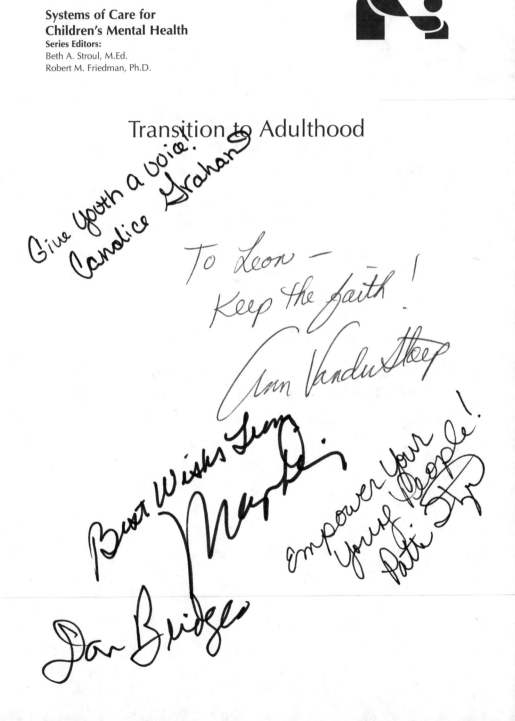

Other Volumes in this Series

*From Case Management to Service Coordination
for Children with Emotional, Behavioral, or
Mental Disorders: Building on Family Strengths*

edited by Barbara J. Friesen, Ph.D., and John Poertner, D.S.W.

*Children's Mental Health:
Creating Systems of Care in a Changing Society*

edited by Beth A. Stroul, M.Ed.

*What Works in
Children's Mental Health Services?
Uncovering Answers to Critical Questions*

by Krista Kutash, Ph.D., and Vestena Robbins Rivera, M.A.

Promoting Cultural Competence in Children's Mental Health Services

edited by Mario Hernandez, Ph.D., and Mareasa R. Isaacs, Ph.D.

Transition to Adulthood

A Resource for Assisting Young People with Emotional or Behavioral Difficulties

edited by

Hewitt B. Clark, Ph.D.
University of South Florida
Tampa

and

Maryann Davis, Ph.D.
University of Massachusetts Medical School
Worcester

Baltimore • London • Toronto • Sydney

Paul H. Brookes Publishing Co.
Post Office Box 10624
Baltimore, Maryland 21285-0624

www.brookespublishing.com

Typeset by Argosy, West Newton, Massachusetts.
Manufactured in the United States of America by
Versa Press, East Peoria, Illinois.

The case studies and personal stories described in this book involve actual people and actual circumstances. Where personal identification exists, it is published with these individuals' permission.

This book was funded in part by the Dean's Office and the Department of Child and Family Studies of the Louis de la Parte Florida Mental Health Institute, University of South Florida; the Center for Mental Health Services Research, Department of Psychiatry, University of Massachusetts Medical School; and the Center for Effective Collaboration and Practice: Improving Services for Children and Youth with Emotional and Behavioral Problems (Grant No. H237T60005). The Center for Effective Collaboration and Practice: Improving Services for Children and Youth with Emotional and Behavioral Problems is funded under a cooperative agreement with the Office of Special Education Programs, Office of Special Education and Rehabilitative Services, U.S. Department of Education, with additional support from the Child, Adolescent, and Family Branch, Center for Mental Health Services, Substance Abuse and Mental Health Services Administration, U.S. Department of Health and Human Services. The views expressed herein do not necessarily reflect the positions of any of the above-named organizations.

Library of Congress Cataloging-in-Publication Data

Transition to adulthood: a resource for assisting young people with emotional
    or behavioral difficulties / edited by Hewitt B. Clark, Maryann Davis.
        p. cm.—(Systems of care for children's mental health)
    Includes bibliographical references.
    ISBN 1-55766-454-4
    1. Youth—Mental health services—United States.   2. Problem youth—
Services for—United States.   3. Problem youth—Rehabilitation—United
States.   I. Clark, Hewitt B.   II. Davis, Maryann.   III. Series.
RJ503.T72 2000
362.2'0835'0973—dc21

                                                                99-047610

British Library Cataloguing in Publication data are available from the British
Library.

Contents

Series Preface

In 1982, Knitzer's seminal study, *Unclaimed Children*, was published by the Children's Defense Fund. At that time, the field of children's mental health was characterized by a lack of federal or state leadership, few community-based services, little collaboration among child-serving systems, negligible parent involvement, and little or no advocacy on behalf of the youngsters with emotional disorders. Since that time, substantial gains have been realized in both the conceptualization and the implementation of comprehensive, community-based systems of care for children and adolescents with serious emotional disorders and their families.

A vast amount of information has emanated from the system-building experiences of states and communities and from research and technical assistance efforts. Many of the trends and philosophies emerging in recent years have now become widely accepted as the "state of the art" for conceptualizing and providing services to youngsters with emotional disorders and their families. There is now broad agreement surrounding the need to create community-based systems of care throughout the United States for children and their families, and the development of these systems has become a national goal. Such systems of care are based on the premises of providing services in the most normative environments, creating effective interagency relationships among the key child-serving systems, involving families in all phases of the planning and delivery of services, and creating service systems that are designed to respond to the needs of culturally diverse populations.

A major need is to incorporate these concepts and trends into the published literature. This need stems from the critical shortage of staff who are appropriately trained to serve youngsters in community-based systems of care, with new philosophies and new service delivery approaches. Of utmost importance is the need to provide state-of-the-art information to institutions of higher education for use in the pre-service education of professionals across disciplines, including the social work, counseling, psychology, and psychiatry fields. Similarly, there is an equally vital need for resources for the in-service training of staff in mental health, child welfare, education, health, and juvenile justice agencies to assist the staff in working more effectively with youngsters with emotional disorders and their families.

This book series, *Systems of Care for Children's Mental Health*, is designed to fulfill these needs by addressing current trends in children's mental health service delivery. The series has several broad goals:

- To increase awareness of the system-of-care concept and philosophy among current and future mental health professionals who will be providing services to children, adolescents, and their families
- To broaden the mental health field's understanding of treatment and service delivery beyond traditional approaches to include innovative, state-of-the-art approaches
- To provide practical information that will assist the mental health field to implement and apply the philosophy, services, and approaches embodied in the system-of-care concept

Each volume in this continuing series addresses a major issue or topic related to the development of systems of care. The books contain information useful to planners, program managers, policy makers, practitioners, parents, teachers, researchers, and others who are interested and involved in improving systems of care for children with emotional disorders and their families. As the series editors, it is our goal for the series to provide an ongoing vehicle and forum for exploring critical aspects of systems of care as they continue to evolve.

Beth A. Stroul　　*Robert M. Friedman*

REFERENCE

Knitzer, J. (1982). *Unclaimed children: The failure of public responsibility to children and adolescents in need of mental health services.* Washington, DC: Children's Defense Fund.

Editorial Advisory Board

About the Editors

Hewitt B. "Rusty" Clark, Ph.D., Professor, Department of Child and Family Studies, Louis de la Parte Florida Mental Health Institute, University of South Florida, 13301 Bruce B. Downs Boulevard, MHC2332, Tampa, Florida 33612

Dr. Clark received his doctoral degree in developmental and child psychology from the University of Kansas in 1972. He is a professor in the Department of Child and Family Studies of the Louis de la Parte Florida Mental Health Institute at the University of South Florida. His research interests and grants focus on evaluating the effectiveness of 1) individualized planning and intervention processes for children with emotional and behavioral difficulties and their families, 2) aftercare services for juvenile offenders, and 3) the transition of youth and young adults into employment, educational opportunities, and independent living. Dr. Clark came to the University of South Florida after directing a comprehensive mental health program for families in Nevada, where he was affiliated with the University of Nevada. Over the course of his professional career, Dr. Clark has developed and researched various innovative programs and has published extensively, with 3 books and more than 80 publications to his credit. He has served as President of the Florida Association for Behavior Analysis and continues to chair the Florida Peer Review Committee, which monitors the quality of treatment programs in developmental disabilities and mental health. Dr. Clark serves on various boards of editors for professional journals and consults nationally and internationally. He was a guest professor at Philipps University in Marburg, Germany, and has presented a series of invited addresses and workshops at conferences in Israel, Peru, Scotland, and Sweden. When Dr. Clark is not conducting research and workshops or teaching, consulting, and developing programs on his topics of professional interest, he enjoys his avocation of sailing the Gulf of Mexico and other seas.

Maryann Davis, Ph.D., Assistant Professor, Center for Mental Health Services Research, Department of Psychiatry, University of Massachusetts Medical School, 55 Lake Avenue North, Worcester, Massachusetts 01655

Dr. Davis received her doctoral degree in psychobiology from Emory University in 1990. She completed her clinical psychology training at Emory University in 1992. She is currently an assistant professor in the Department of Psychiatry at the University of Massachusetts Medical School and a faculty member of the Center for Mental Health Services Research. She has worked in private and public mental health agencies to examine how mental health services for children and adolescents can be improved. Her research interests focus on understanding the interface of the developmental process of entering young adulthood and the service system changes associated with attaining official adult status among young people with emotional or behavioral difficulties. Her current efforts focus on developing an effective model of service coordination for youth in transition. She is also examining the access that adolescents exiting public services have to adult mental health services and their involvement in the adult corrections system. Dr. Davis's work on developing an effective service coordination model and part of her work on this book were supported by a grant from the van Ameringen Foundation. She provides consultation to public agencies on working with individuals making the transition to adulthood and identifying system barriers to and solutions for developing better supports for these individuals.

Contributors

Jane Adams, Ph.D.
Keys for Networking
117 Southwest 6th Street
Topeka, Kansas 66603

Dan Bridgeo, Ph.D.
Transitional Community Treatment
    Team
North Central Mental Health
    Services
1301 North High Street
Columbus, Ohio 43214

Maria A. Brucculeri, Ed.D.
16 Darlene Drive
Southborough, Massachusetts 01772

Michael Bullis, Ph.D.
Department of Special Education and
    Community Resources
University of Oregon
275 College of Education
Eugene, Oregon 97403

Doug Cheney, Ph.D.
Department of Special Education
University of Washington
102 Miller
Box 353600
Seattle, Washington 98195

December Collins
King County Federation of Families
2832 Sunset Lane NE
Renton, Washington 98056

Judith A. Cook, Ph.D.
Mental Health Services Research
    Program
Department of Psychiatry
University of Illinois at Chicago
104 South Michigan Avenue,
    Suite 900
Chicago, Illinois 60603

Cliff Davis
Human Service Collaborative
10800 Springwater Drive
Mount Vernon, Ohio 43050

Nicole Deschênes, M.Ed.
Department of Child and Family
    Studies
Louis de la Parte Florida Mental
    Health Institute
University of South Florida
13301 Bruce B. Downs Boulevard
MHC2337
Tampa, Florida 33612

Kevin Dickens
Parents Helping Parents
594 Monterey Boulevard
San Francisco, California 94127

Lane Falcon
Mental Health Services Research
    Program
Department of Psychiatry
University of Illinois at Chicago
104 South Michigan Avenue,
    Suite 900
Chicago, Illinois 60603

Patrice M. Fetzer, L.S.W.
Child and Adolescent Service Center
1103 McKinley Avenue NW
Canton, Ohio 44703

Kristy Fick
3241 Indianola Avenue
Apartment B
Columbus, Ohio 43202

Genevieve Fitzgibbon
Mental Health Services Research
    Program
Department of Psychiatry
University of Illinois at Chicago
104 South Michigan Avenue,
    Suite 900
Chicago, Illinois 60603

Yati Florida
1208 North High Street
Apartment #7
Columbus, Ohio 43201

Tali Gogol-Ostrowski, Lic.S.W.
Shachaff Eating Disorders Treatment
    Center
Kibbutz Naan
Israel

Candace M. Graham
Child and Adolescent Service Center
150 West State Street
Alliance, Ohio 44601

Renée A. Hatter, M.S.W.
California Department of Education
Diagnostic Center Northern
    California
39100 Gallaudet Drive
Fremont, California 94538

Jeremy Jones
University of South Florida
5109 9th Avenue South
St. Petersburg, Florida 33707

Jamiley Keller
Child and Adolescent Service Center
1103 McKinley Avenue NW
Canton, Ohio 44703

Nancy Koroloff, Ph.D.
Research and Training Center on
    Family Support and Children's
    Mental Health
Graduate School of Social Work
Portland State University
Post Office Box 751
1912 S.W. 6th Avenue, Room 120
Portland, Oregon 97201

Mark J. Kroner, M.S.W., L.S.W.
Self-Sufficiency Services
Lighthouse Youth Services Inc.
1501 Madison Road, 2nd floor
Cincinnati, Ohio 45206

Matthew T. Lee
Southern Oregon University
1361 Quincy Avenue,
    Building 9, Apartment F
Ashland, Oregon 97520

Constance M. Lehman, Ph.D.
Child Welfare Partnership
Graduate School of Social Work
Portland State University
520 S.W. Harrison Street
Portland, Oregon 97201

Jennifer Martin
Cañada College
4200 Farm Hill Boulevard
Redwood City, California 94061

Melissa Nolte
Keys for Networking
1221 Pennsylvania Street
Lawrence, Kansas 66044

Robert Ortiz
Young Adult Independent Living
37 Clinton Street
Redwood City, California 94062

Melissa Platte, M.S.
Mental Health Association of San
    Mateo County
2686 Spring Street
Redwood City, California 94063

Ernie Rodriguez, Ph.D.
Office of Psychological Services
Cañada College
4200 Farm Hill Boulevard
Redwood City, California 94061

Jill Schalansky
Keys for Networking
117 Southwest 6th Avenue
Topeka, Kansas 66603

Justin Sloan
Project Nexus
30 Mystic Street
Arlington, Massachusetts 02174

David Stewart, Ph.D.
Odessa Brown Children's Clinic
2101 East Yesler Way
Seattle, Washington 98122

Chad J. Tehan
Lane Community College
Eugene, Oregon 97405

Ann Vander Stoep, Ph.D.
Department of Psychiatry
Division of Child and Adolescent
   Psychiatry
Children's Hospital and Medical
   Center
Mailstop CH-13
4800 Sandpoint Way NE
Seattle, Washington 98105

Thomas E. West, L.S.W.
Child and Adolescent Service Center
Transitional Community Treatment
   Team
1103 McKinley Avenue NW
Canton, Ohio 44703

Maxine Williford
John Swett Unified/Contra Costa
   Selpa
1650 Crockett Boulevard
Crockett, California 94525

Foreword

While training groups, I often ask them, "How many of you can read at a fourth-grade level?" All members of the audience raise their hands. Most of the young adults in children's mental health services cannot do the same. I then ask, "How many of you have had only one placement in your life [meaning that one or both of your parents raised you]?" Again, most hands go up. Most of the people whom we serve cannot make that claim. "How many of you went to fewer than three elementary schools?" I ask. I view a sea of hands. Most of the young folks we serve could not raise their hands in response to that question. I then ask the group, "How many of you were independent at age 18 [meaning that you left home and stopped getting money from your parents]?" Only a few participants ever raise their hands. None of the young people we work with can raise their hands in response to that question, either, yet. The state usually says to children who have been wards for many years that they should be self-supporting at this age.

According to the 1990 U.S. census, the average age at which children leave home for the last time is age 28. When it comes to the young adults whom we all serve, you can see that there is a large gulf between perception and reality.

Historically, the prevailing attitude in the United States has been that everyone should be able to "pull themselves up by their bootstraps." During the 1970s, the state of Illinois, along with most of the other states in the union, placed thousands of children from the child welfare, mental health, special education, and juvenile justice systems in out-of-state facilities. Many of these young people were between the ages of 17 and 21 and had already experienced numerous placements that included foster care, group homes, shelters, detention facilities, residential centers, institutions, and hospitals. Many of them had lost contact with or had severed their ties to their biological families.

Unfortunately, when children are removed from their own homes and communities and placed far away, state and county officials, who are responsible for them, find it very difficult to supervise the type of care and service interventions that are delivered. In one instance, it was discovered that one of our young people had been chained to a tree for several days as a punishment for bad behavior. The act was discovered by the state, and the governor ordered all of the children and young adults back to Illinois.

It was during this era that we started Kaleidoscope. Kaleidoscope's mission is to serve those children and families who have been neglected, have fallen through the service cracks, and who are considered the hardest to serve. Our goal is to serve anyone referred (if space is available) with an unconditional care, no-decline, no-punitive-discharge philosophy.

Upon learning of our philosophy, the state of Illinois referred many young adults who fit into the older, hard-to-place age category. Most had histories of aggression. Many had run away from at least three placements. Some were adjudicated sex offenders. Some were firesetters. What they all had in common was that they would age out of the system within a couple of years with insufficient training and little or no support to live independently in their own neighborhoods. The young adults did not understand the resources and had lost the relationships that most of us depend on: family and friends. In numerous ways, they were ill equipped to survive.

By traditional standards, these youngsters were not ready to make the transition to adulthood and independence. However, it was our feeling that we needed to force them into independence, regardless of whether they were ready, because we had so little time to work with them. It was obvious that young adults who had many of the challenges previously described could not be placed in the community without a tremendous amount of support.

During the early years of Kaleidoscope's independent living services, we concluded that past attempts to surround the youngsters with "bricks and mortar" had been unsuccessful for the most part. We believed we could increase the success rate by surrounding them with people and services instead of walls. This became one of the first wrap-around approaches in the United States. Kaleidoscope decided to place them in neighborhoods of their choice and to hook them up to existing community resources. We hoped to teach them to survive in their chosen neighborhoods.

We learned many lessons through our efforts to serve this population:

- *Lesson 1:* The young adults tended to stay in the neighborhoods that they had chosen to live in, despite, in some cases, many runaways from previous placements. We experienced only two runaways during the first 13 years of operation.
- *Lesson 2:* When the services were based on young adults' strengths while also planning for their issues, our success rate skyrocketed, and we learned some amazing things about the incredible strengths

and abilities of these forgotten youngsters. For example, if a young person was interested in art, then we would surround her with people who had the same interest. We also worked to enroll the young person in art classes or find her a job that had something to do with her interests.

- *Lesson 3:* We learned that it was imperative that we individualize the service.
- *Lesson 4:* The young people had to be part of the decision-making process.
- *Lesson 5:* Whenever possible, we included their biological and/or extended families.
- *Lesson 6:* Twenty-four-hour crisis intervention services had to be a critical piece of every service plan.
- *Lesson 7:* A team approach was important, not only to prevent staff burnout but also to provide consistency of service providers to youngsters who in the past had formed staff relationships only to have them severed when staff left or the young adult was moved to another agency. The team approach ensured that they were always involved with someone familiar to them.
- *Lesson 8:* We needed to be patient. Often it takes several years of intensive services for some youngsters to be truly independent. Because, like many of us, our first attempts at independence were less than totally successful. Hence, the importance of a no-eject policy.
- *Lesson 9:* Natural consequences played a significant part in the process of moving people toward independence.
- *Lesson 10:* Many of these young people came from different ethnic groups and sometimes from different regions of the United States and thus had been assimilated into American culture to varying degrees. Our cultural competence became an absolute necessity.
- *Lesson 11:* Our main responsibility was to "work our way out of a job" by making sure that the young adults knew how to gain access to community resources.
- *Lesson 12:* Last but not least, a vehicle for after-care services was needed.

These early lessons have become the backbone of Kaleidoscope's independent living services and have given us the opportunity to work with many gifted young adults. These lessons have been operationalized throughout this book at the practice, program, and systems levels. In the 1990s, many states lowered the age bar at which they relinquish guardianship and stop funding and thus stop providing services. We have watched this bar lower from age 21 to age 18 in many states because there is a general, though, I feel, false assumption that young people, many of whom have spent years in restricted settings, can be independent at age 18.

In Kaleidoscope's neighborhood in Chicago there is a fast-food restaurant that very graciously feeds the homeless between 6:00 and 6:30 every morning. I decided to ask the young adults who showed up at the restaurant door about their backgrounds. Twenty-six of the thirty-five people admitted to having been served by our children's human services systems. All admitted to having been victims of violence.

As I have worked and thought about the need to help youth make the transition into adulthood over the past 25 years, it has become clear that no matter how successful our institutions and substitute care systems are, they cannot completely prepare individuals for independence. If we are to turn the tide of homelessness, incarceration, and violence, we must expand our knowledge base about serving this population.

This book's contribution to our knowledge base is particularly important because the authors have focused on the practical. They let us know as family members, service providers, administrators, and policy makers what we can do to help. They have focused on what is unique about the time of life when young people move from adolescence into adulthood and what is unique at this time for those with emotional or behavioral difficulties.

The most vital contribution of this book is that of the professional authors, who, in addition to their own vast experience and research, listened to many of the real experts in this field: the young people who have been served in our systems. At a consensus forum that the book's editors held before any writing took place, young people told them about their experiences and what changes they thought were needed. Most important, at least one young person is a co-author of every chapter. In this way, this book has brought together unique expertise in helping us to better assist these young people to become adults.

I advise us all to read, to listen, and to learn.

Karl W. Dennis
Executive Director
Kaleidoscope

Acknowledgments

We have been privileged to work with some of the most wonderfully insightful young adults throughout the development and preparation of this book. During the National Forum on Transition Practices and Systemic Issues, the young people and parents challenged us to understand their experiences and perspectives. They as well as other young people and parents have contributed to each chapter in ways only their experiences and perspectives would enable. They have enriched the depth of this book and our lives.

Of course, in an edited book, one cannot progress far without the active, wise, and dedicated efforts of the chapter authors. These practitioners, educators, young adults, researchers, parent advocates, and administrators are not, for the most part, the typical academic collaborators who are solicited to write chapters. These are individuals who were selected because the program development and operational activities in which they are involved intimately related to the transition of youth and young adults with emotional or behavioral difficulties. The lead author of each chapter deserves particular recognition for enduring the numerous requests for rewrites to ensure that this book provides the reader with a coherent and comprehensive perspective on the principles, practices, and system issues across chapters.

The series editors, Beth Stroul and Bob Friedman, have helped us in conceptualizing and developing this book. Beth recognized the importance of a practical book on transition for youth and young adults and encouraged the lead editor to develop it. Bob was instrumental in ensuring that we would have the seed funding to initiate the development of the book through the forum. His seed funding enabled us to secure additional collaborative supporters. The following people were helpful in guiding us to parent advocates, young adults, and other professionals with particular interests in this topic as it affects young people and families: Barbara Huff and Trina Osher of the Federation of Families for Children's Mental Health, Brenda Souto of the National Alliance for the Mentally Ill, Terri Eggers of the SEDNET Collaborative of the Florida Department of Education, and David Osher of the Center for Effective Collaboration and Practice.

We were encouraged and supported by David Shern, the Institute Dean, and Greg Teague, Chair of the Department of Community Mental Health, and Bob Friedman and others at the Department of Child and Family Studies, Louis de la Parte Florida Mental Health Institute, University of South Florida. Nicole Deschênes, the Co-principal Investigator of the Transition to Independence Process grant, played a particularly essential role in organizing and executing the forum to plan this book. As with all of our team projects, Mary Irwin provided highly competent clerical assistance, ensuring the accuracy and professional appearance of all of our documents throughout the long, detailed road to publication. Their efforts, along with the invaluable fiscal guidance and management of Maria Peas, Beth Brookfield, and Margie LeHeup, and the technical assistance of Doug Stimac, allowed us to maneuver this project through the bureaucratic minefields that seem endemic in all large organizations.

We were supported at the Center for Mental Health Services Research by Directors Bill Fisher and Chuck Lidz, who provided both the financial support of the center and wisdom regarding the transition issue from the adult system perspective. Fiscal guidance was provided by Mary Handley and Janice Lagace. The many correspondences between the second editor and the contributing authors were assisted by Pat Gordon. Joanne Nicholson, Alexis Henry, and Jeffrey Geller have provided much-needed support, advice, and connections in the second editor's pursuit of providing services to, advocacy for, and the study of young people with emotional or behavioral difficulties.

The development of this book was guided masterfully by several individuals at Paul H. Brookes Publishing Co., including Jessica Allan and Jennifer Kinard (acquisitions editors), Elaine Niefeld (editorial director), and Paul Klemt (book production editor). Each of them was sensitive and flexible with us in the creation of this unique book.

We are indebted to each of these individuals and to others whom we have certainly left unnamed. We wish to acknowledge and express our appreciation to each of them for facilitating the accomplishment of our vision for this book.

Introduction

Hewitt B. "Rusty" Clark and Maryann Davis

This book focuses on practices and systemic strategies for improving the transition of youth and young adults (ages 14–25 years) with emotional or behavioral difficulties who are in the throes of moving from adolescence to young adulthood regarding employment, education, and community life. The issues facing these young people as they leave childhood and children's services and enter adulthood are daunting. They face the challenges that all young people face at this time in their lives yet they carry the added burden of an invisible disability. Few appropriate services exist to support them, and no unified public agency is available to help these young people and their families as they move into adulthood. In addition, special programs and skills are required for service providers to work well with youth and young adults with emotional or behavioral difficulties.

Because this is the first book addressing transition issues specifically for youth and young adults with emotional or behavioral difficulties, experts have come together on these pages to clarify and address the broad spectrum of issues surrounding this topic and to recommend solutions. The purposes of this book are to

1. Familiarize the reader with the characteristics of this population and the challenges they face
2. Describe the recommended practices for best serving the unique individual needs of these youth and young adults
3. Provide examples of the application of these practices within the context of collaborative systems
4. Review the current status of research regarding the transition of these youth and young adults to adulthood
5. Provide perspectives from young people and parents on ways to facilitate successful transitions
6. Provide guidelines for the development and expansion of a system to facilitate the transition of these youth and young adults into greater self-sufficiency

7. Discuss issues related to transition financing, policy and systemic reform, and advocacy

The book is a practical handbook for practitioners, educators, and administrators who work in the child and adult mental health services systems, secondary schools, postsecondary education, child welfare, juvenile justice, vocational rehabilitation, substance abuse, residential programs, homeless and runaway shelters, and children's systems of care. It is also relevant to some private therapists, counselors, pediatricians, and physicians. This book was also developed to inform community and natural support sources such as clergy, extended family members, recreation personnel, and community leaders. Two of the most important functions of this book are to guide parents with regard to which resources or services may be needed for their children in transition and to guide advocates and policy makers in the reform of funding, systems, and policies at the local, state, and federal levels.

To initiate the writing of this book, the editors brought all of the prospective authors together with some additional young adults and parents at a national forum on transition practices and systemic issues.[1] This group consisted of parents, young adults, practitioners, educators, and program managers and represented a broad array of disciplines and child advocacy groups. One of the first issues discussed was how to refer to and describe the young people on whom this book focuses. Many labels have been applied in the past, such as *serious emotional disturbance, emotional and behavioral disorders,* or *young people with mental health needs.* These terms were not acceptable for a variety of reasons, and the group concluded that the book would refer to these young people as having *emotional or behavioral difficulties.* Consensus was reached that the origin of the emotional or behavioral difficulties (i.e., biological versus environmental origin) was largely unimportant to the discussion but that it was important to emphasize that the *primary* difficulty was more psychological than developmental, cognitive, medical, or substance related. The group recognized that the clinical diagnostic system (i.e., *Diagnostic and Statistical Manual of Mental Disorders, Fourth Edition* [DSM-IV]) would not capture all young people who have emotional or behavioral difficulties; thus, this book focuses on

---

[1]In addition to most of the contributing authors' having been present at the forum, the following individuals also participated: Karl Dennis, Barbara Huff, Darryln Johnson, Lois Jones, Julie LaMonaca, Lois Moltane, Angela Nelson, Aaron Parker, Roberta Pettit, Brenda Souto, Greg Teague, and Amin Valentin. These individuals represented the Federation of Families for Children's Mental Health, the SEDNET Projects of the Florida Department of Education, the National Alliance for the Mentally Ill, the Community Action Grants Program of the Center for Mental Heath Services, and an array of other provider and advocacy organizations.

young people whose difficulties are consistent with but are not limited to mood or anxiety disorders, attention-deficit/hyperactivity disorder or disruptive behavior disorders, eating disorders, personality disorders, or psychotic disorders.

Second, the forum participants agreed that this book should focus on young people whose difficulties result in significant functional impairment that begins by age 18. This point was made to emphasize that these are young people whose difficulties begin in childhood or in adolescence. Thus, they face the challenging tasks of making the transition to adulthood while having experienced difficulties that undermine the developmental foundations of childhood and adolescence as well as undermine the fostering of supports such as family and friends that facilitate young adults' functioning. Similarly, forum participants were concerned about the discontinuity in services that most of these young people face when they reach the upper age limitations of public children's services, usually around age 18 (e.g., mental health, special education, child welfare, juvenile justice). For a complete discussion of definitional and population issues, see Chapter 1 and Davis and Vander Stoep (1997).

The practitioners, educators, and program managers heard from young adults and parents in no uncertain terms about the struggles that they have faced through the transition period and either the inappropriate role that most service systems had played in their lives or the absence of such systems in their lives. They also reminded us that young people of this age must be centrally involved in the design and implementation of any program and that they must be the "boss" of their own treatment and service decisions to have ownership of these plans. It was only during the final afternoon of this 2-day forum that the young adults and parents felt that those of us representing various professions had begun to appreciate, in some small way, the experience of their transitions.

The second most significant outcome of the forum was the group's decision to have a young adult co-author involved in writing each chapter. This brought an even broader array of voices into the book, with lead authors inviting young adults from their communities to join them in the formulation and/or writing of the chapters. After the forum, many of the contributing authors said that they would be writing a better chapter after hearing these young adults and parents and through the process of involving young people directly in the writing of the chapters.

During the forum, it was decided to minimize the labeling of the youth and young adults in this book and, of course, necessarily when referring to a classification, to use person-first language (e.g., *youth with emotional or behavioral difficulties*). Also discussed were a number of other terms, such as *transition* and *adulthood*. Transition into adult roles can be examined on a developmental level, as illustrated in the first chapter on developmental and institutional clashes and in the chapter on young adult perspectives. The rest of the chapters provide the practice and systemic framework for the development and operation of a Transition to Independence Process system to facilitate the transition of youth and young adults (ages 14–25 years) into employment, educational opportunities, living situations, and community-life adjustment.

This book brings the perspectives and experiences of young adults, parents, and relevant leaders in the child and adult fields together to provide practical guidance in the practices and systems that address the critical services and supports to improve the transition outcomes for youth and young adults with emotional or behavioral difficulties. The book presents the *state of the art and science* in practice and systemic strategies that appear to be essential to effectively facilitate the transition process with these young people. However, additional research is required to fully test the effectiveness and cost benefits of these strategies.

Along with our contributing authors of young adults, parents, practitioners, educators, researchers, and administrators, we hope that this handbook will assist in inspiring and guiding you to improve the provision of services for these young people in your community. We would value your sharing your experiences in such efforts so that we can learn from your applications of the promising practices presented.[2]

OVERVIEW

This book is organized into five sections. It is designed to be user-friendly for practitioners, educators, transition specialists, parents, advocates, and administrators.

Section I: Developmental and System Perspectives on Transition

The first chapter describes research regarding 1) youth and young adults with emotional or behavioral difficulties, 2) the systems that serve them during this developmental period, and 3) the clashes that occur when these individuals and the service delivery system meet. Chapter 1 presents relevant outcome data regarding the well-being of these young people and their impact on their communities. Chapter 2 provides the reader with a framework for the development and opera-

---

[2]Readers who wish to explore additional information regarding transition practices and systemic strategies should visit the following web site: http://www.fmhi.usf.edu/cfs/policy/tip/tiphp.htm.

tion of a transition system, describing recommended values, practices, and system guidelines necessary for a community consortium to address the needs of youth and young adults in transition. This transition framework is referred to as the *Transition to Independence Process (TIP) system.*

Section II: Transition System: Recommended Strategies and Practices to Facilitate Success Across Domains

Each of the chapters in this section acquaints the reader with empirically based treatment practices and other practical support and intervention strategies that have been refined in the field and are being applied to assist young people in achieving success across the transition domains of employment, education, living situation, and community-life adjustment. The chapters are by practitioners and educators in the field, along with young adults who have already made the transition to adulthood, thus ensuring the relevance and cultural competence of these approaches.

Section III: Young Adult and Family Perspectives

The three chapters of this section build the reader's understanding of young people's and parents' perspectives and the roles of parents, members of the natural support system, and young people themselves in this transition period and process. We are particularly appreciative of the powerful and informative stories that Amin, Jill, and Sean provided in Chapter 9 to assist readers in understanding the firsthand experiences of young people as they wend their way through the transition period. The next chapter illustrates how a program has provided greater voice and leadership for youth and young adults in a system of care to strengthen its transition capacity and capability. Chapter 11 describes the changing role of parents and caregivers during this developmental stage, the importance of programs and their practitioners in engaging parents and other members of natural support systems actively in service planning and support and service interventions, and the continuing role of parents as advocates for their youngsters.

Section IV: System, Policy, and Financing Issues

Providing appropriate services to youth and young adults in transition to adulthood is one of the most difficult funding challenges in the human services and education fields. This dilemma has been the result of both poor policy and lack of funding. Chapter 12 describes funding limitations and outlines mechanisms that can be used to create services and supports for these youth and young adults, tapping resources across the collaborative fields of human services, education, vocational rehabilitation, and corrections at the child and adult levels. The second chapter in this section is of particular interest to parent advocates, administrators, and policy makers who are willing to learn about the facilitative and inhibitory features of policies related to transition. Armed with this knowledge, they will be equipped better to initiate reforms at the local, state, and federal levels that are needed to facilitate the development of transition systems.

Section V: Conclusion

Chapter 14 summarizes and highlights the practice, systemic, policy, and funding issues and provides relevant agendas for future advocacy, policy, and system reform and research that are essential to enhancing collaboration among systems in order to improve transition outcomes of youth and young adults with emotional or behavioral difficulties.

We dedicate this book to those individuals in our lives whom we most value in facilitating our own transitions into adulthood:

I dedicate my efforts in this transition arena to my mother, Margaret Mae Clark Ferris, and my grandmother, Annabel Howe Blystone, for their constant love despite the ebbs and flows of our family circumstances; to Rudy Blakeman's friendship, which carried me through those high school years in a new town; to Ken Nielsen, a lifelong friend who has been my soulmate, always being there for me regardless of where my choices, good and poor, have led me; and to my wife, Rebecca, who has been and continues to be there for me through the adult transitions that have confronted me during the past 27 years and those yet to come.

—Hewitt B. "Rusty" Clark

I dedicate this book to my parents, Jack and Kitty Davis, who danced the turbulent dance of transition with me well and remain a wellspring of inspiration; to my husband, Steve Gatesy, whose humor, sharp mind, insight, and love inspire and sustain me; and to my daughter, Anwyn, whose infancy developed with this book and who inspires my best every day.

—Maryann Davis

Transition to Adulthood

I

Developmental and System
Perspectives on Transition

1

Transition

A Time of Developmental and Institutional Clashes

Ann Vander Stoep, Maryann Davis, and December Collins

Do you remember the exhilaration of reaching the final quarter of your senior year in high school? Or of buying groceries with your first paycheck? Or of standing in line to vote in your first presidential election? The transition to adulthood was an exciting time!

Do you remember the stress of driving to a remote place with a date whom you didn't know well and wondering whether you both had the same expectations about sex? Or of learning that most of your peers were experimenting with drugs and trying to make decisions that were right for you? Or of telling your friends you'd found the perfect apartment and then finding out that you had to pay the first and last month's rent and a security deposit up front? The transition to adulthood was a challenging time!

Each culture recognizes a time of passage from childhood to adulthood. The beginning of this passage is marked by the onset of the physical changes of puberty during adolescence, and the end is marked by the acceptance of the responsibilities and privileges of early adulthood. In American culture, it is a period of life that entails completing school, finding satisfying work, developing a social network,

The authors acknowledge the helpful perspectives of Seattle developmental psychologist and author Laura S. Kastner, Ph.D.

3

contributing to the maintenance and support of a household, and participating as a citizen in a community.

The transition to adulthood is particularly arduous for people with emotional or behavioral difficulties because it is often the very abilities central to a successful transition that are impaired in these individuals (Davis & Vander Stoep, 1997). Imagine yourself in the following real-life situations:

- You are experiencing a deep, debilitating depression in which you cannot find the will to drag yourself out of bed, but you know that if you miss another week of school, you'll fail your classes and won't be able to graduate.
- You periodically have uncontrollable rages in which you break furniture and punch holes in walls, and you know that in this apartment complex your landlord won't give you a second chance.
- You have just started the fourth job you've had in 6 months, and, as in your previous jobs, a co-worker has started to give you a hard time. Although the mean-spirited teasing is nearly unbearable, your parents have put their foot down and said that if you lose this job, too, you can't live at home anymore.
- You have lived your whole childhood in one foster home after another, never having felt the consistent love of any one caregiver. The first young man whom you've liked who says he likes you too is 6 years older than you. He tells you he doesn't want to go out with you anymore unless you have his baby.
- You are getting married and want to start a family. You are told that if you continue to take your medication during your pregnancy, it might harm the baby; but if you stop taking it, you'll be likely to do something very dangerous.
- You turn 22 next month, which means you will no longer be able to live in the transitional home in which you've been living for 2 years after spending a year on the streets. You don't qualify for Social Security, which means that you can't live in an adult residential facility, but you know you don't have the skills to live on your own.

These real-life examples demonstrate the challenges many young adults face in the areas of work, relationships, parenthood, housing, and treatment. Crossing the threshold into adulthood is a major struggle for young people with emotional or behavioral difficulties. They have gone through adolescence with symptoms that have affected their development. Whereas their peers can invest themselves in their own emotional, social, cognitive, and moral growth, adolescents with emotional or behavioral difficulties expend much energy simply struggling with these difficulties. They miss school because they have to be hospitalized. They miss basketball practice because they have counseling appointments. They miss eighth-grade graduation because they are in juvenile detention centers.

The challenge to young adults with emotional or behavioral difficulties is not limited to struggling with debilitating symptoms. Although these young people are found at all socioeconomic levels, in all cultural and ethnic groups, and in strong as well as challenged families, they are more likely than the average young adult to come from families living in poverty (Costello, 1989; McLeod & Shanahan, 1996). A number of conditions associated with poverty, including exposure to violence, family stress, despair, limited access to health and mental health care, and poor-quality schools, exacerbate the challenges of living with mental illness (Bolger, Patterson, Thompson, & Kupersmidt, 1995; McLoyd, 1990). The family's ability to provide financial support in ways such as helping to purchase a first car, to pay tuition, or to move into an apartment is limited.

Raising a child with emotional or behavioral difficulties can drain a family's resources. Parents may have to miss work to care for their child or to participate in meetings about their child (Rosenzweig, Brennan, & Oglivie, 1998). Multiple treatment episodes and medications may be very costly. Although having access to financial resources does not make being or parenting a young adult with emotional or behavioral difficulties easy, it helps. Struggling to meet their child's exceptional needs, parents often experience depletion of their emotional resources. Marital strain is common. Parents' job performance may be weakened. Emotional bonds between young people and families become strained when youth are treated in out-of-home settings.

Participation in informal community networks has been shown to affect the ability of families to navigate transitions (Staff & Catron, 1986); but for a variety of reasons, families with children with emotional or behavioral difficulties may actually *reduce* their extrafamilial contacts and roles (Mallory, 1995). The ritual of launching into young adulthood heightens the discrepancies between families that are raising children with emotional difficulties and other families. Young adults who are developing typically leave home, attend college, find jobs, and get married. Few young adults with serious emotional or behavioral difficulties move through these rites of passage easily. Thus, their families may feel particularly isolated and stigmatized during their child's transition years.

In this chapter, vignettes and studies that depict what the transition to adulthood is like for individuals with emotional or behavioral difficulties are interwoven. The first vignette tells of an adolescent who had struggled with mental illness for many years and was about to "age out" of eligibility for foster care. She still had many challenges that would be difficult to surmount:

Sharan is a 17½-year-old adolescent who has experienced recurring bouts of depression since she was in middle school. Sharan's depressive episodes generally last 2 or 3 weeks, during which time she feels hopeless, exhausted, listless, and unable to concentrate. Her schoolwork and relationships suffer. Sharan lives in a foster home. She and her five brothers and sisters were removed from their natural parents when Sharan was 9. When her birth father died 3 years ago without having left sufficient funds for a proper burial, Sharan became suicidal and had to be hospitalized. Sharan has completed five semesters of high school and worked part time last summer answering the telephone in her foster father's office. She is expecting her first baby in August. Her foster family wants her to move out when the baby comes. Sharan is looking for an apartment with her cousin in a part of town where rent is low. She plans to use 6 months of her lifetime allotment of 60 months of welfare to support herself while she cares for her newborn. When her baby is about 5 months old, she plans to return to school during the day and get a night job. Sharan is hoping the baby's father or her cousin will provide child care while she is away at school and work.

Keeping up an apartment, finishing high school, finding a job, getting to work each day, and paying the bills would be a challenge for any 18-year-old, let alone one who is a single parent with incapacitating emotional difficulties. Young adults who are in situations such as Sharan's need guidance in setting realistic goals and help in finding resources to support them as they make these major transitions to parenthood, independent living, and a vocation.

People who study transition distinguish between developmental transition and institutional transition (Mallory, 1995). In this book, *developmental transition* refers to the natural process of maturation, which begins in late adolescence and never occurs exactly the same way in two individuals. Developmental transition is tied to a culture's expectations of the young adult and is marked by cultural rites of passage. *Institutional transition* refers to changes in legal or bureaucratic status. Institutional transition is marked by abrupt, arbitrary changes in status, whereas the developmental transition involves natural, more gradual psychological and biological changes. For youth with emotional or behavioral difficulties, the contrast between the natural process of development and the arbitrary changes imposed by the institutional systems that are involved in their lives creates a particular burden.

For individuals who have been supported by child welfare, special education, juvenile justice, or mental health programs, eligibility usually ends or changes drastically when they reach 18 or 22 years of age (Vander Stoep, 1995). For many different reasons, systems that serve children seldom prepare these individuals for adult functioning, and systems that serve adults reject them or serve them poorly. Thus, appropriate institutional supports for adolescents with emotional or behavioral difficulties making the transition to adulthood are less available at precisely the time when they are most needed.

The second vignette tells of a young man whose developmental needs were not met by existing adult mental health services, although he did meet eligibility criteria:

Grant is 19 and has a long history of emotional and behavioral difficulties. In his early teens, Grant began to have intermittent violent, explosive outbursts. At the age of 16, Grant was placed in a children's residential treatment facility, where he lived until he was "emancipated" at 18. After discharge, he worked on getting his general equivalency diploma. He was living with his girlfriend and working in a lumberyard when he had an explosive episode. Grant was taken in restraints to the state psychiatric hospital, kept there for 3 months, then released to an adult congregate care facility. The facility had the look and smell of a poorly run nursing home. Heavily medicated middle-age and older adults shuffled through the hallways. Grant, feeling stable and energetic, was eager to get back to work and to his girlfriend. Instead, he stayed inside all day, took his medications, and attended daily group sessions with the other residents. This institutional placement was not appropriate for someone with Grant's developmental needs.

Young adults like Grant need help with creating and implementing appropriate community transition plans. Often they become caught in "snares" that divert them from their quest for full adulthood (Moffitt, 1993). These snares include but are not limited to hospitalization, substance abuse, unplanned pregnancy, and incarceration. Many earnest young adults work successfully at a job or attend college for a period of time, only to be sidelined by a sudden increase in symptoms or an adverse response to new circumstances, leading to hospitalization and job loss or school failure. When such acute episodes subside, these young adults must begin anew their quest for adult independence. Sharan's and Grant's vignettes give us a taste of what the transition is like for adolescents with emotional or behavioral difficulties.

During the 1990s, research investigators (Kutash, Greenbaum, Brown, & Foster-Johnson, 1995; Vander Stoep, 1995; Wagner, Blackorby, & Hebbeler, 1993) concluded that the path to adulthood for many, if not most, adolescents with emotional or behavioral difficulties is indeed rocky. The research findings presented in this chapter address four questions:

1. How many individuals with emotional or behavioral difficulties are making the transition to adulthood?
2. What types of emotional or behavioral difficulties do transition-age individuals typically have?
3. How well are adolescents with emotional or behavioral difficulties meeting the developmental tasks of young adulthood?
4. How well do our institutions support youth through the transition process?

How many individuals with emotional or behavioral difficulties are making the transition to adulthood? To get an accurate estimate of the number of young adults who are affected by emotional or behavioral difficulties, we must first define what we mean by *young adult* and what we mean by *emotional or behavioral difficulties*. The transition phase is variable in the age it begins and how long it lasts. However, a person is typically considered a *young adult* from age 16 to age 25 (Davis & Vander Stoep, 1997). *Emotional or behavioral difficulties* is a more difficult term to define. Researchers who have conducted studies in which they randomly selected households and administered standardized psychiatric diagnostic interviews to children and their families living in communities found that approximately 18%–21% of children meet the diagnostic criteria for a psychiatric disorder (Cohen, Provet, & Jones, 1996). The *prevalence,* or proportion, of the child population living with a psychiatric disorder at any given time increases with children's age (Roberts, Attkinson, & Rosenblatt, 1998). The prevalence of serious emotional disturbance (SED) has been estimated conservatively at 5%–9% (Friedman, Katz-Levy, Manderscheid, & Sondheimer, 1996). The criteria for the SED classification are more stringent than the criteria for psychiatric diagnosis and require the presence of significant functional impairment. In 1997, there were 36 million 16- to 25-year-olds in the United States. If the prevalence estimate of 18% with a psychiatric disorder is multiplied by the number of people of transition age, we come up with the staggering figure of 6.5 million individuals of transition age with psychiatric disorders. Using the more conservative prevalence estimate (5%–9%) for SED reduces the number to between 2 million and 3.2 million. Either way, many young people in the United States are affected.

A small proportion of the transition-age population receives services. One study (Leaf et al., 1996) showed that fewer than one third of youth across four communities who had both a psychiatric disorder and a significant functional impairment received mental health care from specialists. Other studies (Costello & Janieszewski, 1990; Knitzer, 1983; Realmuto, Bernstein, Maglothin, & Pandey, 1992) estimated that between 6% and 20% of children and adolescents who need mental health treatment actually receive such treatment.

What types of emotional or behavioral difficulties do transition-age individuals typically have? The most common types of emotional or behavioral difficulties found among transition-age individuals in studies that were conducted in communities are different from those found in studies that were conducted in service systems. Because studies in both environments have determined primarily how many people meet the criteria for the psychiatric diagnoses found in the *Diagnostic and Statistical Manual of Mental Disorders, Fourth Edition* (DSM-IV; American Psychiatric Association [APA], 1994), *types of emotional or behavioral difficulties* is translated into *types of diagnoses.* Unfortunately, few studies have focused specifically on individuals in this age group. A study (Vander Stoep et al., in press) of 16- to 17-year-olds with psychiatric disorders living in households in communities found the most common diagnoses to be disruptive behavior disorders (12 of 100 individuals studied), substance-related disorders (9 of 100 individuals studied), anxiety disorders (6 of 100 individuals studied), and depressive disorders (4 of 100 individuals studied). A study (Davis & Vander Stoep, 1997; P. Greenbaum, personal communication, March 21, 1995) of 17- to 25-year-olds with SED who had received treatment as children found their most common diagnoses to be substance-related disorders (ranging from 43 of 100 to 49 of 100), anxiety disorders (ranging from 34 of 100 to 36 of 100), and depressive disorders (ranging from 10 of 100 to 18 of 100). The lack of disruptive disorders in the older sample is an artifact reflecting differences in diagnostic criteria for children and adults. In fact, two thirds of the same sample of youth under age 18 met the criteria for a diagnosis of conduct disorder. Studies (e.g., Cohen et al., 1996) have shown that approximately half of all adolescents who meet the criteria for any psychiatric disorder meet the criteria for two or more disorders. These findings give us a rough idea of the types of psychiatric disorders found within the general young adult population and among the small subset of this population who received treatment as children.

Translating these diagnoses back into the lives of real people suggests that many youth in transition struggle with intense feelings of anger and frustration, intense desires to avoid social and other stressful situations, feelings of sadness and worthlessness, and a lack of interest in fun or pleasurable activities. Their behaviors include being socially explosive and inappropriate, using alcohol or other drugs, getting into trouble with the law, withdrawing, escaping through sleep, being inactive, and being anxious in new situations or in particular types of situations.

To enable themselves to enter the world as young adults, most adolescents acquire a supply of developmental competencies that are gained as a result of a combination of innate capacities, experiences, exposures, and relationships (Kastner & Wyatt, 1997). Cognitive development progresses to more abstract, relative, and multidimensional thinking, with an increasing ability for self-reflection and future orientation (Keating, 1990). Social networks expand, and peer relationships involve increasing mutuality, intimacy, and loyalty (Damon, 1983; Selman, 1980; Youniss, 1980). Family relationships change to reflect a delicate balance between the growing need for independence and the continued need for emotional support and guidance (Karpel & Strauss, 1983). Like all 19- and 20-year-olds, individuals with emotional or behavioral difficulties want the status, opportunities, and privileges of young adulthood. Recognizing that their 19- and 20-year-olds are not yet competent to accept this status, caregivers of young adults with these difficulties understandably wish to hold them back for their own protection. This inevitably leads to conflicts, acting out, and often self-destructive acts such as running away or living on the street (L. Kastner, personal communication, July 13, 1999).

Central to adolescent development is the formation of a unique identity. En route to identity formation, adolescents crave adult milestones to enhance a sense of self, prowess, and status (Jessor, 1991). Because their sense of self and self-esteem may be compromised, adolescents with emotional or behavioral difficulties often crave these milestones even more intensely than young adults without these difficulties do (Kastner & Wyatt, 1997). By establishing a sexual relationship or using illegal substances, adolescents are able to mimic their peers or experience a sense of "grownupness." Because experimenting with sex and substances can also provide easy ways to cope with feelings and loneliness, young people can meet these needs while further postponing healthy development.

For most young adults, the adolescent experimentation, risk taking, and oppositionality that are important precursors to identity formation taper off and a more secure and stable identity is established by the time they reach transition age. Identity formation lays the foundation for basic choices such as those regarding gender roles, life goals, committed relationships, parenting, and occupation (Erikson, 1968; Josselson, 1980). Attending college, keeping a job, and maintaining friendships require the ability to plan ahead, to demonstrate social skills consistently, to be conscious of time, to attend responsibly to multiple tasks, and to feel empathy. Yet, for adolescents with emotional or behavioral difficulties, much of their resources and those of their families have gone into coping with the symptoms and stressors that accompany their emotional difficulties. It is not difficult to understand why these youth are likely to fall behind in a number of developmental areas and how this translates into problems in meeting the demands of typical young adult activities. It leaves caregivers to meet the challenge of supplying sufficient opportunities for older youth to experience young adult status without offering more than can be handled.

DEVELOPMENTAL TRANSITION

How well are adolescents with emotional or behavioral difficulties meeting the developmental tasks of young adulthood? Three service system–based longitudinal studies and one community-based longitudinal study broadly described the young adult outcomes of adolescents with psychiatric disorders. Several other smaller studies addressed outcomes in specific areas and were included in a previous review (Davis & Vander Stoep, 1997). The three major service system–based studies are the National Longitudinal Transition Study (NLTS) of 8,408 special education students from secondary schools across the United States, approximately 10% of whom were classified as having SED (Valdes, Williamson, & Wagner, 1990; Wagner et al., 1991; Wagner et al., 1993; Wagner, D'Amico, Marder, Newman, & Blackorby, 1992), the National Adolescent and Child Treatment Study (NACTS) of 812 youth with SED, half of whom were in special education programs and half of whom were in residential treatment programs (Kutash et al., 1995; Prange et al., 1992; Silver et al., 1992), and the McGraw Center Study of 86 adolescents with severe psychiatric impairments who were discharged from a long-term residential facility in Washington State (Vander Stoep, 1992; Vander Stoep & Taub, 1994; Vander Stoep, Taub, & Holcomb, 1994).

Before the results of service system–based studies are presented, some implications of the methods used in the studies cited are considered. Only a small proportion of people with emotional or behavioral difficulties actually receive treatment. Individuals who receive treatment for emotional or behavioral difficulties are different from individuals who do not receive treatment in terms of ethnicity, social class, gender, and urban as opposed to rural residency. Males are overrepresented in special education classrooms, residential treatment facilities, and psychiatric hospitals (Pottick, Hansell, Guttman, & White, 1995; Silver et al., 1992; Valdes et al., 1990). The limited evidence that is available indicates that youth who are African American, Asian American, Hispanic American, and Native American are underrepresented in receiving mental health services (Hoberman, 1992). Studies (e.g., Cohen & Hesselbart, 1993) have shown that middle- and low-income youth with emotional or behavioral difficulties and those living in rural areas are less likely than other youth to receive mental health treatment. Youth who are treated also differ from those who are not treated in terms of the type and severity of their emotional or behavioral difficulties (Leaf et al., 1996). Because of the selection factors that determine which young adults with emotional or behavioral difficulties receive services, it is difficult to generalize from the results of these studies to all transitional youth. The young adult outcomes of individuals with emotional or behavioral difficulties who were identified and treated are likely to be either worse (because those with the most serious emotional or behavioral difficulties are selected for treatment) or better (because of the positive effects of treatment) than the outcomes of adolescents with emotional or behavioral difficulties who did not receive services. To understand the plight of all adolescents with emotional or behavioral difficulties, results from community-based studies must be examined.

The single community-based study (Vander Stoep et al., in press) of transition was part of the Children in Community Study that was carried out in two counties in upstate New York (Cohen et al., 1993). In 1975, 1,141 households with 1- to 10-year-old children were selected randomly for participation in the study. Children and their mothers were interviewed every few years to chart the children's life course through adolescence and into young adulthood. Structured diagnostic interviews were used to identify adolescents with emotional or behavioral difficulties so that young adult outcomes of those with and without emotional or behavioral difficulties could be compared.

The results presented address the following questions: What proportion complete school? What proportion are employed? What proportion are living alone or with their families? What proportion have been arrested? What proportion are pregnant or have given birth? Table 1 consolidates the findings from the Children in Community Study and the three service system–based studies and shows how well young adults with emotional or behavioral difficulties are meeting the developmental tasks of young adulthood compared with young adults in the general population and young adults without emotional or behavioral difficulties. Keep in mind that different cultures within the United States may vary in the value that they place on some of these tasks. For example, moving out of the family home may generally be valued more or less among Hispanic and African American families than among families of European American descent.

The table is arranged in order of severity of psychiatric impairment within the population studied. At the left are data from the McGraw Center Study, whose study population had, on average, the most severe impairments. All young adults in the McGraw Center Study had received long-term residential treatment; half of the young adults in NACTS had received residential treatment and half special education services; and all young adults in the NLTS had received special education services. The last three columns in Table 1 show outcomes for the young adults with emotional or behavioral difficulties in the community-based study, for the U.S. general population based on the U.S. census, and for the comparison group of young adults in the Children in Community Study who did not have emotional or behavioral difficulties.

Table 1. Comparing young adult outcomes across transition studies

Young adult outcome	McGraw study (ages 18–22 years)	NACTS (ages 18–22 years)	NLTS (SED)	CICS PD (ages 18–21 years)	CICS No PD (ages 18–21 years)	U.S. general population
Secondary school completion	23%	26%	48%	61%	93%	81%
Currently employed	46	52	48	59	80	78[a]
Residing with family	43	45	45	68	74	56[a]
Recent police incidents/arrests[b]	37	22	21	24	11	13[c]
Pregnancy in young women	50	38	48	29	14	17[d]

CICS, Children in Community Study; NACTS, National Adolescent and Child Treatment Study; NLTS, National Longitudinal Transition Study; PD, psychiatric disorders; SED, serious emotional disturbance.

[a]Age group = 20–24 years.

[b]CICS measured "trouble with police"; McGraw, NACTS, and NLTS measured "arrests."

[c]Arrests among 17-year-olds in King County, Washington, in 1991.

[d]Age group = 18–19 years.

As can be seen in Table 1, among young adults in the general population (approximately 20% of whom have emotional or behavioral difficulties), surveys have shown that

- 80% finish high school
- More than 75% are employed
- More than 50% live with their families
- 13% have been arrested
- Fewer than 20% of 18- to 19-year-old women become pregnant

According to each of the transition studies discussed in this chapter, young adults with emotional or behavioral difficulties have worse outcomes than their peers without these difficulties. We discuss the findings of these studies in more detail in the subsections that follow.

School Completion

Graduating from high school is an important milestone in the life of a young adult. Accomplishing this task opens the door to further opportunity, and failure to do so raises roadblocks to economic stability and life satisfaction. Rates of school completion for young adults with emotional or behavioral difficulties or SED are alarmingly low (23%–61%), particularly among those receiving services. When the NLTS compared young adults with SED and young adults at each grade level in 10 other disability categories, including mental retardation, multisensory disabilities, and learning disabilities, the dropout rate was highest for those with SED (Wagner et al., 1993). Thus, research confirms that young people with emotional or behavioral difficulties struggle tremendously in facing the day-to-day challenges of being successful in school.

Employment

In light of their low school completion rates, it is not surprising that employment rates of youth with emotional or behavioral difficulties are also low relative to those of young adults without these difficulties. The NLTS showed particularly low employment (39%) for individuals with SED who had dropped out of school. A disturbing aspect of the McGraw Center Study was that the number of youth with emotional or behavioral difficulties who were employed actually decreased as they aged from 18 to 19 to 20 years (Vander Stoep et al., 1994). Many of the young adults in the study had received vocational training during their residential treatment and had been placed in jobs before discharge. Perhaps as time went by, the effects of this boost of training wore off and these youth became less competitive in the job market.

Residential Status

Between the 1970 and the 1990 U.S. censuses, the age at which young people left home increased. The majority of Americans who were 20–24 years old at the time the 1990 U.S. census was taken were still residing with their parents (U.S. Department of Commerce, 1993). What is surprising is that this is less often true for young adults with emotional or behavioral difficulties. They are more likely than their peers without such difficulties to be living on their own. It is not surprising, then, if one considers how challenging it is for young adults to become self-supporting, that young adults with emotional or behavioral difficulties are at high risk of becoming homeless. The McGraw Center Study found that during the 5 years after discharge from residential treatment, 30% of young adults with serious emotional or behavioral difficulties had had at least one episode of homelessness (Vander Stoep, Embry, Evens, Ryan, & Pollack, 1997).

Community Membership

Dropping out of school, being without work, or living on the brink of homelessness places one at risk of turning to illegal activities. Indeed, the transition studies discussed in this chapter showed that a high proportion (21%–37%) of young adults with emotional or behavioral difficulties are engaged in criminal activities. The highest rates of arrest were found in the McGraw Center Study cohort, in which 37% had been arrested during the 3-year interval after discharge from residential treatment. Twenty-one percent had been incarcerated for at least 7 days (Vander Stoep, 1992). Both the NLTS and the community-based study found that criminal involvement was particularly high for young adults with emotional or behavioral difficulties who had not completed school. The NLTS also showed that young adults with SED are the least likely among those in all of the disability categories to belong to social or community groups or to register to vote (Wagner et al., 1992). The cost of untreated emotional or behavioral difficulties can translate into high cost to both those with emotional and behavioral difficulties and society in general.

Pregnancy

Becoming pregnant in early adulthood was a uniformly common occurrence across the service system–based cohorts as well as in the subgroup of individuals in the community-based study who had emotional or behavioral difficulties (29%–50%). Although pregnancy is not a "bad" outcome per se, evidence from the McGraw Center Study and the Children in Community Study indicates that young women with emotional or behavioral difficulties are more likely than their peers without these difficulties to experience multiple pregnancies at a young age and to lose custody of their babies.

Taken together, these studies corroborate what we know from our experience: Many young people with emotional or behavioral difficulties are failing to meet the challenges of young adulthood. Because the service system–based studies did not control for differences that exist between families of youth with emotional or behavioral difficulties and other families in the general population with regard to economic disadvantages, these results could be interpreted as reflecting the effects of economic disadvantages as well as the effects of emotional or behavioral difficulties. However, the community-based study addressed this issue by comparing young people with emotional or behavioral difficulties with other young people of the same gender and social class and found the following with regard to those with emotional or behavioral difficulties:

- The risk of failure to complete school was 14 times greater.
- The risk of not being in college, in vocational school, or employed at ages 18–21 years was 4 times greater.
- The risk of engaging in illegal activities was 3 times higher.
- The risk of a young person's being involved in a pregnancy was 6 times higher.

Although social class (based on mother's education, father's education, father's occupation, and family income) had a strong independent effect on young adult outcomes, it did not diminish the powerful adverse effect of emotional or behavioral difficulties. We have presented strong evidence that many young people with emotional or behavioral difficulties live in our communities and that their difficulties are serious and contribute to their falling behind in the developmental transition to adulthood.

INSTITUTIONAL TRANSITION

How well do our institutions support youth through the transition process? The studies summarized in this chapter showed a failure of young people to navigate the passage to adulthood successfully. We do not know what part of this failure is inevitable and what part can be avoided by the provision of appropriate supports. The research base depicting the clashes between the developmental needs of young adults with emotional or behavioral difficulties and the barriers that they face is inadequate. We know from several studies that the small proportion of individuals receiving services in childhood declines after age 17, 18, or 19 (Cohen & Hesselbart, 1993; Davis, Yelton, Katz-Levy, & Lourie, 1995;

Silver, 1995). It is unlikely that this is due primarily to young adults' rejecting available services. Silver (1995) showed that three times as many 18- to 20-year-olds desired services as received them, and Cohen and Hesselbart (1993) showed that 17- to 20-year-olds were significantly more interested than 10- to 16-year-olds in receiving services. The decline in services is far more likely to be due to barriers to appropriate supports that are raised as youth leave the children's services systems.

Despite the paucity of studies that depict young people's institutional transition to adulthood, young adults and their families and professionals and administrators from across the United States have voiced a number of consistent themes pertaining to the nature of the institutional transition and why it is so difficult:

1. Institutional supports are withdrawn abruptly and are often based on the individual's age alone.
2. Institution-generated transition plans are weak and ultimately are not followed.
3. Continuity of care across child and adult institutions is lacking.
4. Institutional supports are not designed for young adults.
5. Institutions engender mistrust.

The remainder of this chapter is devoted to a discussion of the recurring themes just listed.

Arbitrary Institutional Boundaries
Institutional supports are withdrawn abruptly and are often based on the individual's age alone. There are many stories from youth and families, as well as from service providers and administrators, about young adults who have a great need for continuing supports but whose services end abruptly when they reach a specified age.

Youth who are involved with special education or child welfare lose those services either when they leave school (graduate or drop out) or when they reach age 18 or, under certain circumstances, age 22. These systems do not serve anyone older than specific age limits, nor do they offer continued involvement with individuals once they have exited. At best, these institutions seek other supports for young people in anticipation of their leaving. At worst, little planning is done, and youth and their families are simply cut off when they leave the system or reach the specified age limit. In addition, at the same age at which children's services end, other systems such as the Social Security Administration, insurance companies, Medicaid, Temporary Assistance for Needy Families, the Immigration and Naturalization Service, and public housing programs define these young people as adults. Lacking continuity of care from children's services systems, these young adults are set adrift to navigate the myriad bureaucracies on their own. In the following vignette, a young woman must make an extremely difficult choice between experiencing a severe bout of depression without medical care or lying about the seriousness of her condition:

Rochelle, a 20-year-old parent of an infant, lost her eligibility for Medicaid when she took a job as a receptionist at a dentist's office. Rochelle had been diagnosed with bipolar disorder, and every few months she cycled through dramatic emotional highs and lows. Her health insurance, however, covered only $40 for each of 20 visits to a psychiatrist or a mental health counselor each year. When Rochelle found herself facing a severe depressive episode, she was advised to feign being suicidal so that she could be admitted to the hospital, where she was "covered" for 7 days of inpatient care while her condition stabilized.

For young adults such as Rochelle to be supported adequately, their unique patterns of suffering and their unique health care needs must be taken seriously. Most state mental health agencies have separate, autonomous child and adult systems (Davis, Yelton, & Katz-Levy, 1995). Typically, individuals stop receiving services in the children's mental health services system at age 18. Unfortunately, neither the children's mental health services system nor the adult system has the mandate to provide specific services for individuals who are crossing the transition "border." Most adolescents do not become "cured" by the time their eligibility for children's mental health services ends, and mental health systems rarely provide adequate planning in anticipation of the loss of children's services.

Weak Transition Plans

Institution-generated transition plans are weak and ultimately are not followed. Unlike social policies in many European countries, those in the United States that are directed at children with disabilities are mainly "substitutive" rather than "supportive" in their orientation (Monroney, 1981). This orientation means that only after families have "failed" in their ability to care for children is the state mandated to invest public resources to help such families (Mallory, 1995). A substitutive orientation toward children with special needs does not bode well for the system anticipating their needs during life-cycle transitions. A supportive approach involves creating transition plans that help youth and families realistically face the limitations of systems of care, that identify what their continuing needs will be, and that begin to make resources available or to create new ones. The following vignette describes the situation of a young man who faces pressure from systems and from his family to "emancipate" himself into an adult lifestyle but lacks the requisite life skills to do so:

Jake's mother brought him home from a residential school when he was 18. He had not completed school, but she was very displeased with the program and believed it was doing him more harm than good. His family struggled hard with his explosive, angry, and irresponsible behavior at home. A special day school was located, and a year later he had his diploma. However, because all efforts had been invested in getting him through school, Jake was unprepared to work or to live on his own. He had never shopped for groceries, done laundry, balanced a checkbook, or held a job. An application was made to an adult mental health program; but, despite having a diagnosis of bipolar disorder, Jake did not meet the eligibility criteria, because his behavior problems were seen as his primary mental health issue. Jake did not have the patience to wade through the paperwork at the Department of Vocational Rehabilitation. His family wanted him to move out, but he was utterly unprepared to maintain his own household. Jake was about to begin his adult life both unskilled and unsupported.

Young people like Jake need transitional supports that can help them to gain independent living skills while their families adjust to the unique demands of parenting their transition-age children. Through the education system (under the Individuals with Disabilities Education Act [IDEA] of 1990 [PL 101-476]) and the child welfare system (in the John H. Chafee Foster Care Independence Program [Consolidated Omnibus Reconciliation Act (COBRA) of 1985; reauthorized, COBRA 1993; Foster Care Independence Act of 1999 [PL 106-169]), special steps are to be taken to facilitate the young person's transition to independent living. The IDEA Amendments of 1997 (PL 105-17) specify that transition services for all students with disabilities who are 14 years of age and older must be addressed in an individualized education program (see also *Federal Register,* September 29, 1992, and October 27, 1992).

Transition services are defined as

A coordinated set of activities for a student, designed within an outcome-oriented process that promotes movement from school to post-school activities, including post-secondary education, vocational training, integrated employment (including supported employment), continuing and adult education, adult services, independent living, or community participation. (C.F.R. § 300.18[A])

IDEA requires each agency that provides or pays for the services designated by the individualized transition plan (ITP) to describe its role. Although the IDEA mandate has the potential to provide needed supports for adolescents with SED, implementation of the legislation has been hampered by the fact that no legal requirement exists for states to create a budgetary line item to ensure its full implementation (see also Chapter 13). In the absence of funding, the law has gone largely ignored in many states (see, e.g., Florida Department of Education, 1993).

Furthermore, the mandate targets only adolescents who are in school in special education programs. As described earlier, many youth with SED drop out of school. The mandate also does not extend to students with SED who are being educated outside the public school system in residential treatment facilities, group homes, or detention halls. Nor does it apply to the large proportion of adolescents with emotional or behavioral difficulties who have never been identified by their schools as needing special education services. Thus, although by highlighting entitlement to a written ITP IDEA can serve as a basis for litigation, in actuality it has helped to provide a potential safety net for a very small proportion of the total number of individuals in need (Davis & Vander Stoep, 1997). Within most service sectors other than education and child welfare, transition legislation does not even exist.

Discontinuity of Care
Continuity of care across child and adult institutions is lacking. This discontinuity is reflected in changes in eligibility criteria, cultures, and array of services.

Conflicting Eligibility Criteria   One of the most glaring barriers to continuity of care is the change in eligibility criteria that excludes most youth with emotional or behavioral difficulties from the adult services system. Diagnostic eligibility criteria for the adult mental health system generally screen out all but adults with the most serious and chronic disabling conditions, most of whom typically have their first onset in early adulthood. Adult mental health programs primarily serve adults who have diagnoses of severe mood disorders or schizophrenia and who have chronic functional impairments. A study (Davis, 1995) conducted in Massachusetts showed that among adolescents who received intensive public sector mental health services, individuals with psychotic disorders, mood disorders, or anxiety disorders tended to receive services as adults, whereas those with conduct disorders, substance abuse disorders, and adjustment disorders did not. Adult mental health systems often specifically exclude individuals with conduct or substance use problems from all but emergency psychiatric services. Yet, conduct problems are the most common type of problems addressed by children's mental health services systems. Thus, the strict diagnostic eligibility criteria for access to adult mental health services bar entry of the majority of youth with emotional or behavioral difficulties who are cared for in the children's mental health services system.

In addition, differing eligibility criteria and inflexible and categorical funding streams within children's mental health services systems often contribute to a lack of coordinated care across the special education, children's mental health, child welfare, and juvenile justice systems. In particular, children receiving special education services under the disability category of SED may not qualify for children's mental health services and vice versa, because definitions of SED differ within each system. Thus, many children do not receive special education services and do not have ITPs. Children with emotional or behavioral difficulties who do qualify for services from multiple systems may receive services that are not coordinated. Lack of coordination results in an inefficient, ineffective, and stressful transition process.

Finally, because there is often no linkage between the adult mental health services and children's services systems other than the children's mental health services system, children who are primarily the responsibility of the child welfare system, special education system, or juvenile justice system often have no means of entry into the adult mental health services system. Well-coordinated supports should facilitate successful transitions to school and work from the special education system, to independent living from the child welfare system, and to appropriate emotional or behavioral supports from the children's mental health services system.

In 1982, Knitzer demonstrated that service systems were not taking responsibility for the appropriate care of children with emotional or behavioral difficulties. Across the United States, a very small proportion of such children were receiving services of any kind, and those who did often received care that was not helpful or not generalizable to the child's natural context. In describing this neglected population, Knitzer coined the phrase *unclaimed children*. National initiatives have been mounted to design systems of care that can reclaim responsibility for these children. However, a major oversight continues to be the plight of those children at the upper age range of childhood who are about to lose their entitlement to participate in these improved systems of care. Transitional youth are today's unclaimed children.

Conflict of Cultures Continuity of care is hampered for those who continue to receive services, largely because a great disparity exists between the cultures of the adult and child systems. The federal Child and Adolescent Service System Program (CASSP), established in 1984, has promoted a model system of care for children. CASSP provides grants to states and counties to enable them to implement the principles of the ideal system (Stroul & Friedman, 1986). These principles include provision of comprehensive, coordinated, community-based, child-centered, family-focused, and culturally competent services in the least restrictive, most clinically appropriate environment. Many creative ideas, such as interagency planning and case review, flexible funds, wraparound services, and blended funding pools, have been spawned through the CASSP initiative. Unfortunately, most of these good ideas have not made the transition into the adult services sector. Thus, young adults who have been receiving state-of-the-art care may suddenly find themselves in a less-evolved adult services system.

Array of Services: No One's Mandated Population and No One's Budget No adult counterparts to the special education and child welfare systems exist. Adult mental health agencies are the only state agencies charged with the comprehensive care of adults with mental health needs. Yet, as described previously, in practice this charge is limited to the population of adults with the most severe disabilities. Children's services systems have the greatest stake in helping youth make the transition to adulthood. Relationships have been formed, and time and care have been invested in these youth. Sadly, human services are notoriously underfunded. Although children's services systems might like to continue to provide ongoing support for the young adults they have served as children, their already thin budgets do not allow them to do so. Similarly, the adult mental health services system is usually struggling to provide for its mandated populations. With limited budgets, neither system can extend its reach beyond the individuals who are eligible for its services (see also Chapter 12).

Inappropriate Support

Institutional supports are not designed for young adults. Whereas the children's system generally fails to prepare adolescents for independent living, the adult system generally assumes that a consumer of its services has a preexisting level of adult functioning. The majority of adult consumers are in their 30s and 40s. Many of them drove a car, lived on their own, had families, and pursued careers before their illnesses became debilitating. Thus, adult mental health and vocational services tend to be rehabilitative, focusing on a return to preillness levels of functioning. Many adult service coordinators and other service providers are unprepared to work with youth in transition to adulthood and find that these young adults are unlike the "typical" adults they usually serve. Clubhouses and other adult group support entities are composed of older adults and do not appeal to younger adults. Similarly, adult consumers in these programs often find young adults to be immature at best. The unique developmental needs of youth in transition, who must acquire independent living skills and face adult expectations for the first time, go unattended. This situation is made painfully clear in the story of a 22-year-old woman, who describes her treatment program in this chapter's final vignette:

> *The day treatment program I was assigned to was in the morning. Most days, the program consisted of being handed a piece of paper on a topic such as anger, then reading it to the group. I was the youngest person, 18, while the majority of the people were in their 40s. I felt quite intimidated by those "older" folks and a little scared of them. Because everyone was so much older than me, the staff tended to treat me as a functioning 40-year-old adult, which I was not. I wasn't even a functioning 18-year-old! So I felt very inadequate, and it helped to lower my already low self-esteem. The program I attended wasn't personalized or individualized to my needs. It was the exact same for everyone, so I ended up feeling more like a number than an actual individual. (Davis & Vander Stoep, 1996, p. 85)*

In too many cases, the individualization of care to the unique needs of particular young adults or even to the needs of most young adults—a basic tenet of the ideal system—is absent.

Lack of Tested Interventions

Institutions engender mistrust. Unlike the state of care for many physical illnesses, very few demonstrably effective interventions to improve children's mental health have been developed, tested, and implemented (Kazdin & Weisz, 1998). Many families do not know this. Many caregivers whose job it is to help children with emotional or behavioral difficulties do not explain this. Thus, during years of rearing children with emotional or behavioral difficulties, most families have had their hopes raised repeatedly, only to be disappointed by the ineffective care their children receive. In this way, institutions engender mistrust and hopelessness. Under these conditions of depleted morale, families face the transition to different institutions holding even less promise for adequate support. The dreamed-of "normal life" for their children is moved even farther from their grasp.

As mentioned previously, although participation in informal community networks has been shown to affect the ability of families to navigate transition periods positively (Staff & Catron, 1986), families with children with an emotional disorder often reduce their extrafamilial contacts and roles (Mallory, 1995). Family energy becomes tied up in day-to-day survival and symptom management, so that often no time or energy is left for socializing outside the home. Furthermore, it is embarrassing to expose others to the day-to-day family dramas and face possible stigmatization. Finally, time that may have been spent developing and nurturing connections within the natural community may be overtaken by appointments and contacts with service providers. Isolated, overextended parents can be particularly overwhelmed by the additional individual and family stresses that arise during their child's transition to adulthood.

If the family succeeds in obtaining adult mental health care for their young adult child, the rules pertaining to family participation change. Once their child legally becomes an adult, legal barriers and societal traditions preclude the family from being part of or even from having access to information about the young adult's care. It is not uncommon, for example, for the family home to be designated the recommended residential placement for a young adult but for the parents to be barred from access to information regarding their child's diagnosis and recommended medication regimen. Yet, information, trust, and self-efficacy are necessary ingredients that enable families to provide appropriate advocacy and support.

As this description of developmental and institutional clashes draws to a close, imagine that you are 19, you have a mental illness, and you are being served by a transition program whose mission is "to help young adults to fulfill their dreams." As it stands, families and young adults commonly report that service systems are woefully lacking in vision, creativity, flexibility, and initiative. If "increasing numbers of children in our country are growing up under circumstances of poverty and pervasive adversity" (Jessor, 1991, p. 597) at the same time that institutions are losing their responsiveness, we, as a society, are in trouble. How are we going to revitalize our institutions, our families, and our morale to face the daunting task of building a sturdy bridge of support for the several million adolescents in the United States who are standing at the brink of young adulthood? In the introduction to their book *The Seven-Year Stretch: How Families Work Together to Grow Through Adolescence*, Kastner and Wyatt wrote:

> The seven-year period roughly corresponding with the junior high and high school years is a unique stretch of the parenting journey, which calls for an expanded repertoire of skills and new insights. No longer will a simple technique—like pulling out a popsicle—work to affect the moment positively. Because teenagers are more complex beings, parenting involves greater thoughtfulness, greater creativity, and a deeper understanding of what makes kids this age tick. (1997, p. ix)

The vignettes and studies presented in this chapter show that supporting adolescents with emotional or behavioral difficulties across the threshold into adulthood requires an even more extensive stretch on the part of families, institutions, and communities. Certainly, it will take all of the creative ideas and insights we can generate to help young adults with emotional or behavioral difficulties begin to dream again and then to fulfill their dreams.

REFERENCES

American Psychiatric Association (APA). (1994). *Diagnostic and statistical manual of mental disorders* (4th ed.). Washington, DC: Author.

Bolger, K.E., Patterson, C.J., Thompson, W.W., & Kupersmidt, J.B. (1995). Psychosocial adjustment among children experiencing persistent and intermittent family economic hardship. *Child Development, 66,* 1107–1129.

Cohen, P., Cohen, C., Kasen, S., Velez, C.N., Hartmark, C., Johnson, J., Rojas, M., Brook, J., & Streuning, E.L. (1993). An epidemiological study of disorders in late adolescence and adolescence. I. Age- and gender-specific prevalence. *Journal of Child Psychology and Psychiatry, 34,* 851–867.

Cohen, P., & Cohen, J. (1996). *Values and adolescent health.* Mahwah, NJ: Lawrence Erlbaum Associates.

Cohen, P., & Hesselbart, C. (1993). Demographic factors in the use of children's mental health services. *American Journal of Public Health, 83,* 49–52.

Cohen, P., Provet, A.G., & Jones M. (1996). Prevalence of emotional and behavioral disorders during childhood and adolescence. In B.L. Levin & J. Petrila (Eds.), *Mental health services: A public health perspective* (pp. 193–209). New York: Oxford University Press.

Costello, E.J. (1989). Development in child psychiatric epidemiology. *Journal of the American Academy of Child and Adolescent Psychiatry, 28,* 836–841.

Costello, E.J., & Janieszewski, S. (1990). Who gets treated? Factors associated with referral in children with psychiatric disorders. *Acta Psychiatrica Scandinavica, 81,* 523–529.

Damon, W. (1983). *Social and personality development.* New York: W.W. Norton.

Davis, M. (1995, March). *Mental health service utilization by transitional youth.* Paper presented at the eighth annual research conference: A System of Care for Children's Mental Health: Expanding the Research Base, Tampa, FL.

Davis, M., & Vander Stoep, A. (1996). *The transition to adulthood among adolescents who have serious emotional disturbance: At risk homelessness.* Delmar, NY: National Resource Center on Homelessness and Mental Illness.

Davis, M., & Vander Stoep, A. (1997). The transition to adulthood for youth who have serious emotional disturbance: Developmental transition and young adult outcomes. *Journal of Mental Health Administration, 24,* 400–427.

Davis, M., Yelton, S., & Katz-Levy, J. (1995). *State child and adolescent mental health: Administration, policies and laws.* Tampa: University of South Florida, Florida Mental Health Institute, Research and Training Center for Children's Mental Health.

Davis, M., Yelton, S., Katz-Levy, J., & Lourie, I. (1995). "Unclaimed children" revisited: The status of state children's mental health service systems. *Journal of Mental Health Administration, 22,* 147–166.

Erikson, E. (1968). *Identity: Youth and crisis.* New York: W.W. Norton.

Florida Department of Education. (1993). *Transition: The IDEA way.* Tallahassee: Florida Department of Education, Division of Public Schools, Bureau of Education for Exceptional Students.

Friedman, R.M., Katz-Levy, J.W., Manderscheid, R.W., & Sondheimer, D.L. (1996). Prevalence of serious emotional disturbance in children and adolescents. In R.W. Manderscheid & M.A. Sonnenschein (Eds.), *Mental health United States, 1996* (pp. 71–89). Rockville, MD: U.S. Department of Health and Human Services.

Hoberman, H. (1992). Ethnic minority status and adolescent mental health services utilization. *Journal of Mental Health Administration, 19*(3), 246–267.

Individuals with Disabilities Education Act (IDEA) Amendments of 1997, PL 105-17, 20 U.S.C. §§ 1400 *et seq.*

Individuals with Disabilities Education Act (IDEA) of 1990, PL 101-476, 20 U.S.C. §§ 1400 *et seq.*

Jessor, R. (1991). Risk behavior in adolescence: A psychological framework for understanding and action. *Journal of Adolescent Health, 12,* 597–605.

Josselson, R. (1980). Ego development in adolescence. In J. Adelson (Ed.), *Handbook of adolescent psychology.* New York: John Wiley & Sons.

Karpel, M., & Strauss, E. (1983). *Family evaluation.* New York: Gardner Press.

Kastner, L., & Wyatt, J. (1997). *The seven-year stretch: How families work together to grow through adolescence.* Boston: Houghton Mifflin.

Kazdin, A.E., & Weisz, J.R. (1998). Identifying and developing empirically supported child and adolescent treatments. *Journal of Consulting and Clinical Psychology, 66,* 19–36.

Keating, D. (1990). Adolescent thinking. In S.S. Feldman & G.R. Elliot (Eds.), *At the threshold: The developing adolescent* (p. 54–89). Cambridge, MA: Harvard University Press.

Knitzer, J. (1982). *Unclaimed children: The failure of public responsibility to children and adolescents in need of mental health services.* Washington, DC: Children's Defense Fund.

Knitzer, J. (1983). *The failure of public responsibility to children and adolescents in need of mental health services.* Washington, DC: Children's Defense Fund.

Kutash, K., Greenbaum, P., Brown, E., & Foster-Johnson, L. (1995, March). *Longitudinal outcomes for youth with severe emotional disabilities.* Paper presented at the eighth annual research conference: A System of Care for Children's Mental Health: Expanding the Research Base, Tampa, FL.

Leaf, P.J., Alegria, M., Cohen, P., Goodman, S., Horwitz, S.M., Hoven, C.W., Narrow, W.E., Vaden-Kiernan, M., & Regier, D.A. (1996). Mental health service use in the community and schools: Results from the four-community MECA study. *Journal of the American Academy of Child and Adolescent Psychiatry, 35,* 889–897.

Mallory, B.L. (1995). The role of social policy in life-cycle transition. *Exceptional Children, 62*, 213–233.

McLeod, J.D., & Shanahan, M.J. (1996). Trajectories of poverty and children's mental health. *Journal of Health and Social Behavior, 37*, 207–220.

McLoyd, V.C. (1990). The impact of economic hardship on black families and children: Psychological distress, parenting, and socioemotional development. *Child Development, 61*, 311–346.

Moffitt, T.E. (1993). Adolescence-limited and life-course-persistent antisocial behavior: A developmental taxonomy. *Psychology Review, 100*(4), 674–701.

Monroney, R.M. (1981). Public social policy: Impact on families with handicapped children. In J.L. Paul (Ed.), *Understanding and working with parents of children with special needs* (pp. 180–204). New York: Holt, Rinehart & Winston.

Pottick, K.P., Hansell, S., Guttman, E., & White, H.R. (1995). Factors associated with inpatient and outpatient treatment for children and adolescents with serious mental illness. *Journal of the American Academy of Child and Adolescent Psychiatry, 34*, 425–433.

Prange, M., Greenbaum, P., Silver, S., Friedman, R., Kutash, K., & Duchnowski, A. (1992). Family functioning and psychopathology among adolescents with severe emotional disturbances. *Journal of Abnormal Child Psychology, 20*, 83–102.

Realmuto, G.M., Bernstein, G.A., Maglothin, M.A., & Pandey, R.S. (1992). Patterns of utilization of outpatient mental health services by children and adolescents. *Hospital and Community Psychiatry, 43*, 1218–1223.

Roberts, R.E., Attkinson, C.C., & Rosenblatt, A. (1998). Prevalence of psychopathology among children and adolescents. *American Journal of Psychiatry, 155*(6), 715–725.

Rosenzweig, J.M., Brennan, E.H., & Oglivie, A.M. (1998, March). *How parents balance work and family responsibilities.* Paper presented at the eleventh annual research conference: A System of Care for Children's Mental Health: Expanding the Research Base, Tampa, FL.

Selman, R.L. (1980). *The growth of interpersonal understanding.* San Diego: Academic Press.

Silver, S. (1995, March). *How to promote (and not interfere with) effective transition.* Paper presented at the eighth annual research conference: A System of Care for Children's Mental Health: Expanding the Research Base, Tampa, FL.

Silver, S., Duchnowski, A., Kutash, K., Friedman, R., Eisen, M., Prange, M., Brandenburg, N., & Greenbaum, P. (1992). A comparison of children with serious emotional disturbance served in residential and school settings. *Journal of Child and Family Studies, 1*, 43–59.

Staff, V., & Catron, T. (1986). Networks of social supports for parents of handicapped children. In R.R. Fewell & P.F. Vadasy (Eds.), *Families of handicapped children: Needs and supports across the life span* (pp. 279–295). Austin, TX: PRO-ED.

Stroul, B., & Friedman, R. (1986). *A system of care for severely emotionally disturbed children and youth.* Washington, DC: Georgetown University, Child and Adolescent Service System Program, Technical Assistance Center.

U.S. Department of Commerce, U.S. Bureau of the Census. (1993). *Statistical abstract of the United States* (113th ed.). Washington, DC: Author.

Valdes, K., Williamson, C., & Wagner, M. (1990). *The national longitudinal transition study of special education students. Statistical Almanac: Vol. 3. Youth categorized as emotionally disturbed.* Menlo Park, CA: SRI International.

Vander Stoep, A. (1992, March). *Through the cracks: Transition to adulthood for severely psychiatrically impaired youth.* Paper presented at the fifth annual research conference: A System of Care for Children's Mental Health: Expanding the Research Base, Tampa, FL.

Vander Stoep, A. (1995, November). *Transition to adulthood: Issues of youth with mental illness.* Paper presented at the meeting of the American Public Health Association, Washington, DC.

Vander Stoep, A., Beresford, S., Weiss, N.S., McKnight, B., Cauce, A., & Cohen, P. (in press). Community-based study of the transition to adulthood for adolescents with psychiatric disorder. *American Journal of Epidemiology.*

Vander Stoep, A., Embry, L., Evens, C., Ryan, K., & Pollack, A. (1997, February). *Risk factors for homelessness in youth released from a psychiatric residential treatment facility.* Paper presented at the tenth annual research conference: A System of Care for Children's Mental Health: Expanding the Research Base, Tampa, FL.

Vander Stoep, A., & Taub, J. (1994, February). Predictors of level of functioning within diagnostic groups for transition-age youth with affective, thought, and conduct disorders. In C. Liberton, K. Kutash, & R.M. Friedman (Eds.), *The seventh annual research conference: A System of Care for Children's Mental Health: Expanding the Research Base* (pp. 323–327). Tampa: University of South Florida, Louis de la Parte Florida Mental Health Institute, Research and Training Center for Children's Mental Health.

Vander Stoep, A., Taub, J., & Holcomb, L. (1994, March). Follow-up of adolescents with severe psychiatric impairment into young adulthood. In C. Liberton, K. Kutash, & R.M. Friedman (Eds.), *The sixth annual research conference proceedings: A System of Care for Children's Mental Health: Expanding the Research Base* (pp. 373–379). Tampa: University of South Florida, Louis de la Parte Florida Mental Health Institute, Research and Training Center for Children's Mental Health.

Wagner, M., Blackorby, J., & Hebbeler, K. (1993). *Beyond the report card: The multiple dimensions of secondary school performance for students with disabilities.* Menlo Park, CA: SRI International.

Wagner, M., D'Amico, R., Marder, C., Newman, L., & Blackorby, J. (1992). *What happens next? Trends in postsecondary outcomes of youth with disabilities.* Menlo Park, CA: SRI International.

Wagner, M., Newman, L., D'Amico, R., Jay, E., Butler-Nlin, P., Marder, C., & Cox, R. (1991). *Youth with disabilities: What are they doing?* Menlo Park, CA: SRI International.

Youniss, J. (1980). *Parents and peers in social development: A Sullivan-Piaget perspective.* Chicago: University of Chicago Press.

2

A Framework for the Development and Operation of a Transition System

Hewitt B. Clark,
Nicole Deschênes, and Jeremy Jones

Youth and young adults with emotional or behavioral difficulties face a particularly challenging period in their transition from adolescence through young adulthood. Their unique behavioral or emotional challenges and possible financial hardships, family stress, limited coping and social skills, loneliness, and minimal vocational skills and employment experience create barriers that make the adjustment during this transition extremely difficult (see Chapter 1). The difficulties associated with this transition period are further complicated by the absence of services and the lack of coordination among the children's mental health, child welfare, adult mental health, education, and rehabilitation sectors (Clark & Stewart, 1992; see Chapter 13). In addition, programs that have offered support to this population of young people have traditionally limited their services to one or two areas: employment or independent living (Halpern, 1985, 1992). To improve transition outcomes for youth and young adults, these limitations need to be addressed.

The complex challenges of the transition process of these young people and their unique needs pose a major challenge to parents, practitioners, administrators, and policy makers. It also presents a

This chapter was funded in part by Grant No. 291-26290-90654 to the University of South Florida by the Florida Department of Education, Bureau of Instructional Support and Community Services. The views expressed in this chapter are not necessarily those of the Florida Department of Education.

compelling argument for designing transition systems around a solid framework of promising strategies. This chapter provides such a framework for the development and operation of community-level transition systems. Research findings regarding the values and best practices currently used by a number of promising transition programs in some communities across the United States are the basis for the guidelines presented in this chapter. It is important for the reader to remember, however, that this chapter and this book provide promising practices evolving from research and community applications but that a great deal of research is still required to further refine recommended practice and system strategies.

TRANSITION TO INDEPENDENCE PROCESS (TIP) SYSTEM

The Transition to Independence Process (TIP) system prepares and supports youth and young adults in their movement into adult roles through an individualized process that

1. Teaches community-relevant skills
2. Encourages completion of secondary education
3. Provides exposure to community-life experiences
4. Promotes movement into postschool employment, educational opportunities, living situations, and community life
5. Transcends the age barriers typical of child versus adult services
6. Respects the self-determination of young people

The TIP system promotes independence. However, the concept of interdependence is central to working effectively with young people. This concept nests the focus of independent functioning (e.g., budgeting money, maintaining a job) within the framework of young people's learning that there is a healthy, reciprocal role of supporting others and receiving support from others (i.e., a social support network for emotional, spiritual, and physical well-being).

TRANSITION PROCESS VALUES

Whether they are explicit or implicit, the values that transition staff and administrators in a service system hold determine how the program operates, and they affect features of the program such as support strategies, processes for establishing goals, focus of services, responsiveness to young people, funding plans, hiring and training of staff, and support of staff and young people. Based on an extensive review of community-based transition programs helping youth and young adults move into the world of adult responsibility, Clark, Unger, and Stewart (1993) identified program values and best practices that seem to be important in establishing quality transition programs. These transition process values are similar but not identical to those underlying the children's system of care model (Stroul & Friedman, 1986) and the wraparound process (VanDenBerg, 1993; VanDenBerg & Grealish, 1996). The transition values, which are the underpinnings of the TIP system guidelines, are evidenced in the next section.

TIP SYSTEM GUIDELINES

Six guidelines drive the development and operation of quality transition systems. These guidelines are based on studies of the best practices of transition programs for these youth and young adults (Clark & Foster-Johnson, 1996; Clark & Stewart, 1992; Clark et al., 1993); programs preparing youth for transition (Modrcin & Rutland, 1989); policy issues related to transition (Koroloff, 1990); and transition outcomes (Davis & Vander Stoep, 1996, 1997; Silver, Unger, & Friedman, 1994; Vander Stoep, Taub, & Holcomb, 1994). The following TIP system guidelines embody the underlying transition values and best practices and put them into a framework for the establishment and operation of the system. These guidelines, which have been refined from those published by Clark and Foster-Johnson (1996), are listed in Table 1 and are described in the subsections that follow.

1. **Person-Centered Planning Is Driven by the Young Person's Interests, Strengths, and Cultural and Familial Values**

Improved community outcomes for young people in transition stem from an informal and flexible planning process, driven by the young person's interests, strengths, and cultural and familial values, that allows for the formulation of the individual's goals. The TIP system uses a person-centered planning approach driven by a strength-based assessment of the young person and the young person's environmental situation.

Strength-Based Approach People tend to develop and grow based on their individual interests, aspirations, and strengths (Rapp, 1998). To enhance the young person's motivation during the transition process, a strength-based transition assessment, focused on the young person's skills, competencies, talents, and resources (as opposed to impairments, problems, or pathologies), needs to be conducted (Nelson & Pearson, 1991).

A strength-based transition assessment is a process by which the young person's personal and environmental resources (e.g., natural support system), dreams, and aspirations are explored across the domains of education, employment, living situation, and community life. Strength-based assessments permit the construction of a complete

Table 1. TIP system guidelines

---

1. *Person-centered planning is driven by the young person's interests, strengths, and cultural and familial values.*

    Strength-based approach
    Person-centered planning
    Cultural and familial factors

2. *Services and supports must be tailored for each youth individually and must encompass all transition domains.*

    Transition domains
    Individually tailored services and supports
    Community and natural supports

3. *Services and supports need to be coordinated to provide continuity from the young person's perspective.*

    Coordination of services and supports
    Transition facilitators

4. *A safety net of support is provided by the young person's team.*

    Unconditional commitment
    Hopefulness

5. *Achieving greater independence requires the enhancement of the young person's competencies.*

    Relevant and meaningful skills
    Community-based curricula and instruction
    Teaching strategies for community settings
    Self-advocacy

6. *The TIP system must be outcome driven.*

    Young adult's goals
    TIP system's effectiveness
    Process measures for TIP system improvement

---

profile of the young person and her situation during the transition process. It documents the strengths or competencies that the young person has mastered and those that need to be developed during the transition process to achieve future goals. It also allows for the use of the untapped and unsolicited resources of the young person and those of her natural support system. Strength-based assessments are empowering: They create a sense of personal accomplishment, contribute to satisfying relationships with family members, peers, and adults, and enhance one's personal, social, and academic development during a period of stress and adversity (Epstein & Sharma, 1998; Rapp, 1998; VanDenBerg & Grealish, 1996).

Person-Centered Planning   Person-centered planning has assumed major importance in the special education field and is becoming an important tenet of intervention strategies for youth and young adults during the transition process (Kincaid, 1996; Malloy, Cheney, Hagner, Cormier, & Bernstein, 1998; Menchetti & Bombay, 1994). A person-centered planning approach provides the process and structure that can assist young people in their goal planning and in the development of a means to achieve those goals across the four domains of employment, educational opportunities, living situation, and community-life adjustment. It also allows for younger adolescents (ages 14 and younger) to begin the process of putting their dreams into action, thereby increasing their chance for a successful transition (Koroloff, 1990; Modrcin & Rutland, 1989).

In a person-centered planning approach, a number of people identified as significant by the young person, such as family members, friends, schoolteachers, and athletic coaches, are brought together to help the young person dream, plan, and ultimately achieve his goals. Planning is done and decisions are made in partnership *with* the young person, not *for* him. The involvement of the young person in the planning and decision-making process is considered key to the acceptance of the transition plan and to its eventual success (Bullis & Benz, 1996; Wehmeyer & Lawrence, 1995). Indeed, when their transitions are self-determined, youth and young adults are more committed to the process, take greater ownership of its outcomes, and adjust to their new situations in a more personally meaningful and enduring way (Field & Hoffman, 1998).

Several person-centered strategies exemplify the overall person-centered approach, including Making Action Plans (MAPS; Forest & Lusthaus, 1990; Vandercook, York, & Forest, 1989), Group Action Planning (Turnbull & Turnbull, 1992), Personal Futures Planning (Mount, 1987; Mount & Zwernik, 1988), Dare to Dream (Webb, 1999), *The Real Game Series* (1996), Framework for Accomplishment/ Personal Profile (O'Brien, Mount, & O'Brien, 1991), and Essential Lifestyles Planning (Smull & Harrison, 1992). Although somewhat different, all of these models have similar components, including

1. Creation of a circle of friends or circle of support
2. Focus on talents, strengths, and interests of the individual
3. Identification of the person's dream and development of a long-term vision of what the person really wants to achieve
4. Creation of a plan of action with specific commitments for each team member
5. Empowerment of the young person in the pursuit of her goals

Other chapters in this book (see Chapters 3 and 6) provide more detailed examples of the application of person-centered planning.

Cultural and Familial Factors For the TIP personnel to serve these young people adequately, they need to be *culturally competent*, which means that they must demonstrate sensitivity and responsiveness to individual variation in gender, ethnicity, sexual orientation, social class, and other unique orientations and needs of each transitional youth or young adult and his family. Having parents actively involved in the planning process can also be extremely beneficial in capturing important ethnic and family cultural priorities. Although teenagers and parents are always a challenging mix, parents (or other family members or guardians) typically represent an essential element for the future success of these youth and young adults (Ryndak, Downing, Lilly, & Morrison, 1995). Often, young people have quite different ideas about their futures from those held by their parents. Sometimes transition personnel are able to bring these ideas closer together by working in partnership with both the young people and their parents. At other times, however, all that can be accomplished is to assist parents in understanding the developmental processes that their children will need to experience and the level of support that will be helpful to them.

2. Services and Supports Must Be Tailored for Each Youth Individually and Must Encompass All Transition Domains

Transition Domains The TIP system is comprehensive in scope, encompassing three major environment-based domains—employment, education, and living situation—as well as one community-life adjustment domain that involves the individual skills and activities that are relevant across all of the environmental domains for successful community functioning (see Figure 1 and Table 2). The TIP system provides a comprehensive array of community-based service and support options within each of these domains to accommodate the strengths, needs, and life circumstances of each young person. For example, in the employment domain, it is helpful if a system has access to a range of work opportunities with varying levels of support available, including practicum and paid work experience, transitional employment, supported employment, and competitive employment. Similarly, in the domain of community-life adjustment, supports and services may be needed by some young people for them to learn to manage their anger and function effectively in school, home, and work environments.

Individually Tailored Services and Supports Not every youth or young adult needs assistance across all of the transition domains or requires all of the services and supports related to a given domain. The objective within the TIP system is to meet the particular transitional needs of the young person, customizing the supports and services to the individual's needs and resources rather than basing them on preexisting program requirements. In other words, the types and intensity of supports and services provided during the transition process must match the particular needs and resources of the young person. For some youth, this will mean gaining access to their natural support net-

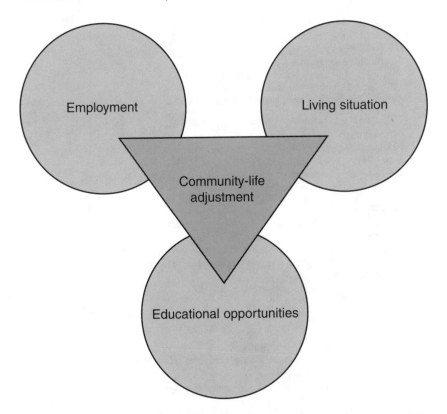

Figure 1. The four transition domains: Three major setting-based domains and one community-life adjustment domain that encompasses the skills and activities that are relevant across all of the domains. (From Clark, H.B., & Foster-Johnson, L. [1996]. Serving youth in transition to adulthood. In B.A. Stroul [Ed.], *Children's mental health: Creating systems of care in a changing society* [p. 536]. Baltimore: Paul H. Brookes Publishing Co.; adapted by permission.)

work during the transition process. It may also involve problem-solving counseling, skill development teaching, advocacy, mentoring, and/or crisis management on the part of transition personnel.

Community and Natural Supports   The TIP model encourages the linking of young people to natural supports within their home, work, school, and community environments whenever possible (Clark & Foster-Johnson, 1996). For example, a mentor might be hired to work with a young adult who needs to be guided away from a drug-involved peer group and into more community-acceptable leisure-time activities. Later, this role might be shifted to a cousin or an uncle with whom a relationship is being renewed. Youth and young adults should be taught to identify and develop use of natural supports in the transition domains of their lives.

Table 2. Components of the transition domains

Employment

Competitive employment
Transitional employment opportunities
Supported employment (individual and enclave)
Work experience opportunities (practicum and paid)

Educational opportunities (career-track training)

Bachelor's degree or beyond
Associate's degree
Vocational or technical certification
High school completion or general equivalency diploma (GED)
Workplace education programs

Living situation

Independent residence (i.e., living where, with whom)
Residing with natural, adoptive, or foster family
Other family situation (e.g., girlfriend's family, extended family)
Semi-independent living (e.g., with non–live-in service coordinator
    assistance)
Supported living (e.g., supervised apartment)
Group or boarding home
Restrictive living environment (e.g., crisis unit, residential treatment
    center, detention center)

Community-life adjustment: Skills
and activities related to functioning across all of the domains

Leisure-time activities and fun
Relationship development and maintenance (e.g., friendships, intimate
    relationships)
Social problem-solving skills (e.g., self-advocacy, assertiveness,
    compromise)
Community social support (e.g., peer groups, community
    organizations)
Emotional/behavioral management (e.g., anger control, relapse
    prevention, self-medication management, self-monitoring,
    self-control)
Safety skills (e.g., prevent victimization, avoid dangerous situations)
Daily living skills (e.g., nutrition, self-care, leasing an apartment,
    money management)
Health care and fitness (e.g., stress management, physical activity,
    health care)
Substance abuse prevention and self-management
Sex education and birth control (e.g., prevention of sexually
    transmitted diseases and unwanted pregnancies)
Parenting skills and resources
Knowledge of community resources and citizenship responsibilities
Knowledge of and access to legal services
Transportation resources and skills
Cultural and spiritual resources

From Clark, H.B., Unger, K.U., & Stewart, E.S. (1993). Transition of youth and young adults with emotional/behavior disorders into employment, education, and independent living. *Community Alternatives: International Journal of Family Care, 5*(2), 22; adapted by permission.

3. **Services and Supports Need to Be Coordinated to Provide Continuity from the Young Person's Perspective**

Coordination of Services and Supports Although the administrators of a transition system may think that their system and its components provide continuity, this attribute of the system must be judged from the "eye of the beholder," that is, the young person. *Continuity* refers to the extent to which the relevant supports and services are provided to a young person in a coordinated fashion. All too often, there is no continuity across services. For example, Jody's school guidance counselor is pushing for her to be placed in a special education program, her psychiatrist has just increased her medication for attention-deficit/hyperactivity disorder (ADHD) despite the fact that it leaves her nauseated throughout the day, her foster care caseworker is seeking to have Jody removed from her foster home of 4 years to be placed in a residential facility because she does not seem to be doing well in the foster home or in school, and Jody's teacher is advocating that she be placed in special education. Clearly, there is not a coherent, coordinated plan in place for Jody.

To ensure access to required community resources and the creation of opportunities across all of the transition domains, collaborative linkages must be established at the young person's level and at the system level. At the young person's level, the TIP system has to assume responsibility to link the young person and his family to the resources, services, and supports that are appropriate to their changing needs. Also indicative of the TIP system's promotion of the continuity of services is the provision of opportunities for young people to maintain and establish valued, positive, and lasting relationships with their natural support system.

At the system level, linkages are required with a broad array of child- and adult-serving systems. Outreach to develop networks of individuals and organizations to assist in working with a young person is also the responsibility of the TIP system. These efforts must include reaching out to ethnic communities so that culturally relevant supports are available to individuals who require them. Recommended approaches to developing these system-level collaborations are discussed under the "Organizational Issues in the Establishment and Operation of a TIP System" heading on page 44.

Transition Facilitators To ensure the coordination and continuity of services and supports, the TIP system is implemented with the assistance of transition facilitators (different sites and service systems use terms such as transition specialist, resource coordinator, life coach, mentor, transition coach, TIP facilitator, and service coordinator) who work with young people to create an array of informal and/or formal supports and services to facilitate achievement of transition goals across the transition domains. From the young person's perspective, access to a transition facilitator allows for system continuity between services that are being provided by different service providers (e.g., school, vocational rehabilitation, mental health). Transition facilitators collaborate first and foremost with the young people with whom they work and secondarily with an array of formal and informal supports relevant to these young people and their transition needs (see Table 3).

4. A Safety Net of Support Is Provided by the Young Person's Team

Unconditional Commitment VanDenBerg and Grealish (1996) defined *unconditional commitment* as never denying services because of extreme severity of disability, changing services as the needs of the child and family change, and never rejecting the child or family from services. Although the TIP team recognizes that young people 18 years or older may refuse services, team members must remain creative and determined to "stick with" them to the extent possible, adjusting services and supports to meet their changing needs.

Hopefulness Unconditional commitment is a powerful expression of the TIP staff's hopefulness and a positive affirmation of the young person's worth and merit (Deschênes & Clark, 1998). This feature is manifested by staff encouraging young people, speaking respectfully, involving youth and parents as partners, respecting youth's choices, and sharing a sense of humor. Young people should be allowed to explore their work and social identities with guidance, support, and acceptance.

Table 3. TIP facilitators collaborate with natural and formal support sources

Natural social supports

Nuclear family or relatives
Mentor from community organizations
Employers, supervisors, and co-workers
Spiritual leaders
Friends
Life mate

Formal support personnel

Service coordinators, case managers
Mentors, co-worker mentors
Teachers, guidance counselors
Employment specialists, job coaches
Job developers
Vocational rehabilitation specialists
School-based transition specialists
Postsecondary education liaisons
Behavior specialists, applied behavior analysts
Mental health counselors and therapists
Psychologists and psychiatrists
Foster care parents and caseworkers
Juvenile justice after-care counselors, probation or parole officers

5. **Achieving Greater Independence Requires the Enhancement of the Young Person's Competencies**

Relevant and Meaningful Skills Competence in a variety of skills is necessary for successful entry into the workplace and independent community living. In a TIP system, skill development means teaching skills that equip youth with the competencies to meet the demands they will encounter upon leaving home, school, and residential environments and should occur in education, work, and living environments within the young person's community. The identification and development of skills are aided by functional assessment, instructional efforts, and curriculum activities focusing on teaching these necessary skills (e.g., budgeting of personal earnings, completion of job applications, anger management, vocational skills) in a context that is meaningful and relevant to the young person (Bullis, Nishoka-Evans, Fredericks, & Davis, 1993; Dunlap, Kern-Dunlap, Clarke, & Robbins, 1991; Horner, Sprague, & Flannery, 1993; O'Neill et al., 1997; Unger, 1994). The application of functional assessment and instruction within group and community settings is described in greater detail in Chapter 6.

Community-Based Curricula and Instruction Creative teachers can make their classroom instruction more community-relevant to students by 1) bringing real-life stimulus materials into their classrooms (e.g., set up student bank accounts), 2) building on young people's preferences and interests in the assignments, and 3) providing youth with effective individualized instruction to teach skills that are relevant to their daily lives. Researchers have found that youth taught with these instruction strategies tend to increase their ability to acquire the necessary skills, become more motivated to learn new skills, generalize learning to other settings, and decrease their problem behaviors (Dyer, Dunlap, & Winterling, 1991; Elliott, Sheridan, Gresham, & Knoff, 1989; Foster-Johnson, Ferro, & Dunlap, 1994; Van Reusen & Bos, 1994). Such strategies can also lead to increased graduation rates for these youth (Frank, Sitlington, & Carson, 1991).

Concrete actions and practice opportunities in real-life daily environments are particularly important for students with emotional or behavioral challenges because many of them have had extremely poor experiences related to traditional classroom instruction (Knitzer, Steinberg, & Fleisch, 1990; Wehman, 1997). In a community-based instruction model, teachers and other transition practitioners work in collaboration to teach selected academic, vocational, and functional life skills in natural community environments, such as worksites, general schools, homes, shopping malls, and recreation areas. Community-based learning is also an interesting means for these students to earn high school credits toward graduation while acquiring relevant experience (Cheney, Hagner, Malloy, Cormier, & Bernstein, 1998).

Teaching Strategies for Community Settings Transition facilitators and other personnel working with transition-age youth and young adults need to be effective teachers as well as counselors, service brokers, collaborators, and mentors. As teachers, they need to be able to recognize "opportunities to teach." This component of teaching is illustrated through a staff training series that the lead author conducted for a new group of five transition facilitators, members of a transition group formed in a large metropolitan area to serve young adults with serious mental health needs. This consultant spent extensive time in the field shadowing facilitators and their young adults during activities in community settings. One of the many occasions that exemplified the need to recognize *opportunities to teach* came when Martha (a facilitator) picked up Rhonda from school to go to a doctor's appointment. Rhonda had missed one of her periods and was concerned that she might be pregnant. Martha conducted some good counseling and problem solving, incorporating humor to soften some of the sensitive issues, while driving to the doctor's office. As they walked into the six-story medical complex, Martha found the building directory and the doctor's suite number, led Rhonda to the elevator, punched the fourth floor button, and, after finding the doctor's suite, announced that Rhonda was here for her checkup.

What a lost opportunity—an opportunity to assess and teach Rhonda how to negotiate a large medical or business complex and obtain required services. These "in situation" opportunities are ideal for assessing an individual's competencies and for providing highly effective teaching. This group of transition facilitators talked "independence" but often missed important opportunities to assess and/or teach community-relevant skills. After a miniworkshop on this issue and some additional field shadowing across the facilitators, they became more effective teachers.

Seasoned transition facilitators operate by two axioms that guide their daily teaching, counseling, and relationship development practices in the field:

1. Maximize the individual's likelihood of success.
2. Allow the individual contact with the natural consequences of life experience.

Facilitators, guided by these axioms, use mentoring, teaching of skills, contingency contracting, counseling, and problem solving to maximize the likelihood of their youth succeeding while recognizing the powerful role that life experience plays in teaching young people through their successes and failures. It may be that a young adult has gone through two social skills training groups, but it is only after being fired from his third job that there is any receptivity to learning how to follow instructions and to problem-solve with authority figures.

In their teaching role, transition facilitators create practice opportunities through simulated situations (e.g., behavioral rehearsal) as well as in natural situations and environments. Facilitators, through their relationship with young people, can serve to reinforce their use of new skills and progress on goals. Skill acquisition and maintenance requires that young people be reinforced in the use of these skills in appropriate situations through social praise, recognition, tangible reinforcers, and natural consequences in community settings. When teaching encompasses these types of "maintenance" or "generalization" strategies (e.g., practice in a variety of settings with various people and situations present, gradually phasing out training from the natural setting, booster training sessions), the acquisition of new skills occurs and the use of these over time and across settings is enhanced (Kazdin, Bass, Siegel, & Thomas, 1989; Lochman, 1992).

Self-Advocacy   One of the goals that is pursued with young people is to assist them in becoming empowered to address and advocate for solutions to issues related to their rights and needs and the provision of essential services and supports. Transition facilitators need to work with the youth to teach and encourage self-advocacy. The facilitators and other personnel involved with the young people provide frequent opportunities for them to express their preferences through choices, decision making, and self-advocacy. An important goal is that young people learn to speak on their own behalf and to gradually assume responsibility for their own futures.

6. The TIP System Must Be Outcome Driven

Young Adult's Goals   The five guidelines discussed previously involve processes that can assist youth and young adults in achieving successful outcomes across the transition domains. For each transition goal established by the young person and his planning team, written measurable objectives should be established so that progress on individualized goals and successes can be tracked over time. For example, Sasha, at $15^1/_2$ years old, may be interested in getting an after-school or weekend job at a veterinarian's office. She and her team may establish four related goals to be completed by the time she is 16 and eligible to work: 1) Sasha will be able to complete job applications with all essential information being 100% accurate across four different forms of applications, 2) Sasha will be able to correctly recognize and label the 25 most common types of dogs and cats from pictures and from viewing them at pet stores, 3) Sasha will complete three consecutive role-play interviews at school and two in the field using at least 90% of the interviewee components, and 4) Sasha will secure at least two interviews with veterinarians.

TIP System's Effectiveness The TIP system's effectiveness should also be assessed. Table 4 provides an overview of TIP system objectives that reflect the types of goal areas that individuals are working on and the transition domain outcomes that the TIP system is attempting to achieve. The effectiveness of the system can be assessed through key outcome indicators that are based on the young adult's outcomes in the four transition domains. For example, aggregation of data regarding individuals' employment goals allows for determination of the percentage of young people who 1) are employed part time and full time, 2) are earning a particular wage per hour, 3) have employer-paid benefits, and 4) are in a job that is on a career track that the young person wants to pursue. These types of key outcome indicators, if tracked over an extended period of time, can provide stakeholders and policy makers with valuable information on the effectiveness of the TIP system.

Table 4. TIP system objectives

The TIP system aims to achieve better transition outcomes across the domains of employment, education, living situation, and community-life adjustment:

Employment
- Employment stability (staying employed, planned changes versus firings and walkouts)
- Wage per hour increases over time
- Career-track–type jobs versus entry-level jobs only
- Benefits increase over time

Education
- High school completion or general equivalency diploma (GED)
- Postsecondary education or training (enrollment and/or degrees or certificates)

Living situation
- Housing arrangement (type of setting: typical home-type environment)
- Stability in housing location (planned moves versus evictions and fleeing to avoid rent)
- Stability in living with a preferred person(s)
- Restrictive placements (e.g., number of days in crisis unit, treatment center, jail)

Community-life adjustment
- Engagement with community (frequency and satisfaction)
- Leisure-time and recreation activities
- Attend community organization activities, support groups, volunteerism
- Daily living skills to function in living environment and other relevant community environments
- Degree to which one can manage budgeting of personal income
- Mobility to gain access to community environments of relevance
- Social support network, friendship contacts (frequency and satisfaction)
- Family/relative contacts (frequency and satisfaction)
- Primary relationship (stability over time and satisfaction)
- Risk behaviors' decreasing over time (substance abuse, violence, criminal activities, arrests, human immunodeficiency virus [HIV] infection risk behaviors [unprotected sex outside long-term primary relationship, injecting illegal drugs, teen pregnancies of girls or fathering a teen pregnancy])
- Public aid support decreasing over time (Temporary Assistance for Needy Families, food stamps, Medicaid, general assistance, housing subsidy)

Transition progress across the domains can be assessed periodically through the use of the Community Adjustment Rating of Transition Success (CARTS) Progress Tracker (Clark, Knapp, & Corbett, 1997). The CARTS Progress Tracker is used to 1) track the progress of youth and young adults (14–28 years of age) into greater independence and 2) provide transition programs with data that may assist program managers in improving the quality and effectiveness of their programs. The CARTS Progress Tracker assesses a young person's progress across the domains of employment, education, living situation, and community-life adjustment. The community-life adjustment domain includes skill competencies, antisocial behavior, and community involvement (e.g., contact with friends, social supports sources, leisure-time recreation activities). The CARTS Progress Tracker also captures satisfaction ratings from a young person regarding his satisfaction with his circumstances. It can also be used to determine the services received and the young person's satisfaction with these services. The CARTS Progress Tracker was designed to be used with each young person at set intervals of every 3 months (by telephone or in-person interviews) to track his progress before, during, and after exposure to his individually tailored TIP program. (For information regarding the CARTS Progress Tracker, refer to the following World Wide Web site: http://www.fmhi.usf.edu/cfs/policy/tip/tiphp.htm.)

Process Measures for TIP System Improvement Unless the TIP values, practices, and guidelines are incorporated adequately, individual and systemic outcomes will never be achieved. Thus, measures of process implementation for system improvement assist stakeholders by providing them with a periodic check of the state of the TIP system's responsiveness in the provision of quality services and supports.

The TIP Case Study Protocol for Continuing System Improvement (Deschênes, Gomez, & Clark, 1999) can be used to assist stakeholders in establishing a profile of the system's areas of strengths and weaknesses. This protocol uses multiple sources of information (e.g., the young person, a family member, a teacher, the transition facilitator, a service provider, record review) to document various components of the transition process (e.g., strengths, needs, transition planning, coordination, supports and services provided, gaps in support/service provision, effectiveness, satisfaction) in a particular environment (e.g., school, school district, community, region). The information provided through the TIP Case Study analysis can be used by administrators, staff, and other interested stakeholders to recognize the strengths of the TIP system and to set the occasion for making modifications to further enhance the service system. (For additional information regarding the

TIP Case Study Protocol for Continuing System Improvement, refer to the following World Wide Web site: http://www.fmhi.usf.edu/cfs/policy/tip/tiphp.htm)

ORGANIZATIONAL ISSUES IN THE ESTABLISHMENT AND OPERATION OF A TIP SYSTEM

TIP Community Steering Committee

The TIP Community Steering Committee serves either as the governing authority or in an advisory capacity for the implementation and operation of the TIP system. The committee assists in the identification of successes and barriers in the TIP system and advises on possible solutions. The Steering Committee representatives also assist in the education of the community regarding the TIP system and promote its acceptance to facilitate a broadening of support for its goals and resources to support its activities, such as access to additional business sites for competitive employment. It also serves in an outreach capacity to strengthen the interagency and community network to improve the availability of and access to transition services and supports appropriate to these youth and young adults.

The TIP Community Steering Committee should be composed of an ethnically diverse membership of representatives from service sectors such as child and adult mental health, public school district, vocational rehabilitation, child welfare, juvenile justice, corrections/probation, housing, homeless/runaway centers, and community colleges. It is also important to involve representatives from consumer and parent advocacy organizations and to include community leaders from corporations and other organizations such as the private industry council, the chamber of commerce, community service organizations, and governmental agencies.

Resource Development

Environmental resources required for young people to achieve their transitional goals across the four transition domains need to be in place within the community. Table 5 lists the employment and educational access and supports that the TIP system should cultivate within the community. These resources need to be provided in full-inclusion environments that allow young people to function alongside individuals without disabilities. It is indeed critical that these youth be offered the same opportunities as their peers to obtain employment with full benefits, to enter postsecondary education programs, and to contribute to community life as active, participatory citizens. To that effect, a number of transition programs are developing contractual agreements with local businesses and companies to provide worksites for internships, training, and employment. Other examples of improving access to community resources include assisting youth and young adults in pursuing their educational goals in general high schools, vocational schools, or community colleges and universities or in facilitating the achievement of their living situation goals, such as moving into an apartment with a roommate of their choice.

At the community system level, there is a need to establish extensive ties and partnerships with child mental health, adult mental health, vocational rehabilitation, and community college, as well as with private sector business and industry to gain access to internships, job training, and employment. At the regional and/or state level, mechanisms may also be required for coordinating policies, interdepartmental resources, and funding streams and for resolving some issues that cannot be dealt with at the local level (Koroloff, 1990).

Table 5. Facilitating access to natural environments

Employment Access

Work experience
    School/program-based practica (credits or wages)
    School/program-sponsored employment
    Summer youth employment
    Transitional worksites
    Competitive employment (supported or independent)

Employment supports
    Remote guidance with young person regarding work activities
    Consultation with employer and supervisor
    Training of co-worker mentor to provide worksite support of young person
    Transition facilitator or employment specialist providing worksite training with the young person regarding job tasks and/or emotional/behavioral self-management
    Job development
        Employer networks
        Job analysis (position requirements, applicant's skills)
        Job carving (e.g., youth crew to load/unload shipments so other skilled workers are not taken away from production duties)

Education Access

Vocational education tracks
    Community-relevant skills
    Prevocational and vocational skills
    Career-oriented versus job-oriented tracks
    Workplace math and English skills
    Job market assessment

Supported education
    Tutorial supports
    Career guidance
    Technical/trade schools
    Community college and beyond

TIP Facilitator Group

Some agencies or communities establish the TIP system by combining several existing personnel lines and/or through the funding of additional personnel lines. When several transition facilitators are in place, it may be advantageous to organize them into a TIP facilitator group. A TIP facilitator group is typically composed of approximately five TIP facilitators and a group supervisor (half-time supervisory and half-time caseload responsibilities). The group serves approximately 28 youth and young adults in *active coaching* status at any one time (i.e., individuals requiring in-person contact daily or every couple of days). Other individuals being served would be in a *maintenance coaching* status requiring one to four in-person contacts per month or in a *follow-along* status with contacts by telephone or in person once per month to once every 3 months. Most groups also have a psychologist, a psychiatrist, a nurse, and peer counselors as part-time members of the TIP facilitator group or available on a consultative or as-needed basis.

The TIP caseload can be assigned to individual facilitators or to the full group of facilitators, with different facilitators seeing a given young person on different days. The one-to-one facilitator–youth assignment may promote relationship development but may also have a negative side effect of maintaining a dependence on one person. Some TIP facilitator groups find that a facilitator–youth rotation system promotes less dependency on the part of the young people and a fairer distribution of the workload and allows for youth to select a facilitator to assist with certain activities (e.g., a female may feel uncomfortable going to a doctor's appointment with a male facilitator). Irrespective of the type of facilitator–youth assignment, the entire TIP facilitator group must have the means to ensure that all of its facilitators are acquainted with all of the young people and their current goals, progress, and any anticipated areas of difficulty. The group shares back-up and on-call responsibilities that can be accomplished only if all of the facilitators have a current knowledge of each young person.

As the facilitators and TIP team members (in collaboration with the young people) are successful in addressing critical transition domain needs, the young people should gradually assume more responsibilities in their plan. As this occurs, they move into a maintenance versus active coaching status. During maintenance, however, the facilitators and team members continue regularly scheduled tracking and monitoring of the individuals to work with the young people to prevent or remediate new or recurring serious problems.

The number of young people assigned per facilitator varies somewhat across programs. Generally, programs have found that a transition facilitator can serve a maximum of 15 young people, with one third being in each of the status categories (i.e., active coaching, maintenance coaching, follow-along) as described previously. The following are some of the factors that may influence caseload assignments across programs:

1. Location of the majority of the young people (e.g., at two schools versus scattered throughout a large area of the community or rural environment)
2. Severity level of behavioral or emotional difficulties
3. Degree of stability in their home, school, and/or employment placements
4. Role of the facilitator as a "primary provider of services" versus being able to serve as a "broker" for many of the required services

The fourth factor is in turn influenced by the availability of relevant supports and services in the community and the amount of flexible funds available to the program.

Some groups find it helpful to have each of the facilitators serve as the "expert" or "liaison" in areas such as job development, housing options, or Social Security benefits. For example, the "liaison" in housing would learn about gaining access to and funding of housing options and would develop working relationships with relevant contacts within organizations such as the local housing authority and the homeless/runaway shelter. The TIP groups function under the system guidelines summarized previously. (For more detail regarding TIP organizational and coordination features, see Chapters 6, 8, and 10.)

Whether the facilitator group is established as a formal or an informal organizational feature may not be as important as ensuring that facilitators have a source of mutual support. They have extremely demanding positions, with daily challenges in their work with young people and the related systems. The ability of facilitators to function competently with unconditional commitment and hopefulness requires that they be provided adequate leadership, consultation, and continuing education and be supported by their associates and administrators. Additional information regarding transition issues is available from the University of South Florida World Wide Web site at http://www.fmhi.usf.edu/cfs/policy/tip/tiphp.htm.

CONCLUSIONS

This chapter provided a framework for the development, expansion, and operation of a TIP system. It is based on research and studies of the best practices of transition programs for youth and young adults with emotional or behavioral difficulties. As discussed, the transition system must be value driven, with policies and procedures that provide a framework that supports the practices and efforts of the TIP facilitators in facilitating the individual goals of their young people. The next chapters in this book present the current best practices in transition efforts with regard to the operation of each component of the TIP system.

REFERENCES

Bullis, M., & Benz, M. (1996). *Effective secondary/transition programs for adolescents with behavioral disorders.* Arden Hills, MN: Behavioral Institute for Children and Adolescents.

Bullis, M., Nishoka-Evans, V., Fredericks, H.D.B., & Davis, C. (1993). Identifying and assessing the job-related social skills of adolescents and young adults with emotional and behavioral disorders. *Journal of Emotional and Behavioral Disorders, 1,* 236–250.

Cheney, D., Hagner, D., Malloy, J., Cormier, G., & Bernstein, S. (1998). Transition to adulthood for students with serious mental illness: Initial results of Project RENEW. *Career Development of Exceptional Individuals, 21,* 17–32.

Clark, H.B., & Foster-Johnson, L. (1996). Serving youth in transition to adulthood. In B.A. Stroul (Ed.), *Children's mental health: Creating systems of care in a changing society* (pp. 533–551). Baltimore: Paul H. Brookes Publishing Co.

Clark, H.B., Knapp, K.S., & Corbett, W. (1997). *Community Adjustment Rating of Transition Success: CARTS Progress Tracker.* Tampa: University of South Florida, Louis de la Parte Florida Mental Health Institute, Department of Child and Family Studies.

Clark, H.B., & Stewart, E.S. (1992). Transition into employment, education, and independent living: A survey of programs serving youth and young adults with emotional/behavioral disorders. In K. Kutash, C.J. Liberton, A. Algarin, & R.M. Friedman (Eds.), *Proceedings of the fifth annual conference: A System of Care for Children's Mental Health: Expanding the Research Base* (pp. 189–198). Tampa: University of South Florida, Louis de la Parte Florida Mental Health Institute.

Clark, H.B., Unger, K.V., & Stewart, E.S. (1993). Transition of youth and young adults with emotional/behavioral disorders into employment, education, and independent living. *Community Alternatives: International Journal of Family Care, 5*(2), 20–46.

Davis, M., & Vander Stoep, A. (1996). *The transition to adulthood among adolescents who have serious emotional disturbance.* Report prepared for the National Resource Center on Homelessness and Mental Illness Policy Research Associates, Delmar, NY.

Davis, M., & Vander Stoep, A. (1997). The transition to adulthood among children and adolescents who have serious emotional disturbance: Part I. Developmental transitions. *Journal of Mental Health Administration, 24*(4), 400–427.

Deschênes, N., & Clark, H.B. (1998). Seven best practices in transition programs for youth. *Reaching Today's Youth, 2,* 44–48.

Deschênes, N., Gomez, A., & Clark, H.B. (1999). *TIP Case Study Protocol for Continuing System Improvement.* Tampa: University of South Florida, Louis de la Parte Florida Mental Health Institute, Department of Child and Family Studies.

Dunlap, G., Kern-Dunlap, L., Clarke, S., & Robbins, R.F. (1991). Functional assessment, curricular revision, and severe behavior problems. *Journal of Applied Behavior Analysis, 24,* 387–397.

Dyer, K., Dunlap, G., & Winterling, V. (1991). Effects of choice making on the serious problem behaviors of students with severe handicaps. *Journal of Applied Behavior Analysis, 23,* 515–524.

Elliott, S.N., Sheridan, S.M., Gresham, F.M., & Knoff, H.M. (1989). Assessing and treating social skills deficits: A case study for the scientist-practitioner. *Journal of School Psychology, 27,* 197–222.

Epstein, M.H., & Sharma, J.M. (1998). *Behavioral and Emotional Rating Scale: A strength-based approach to assessment.* Austin, TX: PRO-ED.

Field, S., & Hoffman, A. (1998). Self-determination: An essential element of successful transitions. *Reaching Today's Youth, 2,* 37–40.

Forest, M., & Lusthaus, E. (1990). Everyone belongs with MAPS action planning system. *Teaching Exceptional Children, 22,* 32–35.

Foster-Johnson, L., Ferro, J., & Dunlap, G. (1994). Preferred curricular activities and reduced problem behaviors in students with intellectual disabilities. *Journal of Applied Behavior Analysis, 27*(3), 493–504.

Frank, A.R., Sitlington, P.L., & Carson, R. (1991). Transition of adolescents with behavior disorders: Is it successful? *Behavioral Disorders, 16*(3), 180–191.

Halpern, A. (1985). Transition: A look at the foundations. *Exceptional Children, 57,* 479–486.

Halpern, A. (1992). Transition: Old wine in new bottles. *Exceptional Children, 58,* 202–211.

Horner, R.H., Sprague, J.R., & Flannery, K.B. (1993). Building functional curricula for students with severe intellectual disabilities. In R. Van Houten & S. Axelrod (Eds.), *Behavior analysis and treatment* (pp. 47–71). New York: Plenum Press.

Kazdin, A.E., Bass, D., Siegel, T., & Thomas, C. (1989). Cognitive-behavioral therapy and relationship therapy in the treatment of children referred for antisocial behavior. *Journal of Consulting and Clinical Psychology, 57*(4), 522–535.

Kincaid, D. (1996). Person-centered planning. In L.K. Koegel, R.L. Koegel, & G. Dunlap (Eds.), *Positive behavioral support: Including people with difficult behavior in the community* (pp. 439–465). Baltimore: Paul H. Brookes Publishing Co.

Knitzer, J., Steinberg, Z., & Fleisch, B. (1990). *At the schoolhouse door: An examination of programs and policies for children with behavioral and emotional problems.* New York: Bank Street College of Education.

Koroloff, N.M. (1990). Moving out: Transition policies for youth with serious emotional disabilities. *Journal of Mental Health Administration, 17,* 78–86.

Lochman, J.E. (1992). Cognitive behavioral intervention with aggressive boys: Three year follow-up and preventive effects. *Journal of Consulting and Clinical Psychology, 60*(3), 426–432.

Malloy, J., Cheney, D., Hagner, D., Cormier, G.M., & Bernstein, S. (1998). Personal futures planning for youth with EBD. *Reaching Today's Youth, 2,* 25–29.

Menchetti, B., & Bombay, H. (1994). Facilitating community inclusion with vocational assessment portfolios. *Assessment in Rehabilitation and Exceptionality, 1,* 213–222.

Modrcin, M.J., & Rutland, A.C. (1989). Youth in transition: A summary of service components. *Psychosocial Rehabilitation Journal, 12,* 3–13.

Mount, B. (1987). *Personal futures planning: Finding directions for change* (Doctoral dissertation, University of Georgia). Ann Arbor, MI: UMI Dissertation Information Services.

Mount, B., & Zwernik, K. (1988). *It's never too early, it's never too late: A booklet about personal futures planning* (Publication No. 421-88-109). St. Paul, MN: Metropolitan Council.

Nelson, C.M., & Pearson, C.A. (1991). *Integrating services for children and youth with emotional and behavioral disorders.* Reston, VA: Council for Exceptional Children.

O'Brien, J., Mount, B., & O'Brien, C. (1991). *Framework for accomplishment: Personal profile.* Decatur, GA: Responsive Systems Associates.

O'Neill, R.E., Horner, R.H., Albin, R.W., Sprague, J.R., Storey, K., & Newton, J.S. (1997). *Functional assessment and program development for problem behavior: A practical handbook.* Pacific Grove, CA: Brooks/Cole.

Rapp, C.A. (1998). *The strengths model: Case management with people suffering from severe and persistent mental illness.* New York: Oxford University Press.

Ryndak, D., Downing, J., Lilly, J.R., & Morrison, A. (1995). Parents' perceptions after inclusion of their children with moderate or severe disabilities. *Journal of The Association for Persons with Severe Handicaps, 20,* 147–157.

Silver, S., Unger, K., & Friedman, R. (1994). *Transition to young adulthood among youth with emotional disturbances* (Report No. 839). Tampa: University of South Florida, Louis de la Parte Florida Mental Health Institute, Research and Training Center for Children's Mental Health.

Smull, M.W., & Harrison, S.B. (1992). *Supporting people with severe retardation in the community.* Alexandria, VA: National Association of State Mental Retardation Program Directors.

Stroul, B., & Friedman, R.A. (1986). *A system of care for severely emotionally disturbed children and youth.* Washington, DC: Georgetown University, Child Development Center, Child and Adolescent Service System Program (CASSP), Technical Assistance Center.

The Real Game Series. (1996). St. Joseph, New Brunswick, Canada: Robinson and Blackmore Publishing.

Turnbull, A., & Turnbull, R. (1992, Fall/Winter). Group action planning (GAP). *Families and Disabilities Newsletter.*

Unger, K. (1994). Access to educational programs and its effect on employability. *Psychosocial Rehabilitation Journal, 17*(3), 117–126.

Van Reusen, A.K., & Bos, C.S. (1994). Facilitating student participation in individualized education programs through motivation strategy instruction. *Exceptional Children, 60,* 466–475.

VanDenBerg, J. (1993). Integration of individualized mental health services into the system of care for children and adolescents. *Administration and Policy in Mental Health, 20*(4), 247–257.

VanDenBerg, J., & Grealish, M. (1996). Individualized services and supports through the wraparound process: Philosophy and procedures. *Journal of Child and Family Studies, 5,* 7–12.

Vander Stoep, A., Taub, J., & Holcomb, L. (1994). Follow-up of adolescents with severe psychiatric impairment into young adulthood. In C.J. Liberton, K. Kutash, & R.M. Friedman (Eds.), *Proceedings of the sixth annual conference: A System of Care for Children's Mental Health: Expanding the Research Base* (pp. 373–380). Tampa: University of South Florida, Louis de la Parte Florida Mental Health Institute.

Vandercook, T., York, J., & Forest, M. (1989). The McGill Action Planning System (MAPS): A strategy for building the vision. *Journal of The Association for Persons with Severe Handicaps, 14,* 205–215.

Webb, K., Repetto, J., Beutel, A., Perkins, D., Bailey, M., Schwartz, S.E., Perry, L.J., & Tucker, V.L. (1999). *Dare to dream: A guide to planning your future.* Tallahassee: Transition Center, Florida Department of Education.

Wehman, P. (1997). *Life beyond the classroom: Transition strategies for young people with disabilities* (2nd ed.). Baltimore: Paul H. Brookes Publishing Co.

Wehmeyer, M.L., & Lawrence, M. (1995). Whose future is it anyway? Promoting student involvement in transition planning. *Career Development of Exceptional Individuals, 18*(2), 68–84.

II

Transition System

*Recommended Strategies and Practices
to Facilitate Success Across Domains*

3

Secondary and Postsecondary Education

New Strategies for Achieving Positive Outcomes

Doug Cheney,
Jennifer Martin, and Ernie Rodriguez

It has been well documented that youth with emotional or behavioral difficulties face significant challenges as they make the transition from high school to adulthood. This diverse group of young people drop out or "age out" of high school at high rates (Cheney & Harvey, 1994; Malmgren, Edgar, & Neel, 1998; Wagner, D'Amico, Marder, Newman, & Blackorby, 1992), have limited enrollment in postsecondary education programs (Frank, Sitlington, & Carson 1991; Malmgren et al., 1998; Neel, Meadows, Levine, & Edgar, 1988), and experience difficulty with obtaining stable employment (Bullis, Nishoka-Evans, Fredericks, & Davis, 1993; D'Amico & Marder, 1991). These young people have limited success in completing high school, whether they receive their education in self-contained programs (Mattison & Felix, 1997) or in general education classrooms (60% dropout rate) (Cullinan, Epstein, & Sabornie, 1992). Despite the best efforts of often dedicated staff and administrators, services at the secondary level typically fail to meet the needs of students and their families in areas essential to successful outcomes in education and employment.

Regarding students at the secondary education level, Unger noted,

> Adolescents with severe emotional disturbances [SED] are often seen as the "difficult" students and are dealt with as disciplinary cases. Although they may create problems in the learning environment, programs that provide personal support, opportunities to build self esteem, and to learn, based on the student's interests and abilities have been successful. (1994, p. 13)

In addition, greater links need to be made between secondary and postsecondary education programs if these young adults are to improve their outcomes in the community (Cheney, Malloy, & Hagner, 1998; Malmgren et al., 1998). As Unger also noted,

> Recent programs that provide support services in the college/ university/technical school environment have shown that youth with mental illness can be successful in the post-secondary environment. Services include tutoring, reasonable accommodations, skill teaching, symptom management, peer counseling, personal support, and mental health services. These services ... should also be available to students with SED at the secondary level. While some of those services are available at the secondary level, most youth with SED do not receive them. (1994, p. 14)

To comply with the Individuals with Disabilities Education Act (IDEA) Amendments of 1997 (PL 105-17), transition planning for students 14 years of age and older should include services relevant to individual students' future goals across the transition domains. In particular, the 1997 IDEA Amendments require that youth with disabilities participate in their own transition planning and that this planning involve representatives from relevant community agencies. The benefit of this federal legislation is that students are encouraged to enter into a discussion of their own transition needs and to offer their statement of vocational preferences, interests, and goals, including their planned course of study.

In addition, effective transition planning should consider the importance of community-based services such as work-based learning as a means to earn high school credits toward graduation (Benz, Yovanoff, & Doren, 1997; Bullis et al., 1993; Cheney, Hagner, Malloy, Cormier, & Bernstein, 1998). Frank and colleagues (1991) suggested that alternative vocational training options are required to increase graduation rates for these youth. These authors also recommended a variety of career and/or vocational programming options, including both classroom- and community-based experiences. Furthermore, linkage to postsecondary education must be emphasized to enhance adult earnings and engagement rates in productive community activities (Carson, Sitlington, & Frank, 1995; Malmgren et al., 1998). To improve this transition, Carson and colleagues (1995) recommended continued system reform in secondary programs so that these students learn the necessary skills to become employed, bridge their high school programs to post-secondary education, receive assistance in finding and maintaining housing, and become more integrated into their local communities.

When such changes are accomplished, these young adults signifi-cantly improve their position in the work force (Hagner, Cheney, & Malloy, 1999). Because the relationship between education and lifetime earnings is well established (Murphy & Welch, 1989), improving edu-cational opportunities for these young people is essential. Involvement in postsecondary education becomes a vehicle to improve the individ-ual's preparation for work and enhance his or her earning power. With fewer than 25% of these young adults enrolled in postsecondary pro-grams, however, the gap in employment and earnings between young people with emotional or behavioral difficulties and young people without these difficulties continues to widen. In essence, these youth reach an employment ceiling prematurely when their involvement in postsecondary learning is curtailed (Blackorby & Wagner, 1996).

The purpose of this chapter is to provide an overview of two inno-vative school-based programs that are beginning to demonstrate positive outcomes for young adults with emotional or behavioral difficulties in the areas of education, employment, and community adjustment. In gen-eral, the approaches described are intended to be both corrective and pre-ventative. These approaches assist in the development of new skills to improve effective transition to an early adult role. In addition, they sup-port positive involvement in social services, such as mental health and vocational rehabilitation services, as well as help these youth and young adults avert involvement in the criminal justice system. Without effective intervention, many of these individuals are likely to become incarcerated and to require extensive support from mental health and other social services systems as they move into adulthood (see Chapter 1).

Support for the strategies used by the two programs reviewed in this chapter comes not only from outcome data but also from the qual-itative experience of young people themselves. This chapter presents the perspective of program participants, in their own words, to facili-tate understanding of the impact of these service support processes. The programs that are reviewed, including initial outcomes and strate-gies, are Project RENEW in Manchester, New Hampshire, and Stepping Stones to Success in San Mateo County, California. Although neither of these programs is situated in an inclusive high school class-room environment, the principles and practices that drive their success are directly applicable to all education environments. These issues are discussed later in this chapter.

PROJECT RENEW

Project RENEW (Rehabilitation, Education, Natural Supports, Empowerment, and Work) is based at New Hampshire Community and Technical College and emphasizes four main goals for its participants: 1) high school completion, 2) continuing and postsecondary education, 3) employment, and 4) community adjustment. Young people between the ages of 16 and 22 who have received special education services and a label of SED from their school district or are diagnosed with a chronic mental illness by a mental health clinic agree to enroll voluntarily in Project RENEW. During the first year of Project RENEW, 17 youth with an average age of 18 years, 11 months were enrolled, including 12 males and 5 females; all were European Americans. At the time of enrollment, six participants (35%) had completed high school or had obtained a general equivalency diploma (GED), and only two participants (12%) were working. Many of the students who enrolled in Project RENEW had little interest in returning to their local high school program, and their first major task was to develop a course of study to earn the necessary credits for high school completion.

Education programs were developed for 11 of the 17 students to earn credits toward high school completion or to prepare for the GED examination. Within 18 months, 7 of these 11 youth were able to successfully complete their high school or general equivalency programs. Of the four young people who did not complete their programs, three were taking classes to complete high school completion requirements or to take the GED examination by June 1998, and one had no plan for high school completion. Thus, 16 of 17 Project RENEW participants (94%) completed high school or the GED program or were expected to complete high school or to receive the GED within the first 2 years of the start of the project.

Developing Education Programs

The positive educational outcomes attained by these students were accomplished by 1) altering conventional academics- and career-oriented secondary education, 2) expanding the curriculum to include the entire community, and 3) linking all of the possible education environments in the area. Project RENEW's education program, therefore, has a continuum ranging from classes to earn a general education diploma to experiences in community-based environments that allow individuals to earn credit toward adult basic education diplomas. This approach requires the students to collaborate with work-based and school-based instructors and tutors to achieve the educational goals as outlined in their education programs. These goals are developed through a process known as

Personal Futures Planning, which includes a realistic assessment of the youth's social, emotional, academic, and physical functioning. The process is adapted from Making Action Plans (MAPS) (O'Brien, Forest, Snow, & Hasbury, 1987; Vandercook, York, & Forest, 1989). In brief, the young adult is asked to discuss his own history, dreams, fears, and immediate objectives in life by writing or drawing these areas on paper with the transition specialist. Malloy, Cheney, Hagner, Cormier, and Bernstein (1998) described the entire Project RENEW process in detail.

Toni's Education and Work Program

Toni qualified for Project RENEW by virtue of her involvement in the Manchester Mental Health Program. When she enrolled in Project RENEW, she was 17 years old and the single mother of a 4-year-old boy, Willie. Willie was diagnosed early in his life as having developmental disabilities and a seizure disorder. Toni's initial demeanor was shy and soft-spoken, but she also possessed a quiet self-assurance. Toni is the oldest of three siblings, and her mother was 15 when she was born. She spent most of her early life in Tennessee with her maternal grandmother and moved to New Hampshire when she was 15 to join her mother. The following is a description of Toni's experience with Project RENEW in her own words:

> *I moved to Manchester, New Hampshire, in March 1996 and finished my sophomore year in high school before working with the Job Corps at the New Hampshire Technical College in the summer. I tried school again in the fall but found myself missing too many days because of problems with my son, Willie, and problems with my mother, who was doing day care with him. The school just felt so big. At the same time, my son and I were just starting to learn about his disabilities. My mental health service coordinator introduced me to Gail [the transition specialist] at Project RENEW. I was attracted to RENEW originally because of educational reasons, and Gail worked hard to make it work for me. Everyone, Gail and another counselor from RENEW and a mental health counselor, came to my first personal futures planning meeting. I expressed my desire to get a GED, a driver's license, and to continue on to college. I wasn't sure about what would happen with my living situation with my mother.*

Gail applied for Supplemental Security Income (SSI) benefits for Toni, who began receiving them as well as educational supports for her son:

With Gail's help, I was able to schedule evaluations for my son from the Moore Center [the area agency for individuals with developmental disabilities], and I applied for and received Temporary Assistance for Needy Families. Willie's day care also got funded under Title XX when I began attending college.

To support Toni's drive toward independence, Gail helped her make the transition through an adult-supported apartment and then to her own apartment that was subsidized by U.S. Department of Housing and Urban Development Section 8 housing. Toni completed her GED program and is studying to become a nurse in the associate's degree program at New Hampshire Technical College:

Right now, I'm completing my liberal arts work by taking 7 credits in the summer and 13 during the fall quarter. I want to specialize in maternity nursing in a hospital setting but realize that I might wind up working in a doctor's office.

In reviewing her involvement in Project RENEW, Toni stated:

Gail was my major connection in Project RENEW. It would have been beneficial to also have a mentor, but then again I like to be independent. It would have been helpful if things had been clearer between Gail and me, but I feel we made the most of our time together. It was obvious to me from the beginning just how busy Gail was, but it did feel like we went from having a lot of time and then to not having enough time. Gail and I did spend a lot of time on the phone and she always knew what was going on with me. Sure, it was frustrating at times, but I see now just how much we got accomplished. I'd recommend a program like RENEW to others. There were frustrations, but Gail showed me how I could help myself and how to get things done. When I look back, it's a pretty good list: driver's license, GED, college, and services for my son. The best advice I could give any young person is to get involved and do it!

Toni's testimony gives credence to the need for community-based, individualized programs to help young people make meaningful educational choices to support their high school completion and postsecondary education goals. In Toni's case, this did not mean returning to the local high school to complete the curriculum there. As she attests, that setting was too large, too impersonal, and not individualized to meet her needs. The transition planning that was supposed to happen did not occur during her high school years. Project RENEW was able to mobilize supports that not only led her to complete the GED program but also allowed her to enter the associate's degree program at the college. Toni is on the road to independence with services for her son, an apartment, and a course of study that will lead her into the profession of nursing.

In the face of unacceptably low graduation rates and during an era of excellence in the academic curriculum, Project RENEW was developed to increase the educational opportunities for these young people. In the Project RENEW approach, clear goals and outcomes are delineated to support youth in completing high school, obtaining meaningful employment, and continuing their education into postsecondary programs. Transition for youth in Project RENEW is not a point in time marked by a graduation or a job. Instead, the transition to adulthood is viewed as an extended time period between ages 16 and 25, with many achievements and failures. Long-term commitment is required to support young adults when they confront extreme failure or barriers. This commitment is predicated on integrated, interagency, community-based planning to improve educational, vocational, and community life outcomes for these young adults. The success that this initial group of young people have had in Project RENEW attests to the fact that education and employment can improve and referrals to residential treatment or incarceration can be averted.

STEPPING STONES TO SUCCESS

The Stepping Stones to Success program is located at Cañada College, a public community college located in Redwood City, California. The Stepping Stones program is supported financially by a grant from the Peninsula Community Foundation, a local foundation, as well as by the San Mateo County Mental Health Services Division and by Caminar, a nonprofit community mental health agency. Support is also provided by the Sequoia Union High School District in the form of liaison staff and advisory committee participation. This interagency partnership results in greater community participation and collaboration. Initial outcome data from Stepping Stones indicated that the strategies described in the subsections that follow are supporting achievement of the overall program goal of improving life skills for more effective adaptation into early adult roles.

During the Spring 1998 semester, 46 students were enrolled in Stepping Stones. Sixty-one percent completed their classes, with an overall grade point average of 3.50 on a 4-point scale. Scores on the quality-of-life measure improved during the semester. For example, in self-evaluations, at the end of the semester 89% of these students judged their overall functioning to be excellent or good, a 30% improvement from the start of the semester. Self-esteem scores also showed improvement during the course of the semester. Seventy-six percent of students strongly or mostly agreed that the program was of value and that they liked the classes they took. Although the data are still preliminary and are based on a small sample, this research indicates movement in a positive direction.

Application of Supported Education and Psychosocial Rehabilitation Principles

As Unger (1994, 1998) indicated, applying supported education principles and practices originally designed for adult students with psychological disabilities to the experience of young people in education environments is of great value. The Stepping Stones program has adapted a number of these strategies for use with students in the program, whose ages range from 14 through 22. The cornerstone of the supported education psychosocial rehabilitation model is a philosophy of hope. The Stepping Stones philosophy statement reads,

> We believe adolescents and young adults with emotional and behavioral difficulties can make progress along a developmental continuum toward adult roles and achieve success in academic, vocational, personal, relational, and community domains, through learning skills and receiving support. (Cañada College, Office of Psychological Services, 1996)

Interwoven throughout this account are portions of Jennifer's story. Jennifer has completed the program's core curriculum, takes classes in an inclusive classroom environment, and serves as a Stepping Stones teaching assistant. Jennifer's own words reflect the lack of hope in her life when she first entered the program:

> *When I first started attending Cañada, I was 16. I left high school during my freshman year. I had been very nearly completely isolated for the next year and a half following that, never venturing much further than the front yard of my parents' house except at night or in the very early morning. I was referred to the Stepping Stones program through my counselor.*

Adult-supported education programs provide a real basis for the hope represented by the philosophy statement quoted above. Experience with adult students confirms that skill building and cognitive reframing, along with contextually determined shifts in behavior, have led many adults with psychological disabilities to experience success in postsecondary community college programs in California (e.g., College of San Mateo, Cañada College).

The strategy of cognitive reframing is implemented in the Stepping Stones classroom curriculum through a process referred to as role redefinition. Young people who are enrolled in the Stepping Stones program are encouraged to think of themselves in the new, more independent, and responsible role of community college student. Students are taught descriptors for this new role that emphasize their value and role as a responsible learner and human being who has much to contribute. Jennifer stated:

> *This program pointed out to me that there was a person of value lying dormant beneath my panic and fears. It honored all of me; in high school if I became afraid I would leave the classroom and then was ashamed to return because of my foolish behavior.*

Special support services are also available for students. These include peer counseling, special academic counseling, classroom teaching teams, a therapeutic classroom model, on-campus mental health counseling and service coordination, disability accommodations, disability assessment services, and a specially developed core curriculum. Jennifer spoke to the value of these supports:

> *When I was in Stepping Stones, I knew that if I left the classroom our support counselor would sit out my panic attack with me and then escort me back to class. Stepping Stones was a safety net where I learned that one incident did not constitute failure and that someone, even my peers, would be there to help me if I fell.*

The curriculum provides classes that focus on skill building. This education for life focus helps students to learn critical life skills. These life skills include relational competence, managing problem behaviors, effective communication, boundary awareness, personal futures planning, social skills, reality testing, and problem solving. After the intake and assessment process designed to ensure accurate placement, students are enrolled in either core level I or more advanced core level II classes. Core level I classes consist of "Introduction to College" and "Building Success." "Introduction to College" helps students to orient themselves to life on campus and to think about their roles as students. "Building Success" focuses on skill building for adaptation. Core level II classes consist of "Life and Career Planning" and "Psychology in Practice." "Life and Career Planning" directs students through a multistage process culminating in a life plan. "Psychology in Practice" allows students to apply their skills in solving real-life problems. Students enrolled in any of the four core classes, if appropriate, may also be enrolled concurrently in a secondary school program or take inclusive community college classes.

Integration with the Local Community System of Care

Effective integration with the local system of care requires community outreach and recruiting, service coordination, and interaction with other service providers and secondary education programs. Members of the Stepping Stones staff participate in local interagency service coalitions such as the San Mateo County Community Rehabilitation Coalition and the School to Work Interagency Transition Partnership (SWITP). Clark, Stewart, and Unger (1993) and Silver and Unger (1992) wrote of the challenges and difficulties related to effective transition planning for these young adults. The SWITP initiative in California is an effort to address the need for effective transition planning for young people with disabilities (Critchlow, 1996). This initiative was launched through a cooperative memorandum of understanding signed by 10 state agencies, including the California Department of Education, California community colleges, the Department of Mental Health, the Department of Rehabilitation Services, and the Social Security Administration. The Community Rehabilitation Coalition provides powerful advocacy for mental health services consumers. It includes mental health service providers and advocacy organizations.

Participating in the local SWITP cooperative allows the Stepping Stones program to interact with secondary schools and a wide range of agencies that support early interagency transition planning for young people. The SWITP model is similar to the model that Clark, Deschênes, and Jones suggest in Chapter 2. They advocate a Transition to Independence Process (TIP) that uses integrated planning that includes supportive, face-to-face meetings with young people in an atmosphere of respect for their interests, goals, and choices.

Maintaining Effective Services to Diverse Populations

Cross, Bazron, Dennis, and Isaacs (1989) and Isaacs and Benjamin (1991) explored the need for effective strategies to provide services to young people with emotional or behavioral difficulties who are from diverse ethnic backgrounds. Stepping Stones serves a diverse group of young people in terms of ethnicity, socioeconomic status, and sexual orientation. The program attempts to build a diversity-focused support system by means of the following strategies:

- Creating extended kinship networks
- Allowing multiple points of entry into the program and multiple sources of support
- Avoiding linear, patriarchal service systems
- Building a sense of community and tribal connection (e.g., ritual, rites of passage, communal activities)
- Encouraging a personalized relational process in which the value of the interaction is based on the connection between individuals rather than on the task that is being addressed (e.g., filling out a form, discussing an assignment)
- Teaching the concepts of worldview and affirmative diversity
- Identifying strengths, skills, and learning styles in a variety of domains: Verbal, affective, interpersonal, and nonverbal
- Providing mentoring by elders
- Empowering voice and self-expression
- Co-creating program process and outcomes within appropriate roles

Philosophically, the concepts of worldview and affirmative diversity are key to the educational experiences of students in the Stepping Stones program. The concept of affirmative diversity supports the inclusion of each individual in appreciation of the value inherent in any difference that she brings to the community (Trickett, Watts, & Birman, 1994).

Dovetailing with the concept of affirmative diversity is the concept of worldview. *Worldview* refers to the particular construct of reality experienced collectively by people who share a common historical and/or cultural heritage. Each individual possesses a worldview that is derived from experience within a particular cultural frame (Ibrahim, 1991; Manoleas, 1996; Sodowsky & Johnson, 1994; Sue & Sue, 1990). Individual worldview is a construct representative of the sum total of experiences the individual has lived over time. As with the concept of affirmative diversity, worldview is at the same time both a philosophical stance and a practical tool. Philosophically, worldview supports equality and respectful appreciation of differences in experience and perception; practically, worldview assessment allows staff in educational settings to explore, in a nonjudgmental, ethnographically sensitive manner, the way in which an individual sees the world as well as the experiential context that gives rise to that perspective.

Culture, which is related to the development of one's worldview, may be understood from the perspective of ethnicity or may be broadened to allow exploration of family culture and the cultures of systems that have affected the life experiences of each student. In this regard, the culture of secondary schools, psychiatric hospitals, and institutions often have a profound effect on a student's worldview. Teachers in the Stepping Stones program actively seek to develop an understanding of the worldview of each student and to help each student develop consciousness of the elements of his or her own worldview as well as those of fellow students.

An activity that illustrates a number of these diversity-focused components is an in-class group process experience led by one of our elder mentors, who uses a transpersonal shamanic model designed to facilitate rites of passage for youth. This activity involves each student's making a shield decorated with symbols that illustrate his or her life journey. After the work of shield making, students participate in the ritual sharing of their personal journeys by presenting their shields and explaining the meanings of the symbols used. The sense of community created through these diversity-focused strategies is illustrated in the following comments of Jennifer:

> I knew, also, that I would be expected to support those in the program that I came to care so much for. Where once I couldn't even trust myself to take care of myself, I found that I could not only take care of myself but could be depended on by other people as well.

A Range of Outcome Options
Because the overall goal of Stepping Stones is to assist students to develop more effective adaptation to early adult roles, it is necessary for the program to support students in exploring a range of options for the future. The Stepping Stones program counselor works to develop an individualized education program with each student. The education program allows each student to move ahead at his or her own pace and toward goals that have meaning for that student. The following are some of the common transition goals of the core curriculum:

- Return to high school to complete the program and graduate
- Attend community college classes to obtain an associate's degree or transfer to a 4-year college
- Attend community college classes to improve skills and increase competence
- Referral to Workability III, an on-campus school-to-work program at Cañada College for students with disabilities developed through a contract with the California State Department of Rehabilitation Services in which students receive job skills training, vocational

assessment, job development and placement services, and job coaching

Students in the program achieve good grades and demonstrate mastery of the curriculum. They seem to experience greater hope for the future. Again, this sense of hope is expressed powerfully in Jennifer's own words:

Participating in the Stepping Stones program, returning to a classroom setting, was probably one of the most traumatic experiences of my life. Can you try to imagine the shock of it? Can you just close your eyes and try to feel as frightened, lonely, and hollow as I felt? Where you once could hide, now you were exposed and vulnerable. Buried underneath the sweltering exhaustion of those emotions is a horrible aching need to be wanted and supported, to belong, to be part of something, anything. Here you are and if the hope invested in this program is disappointed, then there is just nothing else for you. You might as well resign yourself to spending the rest of your life just wasting time. Luckily, it did work out for me. Today I work, live independently, and, most importantly, attend school full time. Stepping Stones taught me how to function again. It taught me how to become a whole person and not just my fears and insecurities.

ENHANCING SECONDARY EDUCATION AND VOCATIONAL SERVICES

A key element in the success of Project RENEW and Stepping Stones has been the placement of these programs in a normalizing postsecondary campus environment. The campus setting and the staff available for support have provided a hospitable and welcoming climate for students. Although it may be difficult to replicate these settings at the secondary level, positive, accepting environments must be developed that meet the primary need of belonging and acceptance for these young people. The following suggestions are offered to enhance secondary programs that desire to improve personal, educational, and vocational outcomes for youth with emotional or behavioral difficulties.

Student-Centered Planning and Direction

Secondary programs work with students who are in a developmental period that involves searching for autonomy and healthy interdependence. To meet this developmental task, programs must allow for input regarding the students' interests in both academic and vocational goals. These programs must consider the students' broader environment and use the community as an extension of the school. Diploma earning should remain central to the curriculum so that students can complete their secondary programs in a timely manner. Students who earn these diplomas are much more likely to continue their education in postsecondary environments. The experiences of young adults in Stepping Stones and Project RENEW suggest that these students are interested in community colleges when the pathway is provided. Others are more amenable to a combined cooperative education program that emphasizes school- and community-based learning in conjunction with employment. This learning seems to provide considerable meaning and relevance in the lives of young people.

Goals for both academically and vocationally oriented students should be self-determined. Throughout the school year, transition specialists should use the personal futures planning process with their students. Malloy, Cheney, Hagner, and colleagues (1998) outlined this process in detail. The personal futures planning process leads students and staff to explore the vocational interests and dreams of young people. In brief, its steps include the following:

1. Writing a student's history
2. Identifying family, friends, and community social supports
3. Determining a student's dreams and fears
4. Translating dreams into goals
5. Developing quarterly actions to move toward goals
6. Evaluating movement toward goals every quarter

This process has been used in Project RENEW and Stepping Stones to develop realistic plans for young adults' academic and vocational interests. Furthermore, the personal futures plan is an ideal means for developing goals and objectives in the student's individualized education program and transition plan. The personal futures plan process, therefore, should continue throughout the student's secondary and postsecondary experience.

School structures must be developed that support the value of self-determination programs for youth. In particular, administrators and teachers must advocate program alternatives and resources that support collaborative teams in developing individualized services. Administrative support provides school teams the license to seek effective program planning for students and to bring flexibility to what can be rigid high school policies regarding credit earning. Programs for youth with behavioral or academic difficulties within a high school

must 1) have low student–staff ratios (1:15) and low program enroll-
ments (25–50 students), 2) be autonomous regarding their ability to
offer credit-earning courses, 3) promote staff investment in and unconditional care for all students, and 4) create a positive peer culture that
enhances a student's school bonds and commitment to complete high
school (Bullis & Cheney, 1999; Wehlage, Rutter, & Turnbaugh, 1987).

The personal futures plan of a young person should be the pre-
cursor to developing goals, objectives, and activities in a student's transition plan. The student should present his or her goals from the
personal futures plan to school staff, in collaboration with community
business, mental health, and vocational rehabilitation personnel, who
have the responsibility for the student's job development. The personal
futures plan also identifies natural circles of social support (family
members and friends) that can help the youth with job development.
Programs that focus on natural supports in the workplace frequently
call on relatives and friends to help young people obtain employment.
Employment sites then serve as credit-earning sites.

High School Curriculum

The high school curriculum should also offer coursework in such areas
as interpersonal and personal problem solving, work-related classes,
and remedial academics (Johns et al., 1996). For example, secondary
programs for youth with mild disabilities should consider tutorial support and learning strategies for young people who are integrated into
inclusive classrooms. Furthermore, this should always be linked to
their interpersonal needs and vocational interests (Cole & McLeskey,
1997). Separate classes are not always the answer to providing these
supports because students with behavioral difficulties need increased
opportunities and exposure to a rich curriculum, cooperative learning
experiences, and classroom discussions that stimulate learning (Cole &
McLeskey, 1997).

Students involved in a general education curriculum must be able
and successful in two areas (Zigmond, 1990). First, they must be able to
maintain academic credits for graduation. Second, they should be
counseled to stay on track to meet the requirements of postsecondary
admission. This typically requires credit earning in language arts, math,
history and social studies, science, and electives. In addition, these students need to pass state learning assessments (Ysseldyke & Olson,
1999). Some content areas, as well as preparation for learning assessments, need to be modified by the special educator. Classes in special
education should supervise closely the writing assignments and study
skills necessary for completing homework. Ideally, such a class should
be scheduled during the last period of a student's school day.

Young people with the interest and abilities should be able to obtain many credits in the general education setting. This work needs to be closely monitored in classrooms because the day-to-day emotional or behavioral issues of these youth can interfere with assignment completion and result in lower grades. An approach that monitors daily performance in academics and social behavior is recommended. Any failure on assignments should be linked to the personal futures plan for review and reality check.

Exposure to Community Experiences
As students enter their final years in public education, it is imperative that learning options be expanded to include work- and community-based opportunities. Given the frequently mentioned problem of discipline in high schools, community-based programming decreases the level of peer influence in school and allows for closer supervision in the workplace for students with vocational interests. Work- and community-based learning also meets the intent of transition programming and school-to-work initiatives. This should not be viewed as a devalued program for youth but should be marketed to youth as a pathway toward success in the community.

For students ages 14 and older, both the legal mandates for transition planning and the developmental needs of youth suggest that a community-wide system of care be developed and implemented. Personnel from community agencies must find the time and the means to create collaborative interagency partnerships. Determination of who should manage this coordination of services should be done at the local level, but it seems that transition coordinators are typically school district employees. Provision of a wider range of support services at the secondary level requires interagency planning and redesign of service delivery models. Unger (1994) identified important support services that assist students at the secondary level to achieve positive educational outcomes. The knowledge base for interagency service delivery has expanded rapidly, and its use is viewed as an efficient and cost-effective approach to transition planning for students with emotional or behavioral difficulties (Epstein, Kutash, & Duchnowski, 1998).

Alternative programs have typically played an important role for students ages 16 and older who demonstrate low skills in reading or math or who have behavioral problems that interfere with their own or others' learning in general education classrooms (Zigmond, 1990). Students in this group are at high risk for leaving school without graduating unless an alternative program can capture their interest. Alternative programs for this group of students often focus on positive climate, interpersonal relationship building, relevant curriculum that bridges academics and vocational interests, behavioral management skills, social skills, and community survival skills (Johns et al., 1996). Outcome goals for this group should target employment, high school completion, interagency support with community services, and housing supports. Again, the personal futures plan must continue to address student goals and immediate objectives in all of these areas.

Young Adulthood

As youth move into the developmental period of young adulthood, community and technical colleges should serve as a valuable resource to students and high schools. For individuals who have not completed their high school programs, credit earning can be provided if the local high school is amenable to such a curriculum expansion. Community colleges can also provide optional programs such as adult basic education and general equivalency diplomas for high school completion. In both Stepping Stones and Project RENEW, community colleges have been able to deliver classes and tutorial programs that are credit bearing for students pursuing their secondary diplomas. Students who have completed their high school programs can be immediately linked to associate's degree programs for 4-year college preparation, trades, and service and professional occupations.

Programs such as Project RENEW (Hagner et al., 1999) and the Career Ladder program (Siegel, Robert, Waxman, & Gaylord-Ross, 1992) have demonstrated the impact that such programs can have on student high school completion and employment rates. RENEW's graduation rates for youth 16–20 years of age have been greater than 90%, and the Career Ladders program had employment rates in excess of 80% for its youth. Attaining these high success rates has been dependent on the development of a continuum of community-based services and supports. A central figure, such as a transition specialist, seems to be essential in monitoring a student's progress toward goals.

A FOCUS FOR THE FUTURE

In this chapter, we have shared work-based, school-based, and individualized components for expanding education programs for young people. The information provided is useful for individuals who work to meet the needs of young people. For more information regarding education issues and exemplary programs, please visit the following World Wide Web site: http://www.fmhi.usf.edu/cfs/policy/tip/tiphp.htm. Parents, educators, practitioners, and policy makers need to work in concert to assist systems to develop the flexibility and courage to explore new possibilities to brighten the lives and futures of young people. These young adults often present a touching paradox. On the one hand, the problems and struggles that permeate their lives are readily apparent. On the other hand, educators and parents are often touched by the intelligence, sensitivity, and creativity of many of these students. It is imperative that continued efforts be made to open doors to their potentials and possibilities. Both the young people affected and American society as a whole will benefit from their success.

REFERENCES

Benz, M., Yovanoff, P., & Doren, B. (1997). School-to-work components that predict postschool success for students with and without disabilities. *Exceptional Children, 63,* 151–165.

Blackorby, J., & Wagner, M. (1996). Longitudinal postschool outcomes of youth with disabilities: Findings from the National Longitudinal Transition Study. *Exceptional Children, 62,* 399–413.

Bullis, M., & Cheney, D. (1999). Vocational and transition interventions for adolescents and young adults with emotional or behavioral disorders. *Focus on Exceptional Children, 31*(7), 1–24.

Bullis, M., Nishoka-Evans, V., Fredericks, H.D.B., & Davis, C. (1993). Identifying and assessing the job-related social skills of adolescents and young adults with emotional and behavioral disorders. *Journal of Emotional and Behavioral Disorders, 1,* 236–250.

Cañada College, Office of Psychological Services. (1996). *Stepping Stones program philosophy and goals statement.* Redwood City, CA: Author.

Carson, R.R., Sitlington, P.L., & Frank, A.R. (1995). Young adulthood for individuals with behavioral disorders: What does it hold? *Behavioral Disorders, 20,* 127–135.

Cheney, D., Hagner, D., Malloy, J., Cormier, G., & Bernstein, S. (1998). Transition to adulthood for students with serious emotional disturbance: Initial results of Project RENEW. *Career Development for Exceptional Individuals, 21,* 17–32.

Cheney, D., & Harvey, V. (1994). From segregation to inclusion: One district's program changes for students with emotional and behavioral disorders. *Education and Treatment of Children, 17,* 332–346.

Cheney, D., Malloy, J., & Hagner, D. (1998). Finishing high school in many different ways: Project RENEW in Manchester, New Hampshire. *Effective School Practices, 17*(2), 45–52.

Clark, H.B., Stewart, E.S., & Unger, K.V., (1993). Transition of youth and young adults with emotional/behavioral disorders into employment, education and independent living. *Community Alternatives: International Journal of Family Care, 5*(2), 19–46.

Cole, C., & McLeskey, J. (1997). Secondary inclusion programs for students with mild disabilities. *Focus on Exceptional Children, 29*(6), 1–13.

Critchlow, J.E. (1996, November). *Breaking through: Best practices for building interagency teams.* Sacramento: California School to Work Interagency Transition Partnership.

Cross, T.L., Bazron, B.J., Dennis, K.W., & Isaacs, M.R. (1989). *Towards a culturally competent system of care: A monograph on effective services for minority children who are severely emotionally disturbed.* Washington, DC: Georgetown University, Child Development Center, Child and Adolescent Service System Program (CASSP), Technical Assistance Center.

Cullinan, D., Epstein, M., & Sabornie, E. (1992). Selected characteristics of a national sample of seriously emotionally disturbed adolescents. *Behavioral Disorders, 17,* 273–280.

D'Amico, R., & Marder, C. (1991). *The early work experiences of youth with disabilities: Trends in employment rates and job characteristics.* Menlo Park, CA: SRI International.

Epstein, M., Kutash, K., & Duchnowski, A. (1998). *Outcomes for children and youth with behavioral and emotional disorders and their families.* Austin, TX: PRO-ED.

Frank, A.R., Sitlington, P.L., & Carson, R. (1991). Transition of adolescents with behavioral disorders: Is it successful? *Behavioral Disorders, 16,* 180–191.

Hagner, D., Cheney, D., & Malloy, J. (1999). Career-related outcomes of a model transition demonstration for young adults with emotional disturbance. *Rehabilitation Counseling Bulletin, 42,* 228–242.

Ibrahim, F.A. (1991). Contribution of cultural worldview to generic counseling and development. *Journal of Counseling and Development, 70,* 13–19.

Individuals with Disabilities Education Act (IDEA) Amendments of 1997, PL 105-17, 20 U.S.C. §§ 1400 *et seq.*

Isaacs, M.R., & Benjamin, M.P. (1991, December). *Towards a culturally competent system of care: Vol. II. Programs which utilize culturally competent principles.* Washington, DC: Georgetown University, Child Development Center, Child and Adolescent Service System Program (CASSP), Technical Assistance Center.

Johns, B., Guetzloe, E., Yell, M., Scheuermann, B., Webber, J., Carr, V., & Smith, C. (1996). *Best practices for managing adolescents with emotional/behavioral disorders within the school environment.* Reston, VA: Council for Exceptional Children.

Malloy, J., Cheney, D., & Cormier, G. (1998). Interagency collaboration and the transition to adulthood for students with emotional or behavioral disabilities. *Education and Treatment of Children, 21,* 303–320.

Malloy, J., Cheney, D., Hagner, D., Cormier, G., & Bernstein, S. (1998). Personal futures planning for youth and young adults with emotional and behavioral disorders. *Reaching Today's Youth, 2,* 2–30.

Malmgren, K., Edgar, E., & Neel, R. (1998). Postschool status of youths with behavioral disorders. *Behavioral Disorders, 23,* 257–263.

Manoleas, P. (1996). *The cross-cultural practice of clinical case management in mental health.* New York: Haworth Press.

Mattison, R.E., & Felix, B.C. (1997). The course of elementary and secondary school students with SED through their special education experience. *Journal of Emotional and Behavioral Disorders, 5,* 107–118.

Murphy, K., & Welch, E. (1989). Wage premiums for college graduates: Recent growth and possible explanations. *Educational Researcher, 18,* 27–34.

Neel, R.S., Meadows, N., Levine, P., & Edgar, E.B. (1988). What happens after special education? A statewide follow-up study of secondary students who have behavioral disorders. *Behavioral Disorders, 13,* 209–216.

O'Brien, J., Forest, M., Snow, J., & Hasbury, D. (1987). *Action for inclusion.* Toronto: Frontier College Press.

Siegel, S., Robert, M., Waxman, M., & Gaylord-Ross, R. (1992). A follow-along study of participants in a longitudinal transition program for youths with mild disabilities. *Exceptional Children, 58*(4), 346–356.

Silver, S.E., & Unger, K.V. (1992, March). *The transition from adolescence to young adulthood of youth with serious emotional problems.* Paper presented at the fifth annual research conference: A System of Care for Children's Mental Health: Expanding the Research Base, Tampa, FL.

Sodowsky, G.R., & Johnson, P. (1994). World views: Culturally learned assumptions and values. In P. Pedersen & J.C. Carey (Eds.), *Multicultural counseling in schools: A practical handbook* (pp. 59–79). Needham Heights, MA: Allyn & Bacon.

Sue, D.W., & Sue, D. (1990). *Counseling the culturally different: Theory and practice* (2nd ed.). New York: John Wiley & Sons.

Trickett, E.J., Watts, R.J., & Birman, D. (1994). Toward an overarching framework for diversity. In E.J. Trickett, R.J. Watts, & D. Birman (Eds.), *Human diversity: Perspectives on people in context* (pp. 7–26). San Francisco: Jossey-Bass.

Unger, K.V. (1994, October). *The transition process for adolescents with serious emotional disturbance and young adults with mental illness.* (Report prepared for Division of Demonstration Projects, Center for Mental Health Services, U.S. Department of Health and Human Services.)

Unger, K.V. (1998). *Handbook on supported education: Providing services for students with psychiatric disabilities.* Baltimore: Paul H. Brookes Publishing Co.

Vandercook, T., York, J., & Forest, M. (1989). The McGill Action Planning System (MAPS): A strategy for building the vision. *Journal of The Association for Persons with Severe Handicaps, 14,* 205–215.

Wagner, M., D'Amico, R., Marder, C., Newman, L., & Blackorby, J. (1992). *What happens next? Trends in postschool outcomes of youth with disabilities.* Menlo Park, CA: SRI International.

Wehlage, G., Rutter, R.A., & Turnbaugh, M. (1987). A program model for at-risk high school students. *Educational Leadership, 44*(6), 70–73.

Ysseldyke, J., & Olson, K. (1999). Putting alternate assessments into practice: What to measure and possible sources of data. *Exceptional Children, 65,* 175–186.

Zigmond, N. (1990). Rethinking secondary school programs for students with learning disabilities. *Focus on Exceptional Children, 23*(1), 1–22.

4

Vocational Rehabilitation
Approaches for Youth

Genevieve Fitzgibbon,
Judith A. Cook, and Lane Falcon

Young people with emotional or behavioral difficulties face a series
of challenges in today's society. These include an uncoordinated
and unresponsive service system, a culture that stigmatizes them for
being different while overlooking their strengths, and lowered self-
esteem coupled with limited peer acceptance, making it difficult to
seek or accept help. Youth coping with these problems often encounter
challenges finding and keeping jobs, which contributes further to their
feelings of low self-worth and their degree of alienation from peers,
families, and the larger society. This chapter briefly describes studies
showing that young people with emotional or behavioral difficulties
encounter serious problems obtaining and maintaining employment.
We then propose a series of service delivery principles that can help to
overcome these obstacles. Writing from the perspectives of a
researcher, a vocational services designer, and a young person who has
coped with emotional problems, we detail ways in which services can
better meet the needs of youth and young adults who pursue their
dreams of meaningful work and occupational success.

This chapter was supported by the National Institute on Disability and
Rehabilitation Research of the U.S. Department of Education and the Center for Mental
Health Services of the Substance Abuse and Mental Health Services Administration,
U.S. Department of Health and Human Services, under Cooperative Agreement
#H133B50004. The opinions expressed herein do not necessarily reflect the position, pol-
icy, or views of either agency, and no official endorsement should be inferred.

HISTORICAL DEVELOPMENT

In the early 1980s, the field of vocational rehabilitation began to reexamine and question the effectiveness of special education services in promoting the transition of youth with disabilities into adulthood (Will, 1983). At that time, the tremendous expenditure of tax dollars for public education of young people with special needs had yielded disappointing results (Will, 1985). After years of special education, youth exited high schools poorly prepared for the transition to employment or to postsecondary education (Bellamy, Wilcox, Rose, & McDonnell, 1985). Moreover, the field of vocational education had relied on overly restrictive models such as sheltered workshops, which offered piece-rate wages and limited opportunities for integration with peers without disabilities (Wehman, Kregel, & Seyfarth, 1985). To address these issues, the U.S. Department of Education's Office of Special Education and Rehabilitative Services (OSERS) funded a series of national model demonstration programs designed to develop services to facilitate the transition to work of young people with disabilities.

A central feature of these programs was supported employment using a place-then-train approach (Wehman, 1985) to provide youth with jobs in inclusive environments for minimum wage or higher with ongoing support to maintain employment. After research had demonstrated the utility of this model, federal legislation was enacted in 1990. The Individuals with Disabilities Education Act (IDEA) of 1990 (PL 101-476) mandates the development of an individualized transition plan (ITP) for every young person by age 16 if the student receives special education services. (Reauthorization of IDEA in 1997 set the age at 14 years.) One component of ITP includes specific services and time frames for the transition into the world of work. Thus, the stage was set as never before for cohorts of youth with special needs to receive services that are focused specifically on helping them make successful transitions to adulthood.

Also during the 1980s, it was increasingly being acknowledged that youth with emotional or behavioral difficulties faced unique disability-related obstacles, including stigma, along with an unresponsive and poorly coordinated service system, resulting in lowered chances of employment success. The National Longitudinal Transition Study (NLTS), a survey of young people exiting special education programs across 303 nationally representative school districts (Wagner, 1989), found that youth classified as emotionally disturbed had the highest percentage of high school dropouts and failing grades. One to two years after exiting high school, only 18% were employed full-time and another 21% worked part time. In a number of other follow-up studies, special education students with emotional or behavioral difficulties had significantly lower rates of employment and productive activity than comparison groups (Carson, Sitlington, & Frank, 1995; Mithaug, Horiuchi, & Fanning, 1985). For example, a follow-up study of 21 school districts in the state of Washington (Neel, Meadows, Levine, & Edgar, 1988) compared former special education students diagnosed as having behavior disorders with their counterparts who did not have disabilities. This study found that a higher proportion of youth with emotional or behavioral difficulties was unemployed, a much lower proportion was attending postsecondary school or training, and a higher proportion was engaging in neither work nor educational pursuits.

Little is known about the job-leaving patterns of youth with emotional difficulties, although high job turnover seems to be a feature of the youth labor force in the general population (Osterman, 1980; Reisman, 1985). The NLTS also found that young people classified as emotionally disturbed had work experiences characterized by greater instability than all other disability groups (Wagner, 1993). In one study of youth (ages 16–21) and adults (ages 22 and older) with emotional or behavioral difficulties receiving supported and transitional employment services, youth were more likely than adults to be fired from their jobs (Cook, 1992). In another study of first and second jobs held by youth in the same program, only 15% moved forward (obtaining higher-paying, more independent employment) after their first job placement, whereas 54% made lateral moves (to jobs similar in pay and autonomy) and another 31% made backward moves (remaining unemployed or holding lower-paying, less autonomous jobs) (Cook, Solomon, & Mock, 1989).

In addition to vocational challenges, numerous reports and studies have documented a lack of coordination between mental health, education, vocational rehabilitation, and child welfare systems (Stroul & Friedman, 1986). A concomitant lack of coordination exists between the youth services sectors and adult systems, which are not designed to interact with each other. Often, youth experience a discontinuity or even a cessation of vocational services as they "age out" of the youth services sectors. Vocational rehabilitation systems tend to focus on adults and have a poor track record in serving young people with disabilities (Bellamy et al., 1985). Young people and their families often find that there is nowhere to turn for the help they need. Despite this situation, a number of successful service delivery programs have been designed to help young people find and keep jobs. Many of these programs were identified in a national review of exemplary services for transition-age youth with emotional or behavioral difficulties (Clark,

Unger, & Stewart, 1993), and others have emerged since that study appeared (Cook, Solomon, Farrell, Koziel, & Jonikas, 1997; Donegan, 1998). In what follows, we describe and illustrate some key principles underlying these successful service delivery programs.

KEY PRINCIPLES

This section describes a series of service delivery principles that can help young people overcome obstacles to obtaining and maintaining employment. Although the focus of this chapter is on early work experience and employment, this is accomplished in the context of person-centered planning (see Chapters 2 and 6), effective treatment and service coordination (see Chapters 7 and 8), community- and worksite-based instruction stratgies (see Chapter 6), and career development through completion of secondary school and pursuit of postsecondary training and education (see Chapter 3).

Early Identification and Supports

The earlier the age of first psychiatric hospitalization, the poorer a young person's posthospital employment record and the greater his chances of rehospitalization (Bloom & Hopewell, 1982; Zigler & Levine, 1981). Yet, without early identification of the emotional or behavioral needs of youth, appropriate services will not be provided and opportunities to conduct career awareness, exploration, and person-centered planning may be lost. The later a youth's vocational interest, training, and employment issues are identified, the more diffi-cult it is for him to catch up; damage will already have been done to his sense of attachment to the labor force, and setbacks will have restricted his self-image as a worker. At the same time, providers must avoid the tendency for early identification to lead to early stigmatization when they focus more on managing symptoms and eliminating acting-out behaviors than on building the competencies and confidence necessary for early career development. One young adult with experience in the mental health system stated that she found that caseworkers and group home staff were more focused on helping young people understand illness-related issues such as symptoms and why they had to take med-ications than on helping them build confidence and learn the skills they needed to get and maintain jobs.

Poor transitional outcomes begin early, often with the youth drop-ping out of school; as mentioned previously, young people with emo-tional difficulties are especially likely to leave high school early. The absence of a high school diploma can further hinder a young person's vocational development. A World Wide Web site created by the National Alliance for the Mentally Ill (NAMI) (1998) suggests that parents should encourage their children with emotional difficulties to begin working at volunteer or paid jobs in the home or community as early as age 12 to develop good work habits early in life. At the Coordinated Employment Supports (CEO) Project for youth with emotional or behavioral difficulties in Hartford, Connecticut, project staff have found that career education and support must be provided at earlier ages than is currently done (e.g., when youth make the transition *to,* rather than *from,* high school). This can help to prevent dropping out and encourage the development of positive behavior patterns and work-related skills. By the time a young person has reached the teen years, it is often too late.

Comprehensive and Integrated Services

To be truly helpful, all stakeholders in the process of employment of youth with emotional or behavioral difficulties (the young people themselves, their families, their teachers, and their service providers) need to develop a shared vision that leads to interventions incorporating a wide range of services emphasizing a strength-based, family-focused, culturally competent, collaborative, and outcome-oriented approach (see Chapter 2). Everyone involved needs to be in agreement about a young adult's goals and abilities and what it will take to be of help. This means, for example, that a mental health therapist must be willing to talk about problems at work and offer practical suggestions about how to handle workplace dilemmas. One young man was seeing a psychologist who refused to talk about job issues during therapy sessions, insisting that the young adult take his work problems to his job coach. This also means that teachers need to be aware of and responsive to the emotional challenges faced by young people who are working. Teachers should understand how the knowledge they impart in the classroom can be translated by young people into job skills that employers value. Vocational counselors need to understand what it is like to be a young worker balancing school, studies, and social life while coping with emotional or behavioral difficulties.

Beyond understanding and more important is that service providers need to communicate with each other and to work collaboratively with young people and their families. Youth and their families need assistance that is broad and flexible, frequently reaching beyond mental health services to include services or supports in education, recreation, employment, physical health, transportation, and housing (Substance Abuse and Mental Health Services Administration [SAMHSA], 1998). A very important component within this mix is the use of natural and community supports whenever and wherever possible. Moreover, this assistance must be integrated, efficient, and congruous. One young adult explained:

It was very helpful to me when my caseworker, my mother, and I all got on the same page. We worked really well together, and this made me feel that we had a good plan. As a result, I felt pretty secure, and this helped me gain some of the confidence I needed to go out and get my first volunteer job at an animal shelter. I'm lucky that the support I've received from my family over the years has been so great. Without it I'm not sure where I'd be today. It has been especially nice at those times when everyone was working together. My parents have known me my entire life, so it just makes sense that my caseworker should try to involve them in what's going on with me. And the times when my caseworker, teachers, doctors, parents, and myself have not been on the same page.... Those were difficult times.

In practice, being on the same page means that schools, the vocational rehabilitation system, and mental health service providers must collaborate. One example of such a collaboration is the Summer Youth Employment and Training Program at the Maine Medical Center. This program has worked for years to promote collaboration between youth and families, vocational programs for young people, the educational system, and the state vocational rehabilitation system. Schools are involved in identifying, screening, and referring students to the program and in helping students learn community- and work-related skills and build on their strengths to prepare for jobs after graduation. Local vocational rehabilitation providers identify jobsites, match students with employers, help students find transportation to their jobs, and visit jobsites to offer support to workers and employers. The Maine Medical Center provides job opportunities, supervision, feedback, and evaluation of job performance. State agencies (the Bureau of Mental Health, the Bureau of Rehabilitation, and the Department of Education and Cultural Services) work with the program by making direct or joint referrals, following students' progress through on-site visits, and planning future training and employment strategies. These partners work closely with young people and their families to ensure that coordination results in vocational success.

It is very important for programs that work with youth to communicate with employers, teaching them about the needs of young workers with emotional or behavioral difficulties. For employment to be successful, the employer may need support and education as well. Because there is evidence that employers are willing to make accommodations for young people with emotional difficulties (Solomon,

1993), services need to nurture this process so that there is a good job–worker "fit." It also is important to teach young workers about the needs of their employers. One young adult was surprised to learn that her supervisor's request for her to work late one night was a reasonable request. This young woman had equated a request to work late with being forced to stay late after school as punishment for bad behavior. Once she understood that employers facing production deadlines often need to ask their workers to put in extra hours, she felt flattered to know her boss needed and valued her work. This is an example of how each side needs to appreciate and understand the perspective of the other.

Individualized Assistance

A "one size fits all" approach to vocational rehabilitation is not effective or user-friendly in the eyes of youth or their families. Young people need to feel that their vocational services plan is uniquely suited to them and responds to their strong points as well as their needs. Such a principle stems from the notion that promoting growth and change in a system of care includes a strong focus on individualized services (SAMHSA, 1998). One young adult commented on the negative effects of nonindividualized assistance:

I have always been inquisitive and, I would say, intelligent, but I struggled through several "alternative" high schools because of the environment I was surrounded by. Although I graduated early, it didn't seem soon enough. Many of the students in the schools I attended were mentally retarded, and I was very different from them. The teachers didn't always seem to know what to do with those of us who were coping with emotional difficulties. It felt like they were trying to use the same plan for all of us, but we were all so different. This also seemed to be the case in a group home I lived in for 2 years. I had a hard time relating to the other kids I lived with. They had a lot of behavioral issues and did things like biting or hitting. It was scary sometimes and I was afraid to go to sleep. And even when two people are diagnosed with the same disorder, it doesn't mean that they will have the same needs. I feel it is very important that services fit the person they are intended to help. It is also important for service providers to remember that if they are making an effort to tailor services to a specific young person, they don't give up when the kid has a bad day or is in a bad mood. Sometimes the staff will get discouraged and feel like giving up, but continued motivation is really what

> *I needed. People who work with young adults need to help them grab onto their vocational dreams and pursue their goals. And staff really need to get to know the kids they're working with and inspire trust by showing that they believe in them.*

As is evident from the foregoing example, engaging these youth is the key. Services should respect, advocate, and empower young people. The Young Adult Employment Supports project at Matrix Research Institute in Philadelphia is one of many programs that place special emphasis on engagement in working with a young person. This occurs through an emphasis on engagement as soon after referral as possible. The general rules of engagement involve developing trust between the transition facilitator and the young person by promoting respect, consistency, individualization, honesty, and positive expectations. Finding ways to engage each young person in the program means that, invariably, staff take an individualized approach. This may mean learning to wait until youth are ready to take their first steps toward employment. Once ready, young people should be helped to choose their own unique employment direction. It is essential to listen to youth at this stage as they express their anxieties and then to help them break down their concerns and issues into manageable portions by encouraging the use of structured problem solving, stress management techniques, and peer supports.

Programs should provide unconditional and unwavering support, allowing for mistakes and failures, because these provide learning experiences, which are part of life. Part of providing individualized services means allowing young people to express their individual preferences, which may mean allowing them to express their dissatisfaction with a job by quitting. Leaving a job voluntarily should not automatically be viewed in a negative light, especially given studies showing that youth in the general population move in and out of jobs in the early stages of their employment careers. Job changing, job satisfaction, and career goals need to be understood as individual choices motivated by a young person's unique life experiences and social context. The key to individualized services is respect for these forms of individual expression.

One program that exemplifies this principle is the Transitional Rehabilitation Services project at the Center for Psychiatric Rehabilitation in Boston. Transitional Rehabilitation Services outreach workers give individualized attention and support to each young adult they serve. Individualized services also offer the advantage of gaining the trust of the young adult and offering a service provision environment over which she has choice. The CEO Project at the Capitol Region

Education Council in Hartford also focuses on person-centered service coordination, with the additional services of round-the-clock beeper access to one of two employment coordinators. The trust established through this ongoing contact has been invaluable in engaging a difficult-to-serve population over a long period of time. The one-to-one consistency provided through this method can be a key component that is often missing in the services provided to youth and young adults during these transitional years.

Use of Peer Support

The paramount importance of the peer group has been well documented for youth in their transitional years (Feather, 1980), and young people with emotional difficulties are no exception. Some programs are built on the notion that the peer group can be a primary agent of change for young people with emotional difficulties (Farrell, 1992). For example, the Thresholds Loren Juhl Young Adult Program in Chicago places a great deal of emphasis on peer support and self-help. Members of this program act as job coaches, trainers, and support sources for their co-workers in a variety of employment settings in the community. One youth believed that he could not handle the stress of a part-time job until he visited another program member at his place of employment. Having young people train new workers offers role-modeling opportunities along with the chance to learn from someone who is especially sensitive to issues faced by the "new kid on the block." It is important, however, that peer mentoring happen in a productive fashion. Some youth resist peer mentorship and other self-help approaches, not wanting to seem different from their peers without disabilities. Youth with emotional or behavioral difficulties may befriend others who are on the fringe of peer acceptance; thus, their peer models may not demonstrate and/or emulate behavior that will help them succeed. Efforts should focus on helping youth establish the kinds of peer relationships they value and helping to ensure that these peers are supportive and positive influences in both job and other arenas.

Place-Then-Train Approach

Some vocational rehabilitation approaches engage youth in unpaid vocational skills training activities for several months to assess job readiness. A place-then-train approach stems from the idea that many youth do better when they are placed in a "real" job, receiving minimum-wage or higher pay, and are then trained and supported while they work (Wehman, 1985).

Youth need real-world experiences in which they can be supported while they try out new roles, expand their capabilities, and engage in the risk taking required by vocational growth. This allows them to build competence and confidence that comes from training in normalized environments, making integrated employment as soon as possible an important goal. Youth especially want to receive services while they are pursuing goals in nonstigmatizing environments, such as the workplace or college, meaning that they often benefit most from community-based vocational services. One young adult who spent many months working on an unpaid crew at a psychosocial rehabilitation agency, followed by a volunteer position, and then paid employment, stated that it was much more beneficial to receive feedback and suggestions for improvement from a supervisor who was paying for the work than from a caseworker "pretending" to be an employer.

One approach to providing real-world employment experiences to youth is through business partnerships. This involves establishing ongoing relationships with community employers. The Camden Work Experience, Rehabilitation, and Collaborative Services (CamWercs) project at the Mental Health Association of Southwest New Jersey uses a place-then-train design. The young adults served by this project most often have no work experience. The CamWercs staff receive referrals from schools, mental health service providers, and parents. Vocational specialists work with youth to identify their job interests and to help them develop their employment goals. The next important step involves the brokering of internships at businesses that match the young adults' goals. CamWercs funds 4- to 12-week internships or placements at companies willing to enter into this type of partnership. During the internship period, CamWercs staff provide on- and off-the-job support and training, after which the young adult is evaluated by the employer and the vocational staff. Some of the internships turn into full-time jobs. Other young people are provided assistance in their own search for full-time employment at other organizations.

Part of helping to provide youth opportunities to work in real-world environments involves assessing their skills there as well. The most informative evaluation of a youth's vocational potential occurs when she is observed at a "real" community job working for pay. It is critical that agencies not arbitrarily exclude youth from vocational services solely on the basis of written test scores. For example, the CEO Project uses paid internships in competitive work settings for 1–2 weeks as settings for situational assessments.

Availability of Ongoing Supports

Youth with emotional or behavioral difficulties typically require ongoing supportive services without arbitrary time limits to establish and maintain employment (Cook et al., 1997). Vocational supports should be provided on an as-needed basis for as long as a youth requires them.

Research from the Thresholds Loren Juhl Young Adult Program found that the ongoing provision of support was needed by some, but not all, of the youth served in the program. Some young people chose to terminate services with the program once they had achieved their goal of community employment. However, others remained in the program and took advantage of evening services for employed individuals, became peer job coaches and job trainers, and participated in a Community Scholar Program designed to help them secure college or postsecondary vocational training to improve their job skills (Cook & Solomon, 1993). They continued to use vocational services as they sought to cope with new issues that arose in the workplace over time or as they coped with leaving one job and finding another. In some cases, the youth who achieved the highest levels of success were those who needed the most support to maintain their jobs. The continuity of long-term supports also becomes critical as young people age out of youth services and become vulnerable to falling through the cracks as they move into the adult mental health and vocational rehabilitation services systems. Many young adults find that their families are the only consistent sources of support as providers come and go in their lives.

Cultural Diversity and Gender Awareness
Many providers note that minority youth experience disproportionately poorer vocational outcomes than their nonminority counterparts. Everyone involved in service delivery to these young people must be alert for potential discrimination and cultural issues that affect school and work life (see Chapter 11). Although little information exists on mental health service utilization for youth of color, particularly by specific ethnic or cultural group, it seems that their service utilization is limited and that higher rates of out-of-home placement, less social service support for their parents, and routing through the juvenile justice system are common (Hoberman, 1992).

Also, these youth face the same kinds of prejudice and discrimination in finding and maintaining employment that any person of color experiences. Coming from a minority community may mean that these youth have less attachment to the labor force because of the unemployment faced by family members and others in their communities. When service providers operate on the basis of values such as "everyone works" or "employment is a lifelong adult goal," some youth may feel that services are not congruent with their own or their families' experiences. Service providers need to be aware of the cultural issues and concerns of the population with which they work and sensitively incorporate them into service delivery. Encouraging participation and feedback from family members, friends, and advocates from young people's own communities is an excellent way to increase one's awareness of the differing needs of the cultural population of youth being served. Service accessibility is also important. Location, hours, availability, and length of time the young person must wait before receiving services all determine a service's accessibility. Accessibility is also determined by the responsiveness of services to members of various racial and ethnic groups, to males and females, and to families of varying socioeconomic statuses (SAMHSA, 1998). Two lessons learned from the CEO Project were 1) the importance of hiring people from minority backgrounds who are able to provide culturally appropriate services to engage minority youth and young adults and 2) the value of staff with experience living and working in the local community and who have established networks and credibility that can be useful to young people seeking employment.

Previous research has shown that among young adults with emotional or behavioral difficulties, females have significantly poorer vocational outcomes than males (Silver, Unger, & Friedman, 1994; Wagner, 1992; Wagner, Blackorby, Cameto, Hebbeler, & Newman, 1993). Several large-scale surveys of youth with emotional or behavioral difficulties have found that young men were more likely to be employed than young women (Silver et al., 1994; Wagner, 1992). For example, the NLTS found that 3–5 years after school exit, 57% of young men with serious emotional disturbance were working but only 19% of young women were employed (Wagner et al., 1993). The unique educational and vocational needs of female youth must be addressed. Given the connections between continuing mental health problems and poverty, and the relatively poor vocational outcomes of young women, developing ways to help these young women gain competitive employment and develop meaningful careers is paramount. Offering skills training and support groups to increase self-esteem, assertiveness, school and work motivation, and job-finding opportunities could be especially effective in helping these young women to go back to or stay in school and to become vocationally prepared. Providing child care in schools and treatment programs to help young women with emotional difficulties finish school or obtain employment also is essential, given their high rates of parenthood. For example, in the NLTS, close to half (48%) of young women with severe emotional disturbance had become mothers within 3–5 years after leaving school, compared with 28% of females in this age group in the general population (Wagner, 1992). As one young adult put it, "All the girls I knew were always hanging on boys rather than thinking about a job. Three of them got pregnant in 1 year. I also think it's harder for women to get jobs."

CONCLUSIONS

Vocational services for youth and young adults with emotional or behavioral difficulties need to take into account the unique nature of their individual challenges as well as the services system barriers they and their families confront. High levels of stigma are especially hard to cope with during the adolescent years, when peer acceptance is so important. Services such as job coaching and workplace support need to be provided in the least obtrusive way possible so that young people do not feel labeled by their co-workers without disabilities. Because many youth with emotional or behavioral difficulties exhibit low self-esteem, vocational services must be designed to limit the amount of induced stress that accompanies employment while offering employment that is status enhancing and esteem building.

Also needed is a commitment to the improvement and coordination of services on the part of all organizations involved and by all of the people who make up those organizations. This requires that the organizational leadership be committed to the principles outlined in this chapter and to providing their staff with the training and support that is necessary to work effectively across programmatic and disciplinary boundaries. The genuine involvement of young people and their families, coupled with effective interorganizational planning and service delivery, makes demands on staff that must be recognized and addressed. The overriding component that seems to make interventions successful is commitment on the part of staff and family to facilitate the young person's transition to adulthood.

REFERENCES

Bellamy, G., Wilcox, B., Rose, H., & McDonnell, J. (1985). Education and career preparation for youth with disabilities. *Journal of Adolescent Health Care, 6,* 125–135.

Bloom, R., & Hopewell, L.R. (1982). Psychiatric hospitalization of adolescents and successful mainstream reentry. *Exceptional Children, 48,* 352–357.

Carson, R.R., Sitlington, P.L., & Frank, A.R. (1995). Young adulthood for individuals with behavioral disorders: What does it hold? *Behavioral Disorders, 20,* 127–135.

Clark, H.B., Unger, K.V., & Stewart, E.S. (1993). Transition of youth and young adults with emotional/behavioral disorders into employment, education and independent living. *Community Alternatives: International Journal of Family Care, 5*(2), 19–46.

Cook, J.A. (1992). Job ending among youth and adults with severe mental illness. *Journal of Mental Health Administration, 19,* 158–169.

Cook, J.A., & Solomon, M.L. (1993). The Community Scholar Program: An outcome study of supported education for students with severe mental illness. *Psychosocial Rehabilitation Journal, 17,* 83–97.

Cook, J.A., Solomon, M.L., Farrell, D., Koziel, M., & Jonikas, J. (1997). Vocational initiatives for transition-age youths with severe mental illness. In S.W. Henggeler & A.B. Santos (Eds.), *Innovative approaches for difficult-to-treat populations* (pp. 139–163). Washington, DC: American Psychiatric Press.

Cook, J.A., Solomon, M.L., & Mock, L.O. (1989). What happens after the first job placement? Vocational transitioning among severely emotionally disturbed and behavior disordered adolescents. *Programming for Adolescents with Behavioral Disorders, 4*, 71–93.

Donegan, K. (1998, April). *Addressing employment needs: Findings from Project YES in Philadelphia: School-to-work transition services for youth with emotional disturbances.* Paper presented at Facilitating Careers for Mental Health Consumers: A National Vocational Rehabilitation Conference, Chicago.

Farrell, D. (1992). The missing ingredient: Separate, specialized programming for adolescents with mental illness. *Psychosocial Rehabilitation Journal, 15,* 97–99.

Feather, N.T. (1980). Value systems and social interaction: A field study in a newly independent nation. *Journal of Applied Social Psychology, 10,* 1–19.

Hoberman, H.M. (1992). Ethnic minority status and adolescent mental health services utilization. *Journal of Mental Health Administration, 19,* 246–267.

Individuals with Disabilities Education Act (IDEA) of 1990, PL 101-476, 20 U.S.C. §§ 1400 *et seq.*

Mithaug, D.E., Horiuchi, C.N., & Fanning, P.N. (1985). A report on the Colorado statewide follow-up survey of special education students. *Exceptional Children, 51,* 397–404.

National Alliance for the Mentally Ill (NAMI). (1998, July 6). *Transition from school to adult life: Preparing your youngster for the future* [On-line]. Available http://www.nami.org/youth/transb.html.

Neel, R.S., Meadows, N., Levine, P., & Edgar, E.B. (1988). What happens after special education? A statewide follow-up study of secondary students who have behavioral disorders. *Behavioral Disorders, 13,* 209–216.

Osterman, P. (1980). *Getting started: The youth labor market.* Cambridge, MA: MIT Press.

Reisman, J. (1985, August). *Quits and firings among adolescent workers.* Paper presented at the annual meeting of the American Sociological Association, Washington, D.C.

Silver, S., Unger, K., & Friedman, R. (1994). *Transition to young adulthood among youth with emotional disturbance* (Rep. No. 839). Tampa: University of South Florida, Louis de la Parte Florida Mental Health Institute, Research and Training Center for Children's Mental Health.

Solomon, M.L. (1993). Is the ADA "accessible" to people with disabilities? *Journal of Rehabilitation Administration, 17,* 109–119.

Stroul, B.A., & Friedman, R.M. (1986). *A system of care for children and youth with severe emotional disturbance.* Washington, DC: Georgetown University, Child Development Center, Child and Adolescent Service System Program (CASSP), Technical Assistance Center.

Substance Abuse and Mental Health Services Administration (SAMHSA), Center for Mental Health Services. (1998). *Fitting the pieces together: Building outcome accountability in child mental health and child welfare systems.* Washington, DC: Author.

Wagner, M. (1989). *The transition experiences of youth with disabilities: A report from the National Longitudinal Transition Study.* Menlo Park, CA: SRI International.

Wagner, M. (1992). *Being female: A secondary disability? Gender differences in the transition experiences of young people with disabilities.* Menlo Park, CA: SRI International.

Wagner, M. (1993). Trends in postschool outcomes of youths with disabilities: Findings from the National Longitudinal Transition Study of special education students. *Interchange, 12,* 2–4.

Wagner, M., Blackorby, J., Cameto, R., Hebbeler, K., & Newman, L. (1993). *The transition experiences of young people with disabilities: A summary of findings from the National Longitudinal Transition Study of special education students.* Menlo Park, CA: SRI International.

Wehman, P. (1985). Supported competitive employment for persons with severe disabilities. In P. McCarthy, J. Everson, S. Moon, & M. Barcus (Eds.), *School-to-work transition for youth with severe disabilities* (pp. 167–182). Richmond: Virginia Commonwealth University.

Wehman, P., Kregel, J., & Seyfarth, J. (1985). Employment outlook for young adults with mental retardation. *Rehabilitation Counseling Bulletin, 29,* 90–99.

Will, M.C. (1983). *OSERS programming for the transition of youth with disabilities: Bridges from school to working life.* Washington, DC: U.S. Department of Education, Office of Special Education and Rehabilitative Services.

Will, M.C. (1985). Opening remarks. *Journal of Adolescent Health Care, 6,* 79–83.

Zigler, E., & Levine, J. (1981). Age of first hospitalization of schizophrenics: A developmental approach. *Journal of Abnormal Psychology, 90,* 458–467.

5

Community Housing and Related Supports

Melissa Platte, Mark J. Kroner, and Robert Ortiz

Housing provides the stability that makes it possible for an individual to live, learn, and work productively in the community. Without housing, much of an individual's existence is dictated by the need to find shelter, meals, and other items necessary for survival. Current estimates indicate that a homeless individual spends upwards of 60 hours per week securing shelter and food. This becomes a full-time job. In the community context of providing support for a young adult in transition, priority must be given to ensuring that the young adult has a safe housing arrangement in the community plan. Only after an individual is safely housed can other critical issues such as education, vocational goals, and mental or physical health problems be addressed effectively.

One of the most significant rites of passage for every young adult is the move from the family home. Typical 17-year-olds dream of living independently, and most 18-year-olds make plans, realistic or not, for such a move. For young people with mental health issues or those unable to live with their biological families, this transition is even more challenging. Although some are moving from wonderfully supportive situations, many are moving from treatment programs, foster care, detention, or family situations that are stressful at best and that dictate when the young people must leave; they have no real choice about whether to stay or go.

According to the 1990 Census Report (Bryson & Casper, 1997), the majority of young adults are not totally financially independent until the age of 27. Young people usually leave the services system much earlier and face monumental challenges, both personal and financial, that other young adults with intact networks of support are better equipped to handle. Young adults in some programs have compared this transition to moving from a cocoon-like environment into a fast-moving and very cold river. Studies have found that many people in the adult shelter system had some out-of-home placements during childhood (Pettiford, 1981; Shaffer & Caton, 1984).

Many young people spend lengthy periods of time "on the streets," in jails, or wandering from place to place before they officially become involved in the adult system of supportive housing. Most communities lack a bridge between the child welfare, juvenile justice, special education, and children's mental health systems and the adult systems that would permit a more humane transition to adulthood. Often, an extreme event such as a suicide attempt, domestic violence, or a crime is what alerts a community to a person's need for basic housing.

Housing is critical to the process of moving young adults into the community. The availability of suitable, affordable, and desirable housing can provide the motivation for youth to connect with programs that provide the skill building and training necessary to make the transition from adolescence to adulthood.

The Lighthouse Youth Services Independent Living Program in Cincinnati, Ohio, in operation since 1981, has a saying: "Independent living [training] without housing is like driver's training without the car." The agency starts its independent living and transitional living services by providing a place to live and then begins to include support services. With housing—and, better yet, with desirable housing—the outreach and connection with young adults is much easier. In addition, and significantly, if a program houses young people, program personnel know where to find them, which makes it easier to provide support services and avoid crises.

The purpose of this chapter is to review existing models of housing and discuss new and emerging trends as well as to provide practical advice on how to set up a housing program that can be tailored to the unique needs of young people with emotional or behavioral difficulties. Robert Ortiz is one of several young adults who worked to develop a network of services for adolescents and young adults in transition. He was instrumental in helping San Mateo County Mental Health Services Division service providers understand the housing needs of young adults. Robert stated:

I became involved in the Young Adult Independent Living [YAIL] program in San Mateo County, California, when I was 19 years old. I finally admitted I had a mental illness and was ready to leave my family home because I needed to get away from the state of hopelessness. I had become a full-blown alcoholic and drug addict and was paranoid about monsters and ghosts. I was ready to move. The YAIL program gave me reason to believe that I was never going back to the darkness.

TYPES OF HOUSING OPTIONS AND YOUNG ADULT PREFERENCES

Young adults want to be able to choose their own housing opportunities. They would like to match a type of housing and level of support to their own perceptions about their skill levels and needs.

Types of Housing Options

For the sake of consistency, a list of working definitions for terms used in this chapter is necessary. Some of the terms (e.g., "transitional living") mean something different to everyone who uses them. A given region might have different terms from those used in Table 1, but having working definitions will facilitate the discussion and assist agency personnel when seeking grants.

Tailoring Individual Supports:
Maximizing Success in Community Housing Options

To effectively serve young people in the types of housing they typically prefer (e.g., semisupervised apartment, independent with support, and independent), program personnel need to provide effective and individually tailored support services. Some individuals are ready for an independent living situation that offers only minimal support. Others may truly want a community program that mimics much of the institutional structure they have known. In some cases, providers may find that they need to do problem-solving counseling with young adults to assist them in examining the short-term and long-term benefits of progressing from a more structured setting (e.g., supervised apartment) to moving directly into a scattered-site apartment to live on their own. Robert Ortiz, the young man already introduced in this chapter, stated:

I became involved in the YAIL program and got to live in the fourplex which houses the program. Until then I had never lived in any community or had friends. Everything was a whole new experience. I had never held a steady job or been on dates with women. I had to learn how to live with myself, how to handle feelings, and how to take care of myself. I began by very slowly discovering where I began and ended and the real world starts.

Table 1.   Working definitions of housing types

Boarding home	A facility that provides individual rooms, often with shared facilities and minimal supervision
Community-based group home	A house in the community that serves a small number of individuals and uses existing community services but provides some treatment around the clock by trained staff
Group treatment settings	Environments that are usually transitional in nature and typically emphasize skill building and training
Host home	A situation in which a young person rents a room in a family's or a single adult's home, sharing basic facilities and agreeing to basic rules while being largely responsible for her own life
Independent with support	An individual lives independently in an apartment or home that is not agency operated, and the person receives non–live-in support
Independent	A situation that does not require the young person to accept other support services
Institution	A large, structured facility or group of facilities housing up to several hundred individuals with most services being provided on the grounds
Live-in mentor	A situation in which a young person shares an apartment with an adult or a student who serves as a mentor or role model; the apartment can be rented or owned by either the adult or the agency
Residential treatment center	A facility or group of facilities using a combination of on-site and community-based services
Semisupervised apartment (*scattered-site apartments*)	A privately owned apartment in which a young adult lives independently or with a roommate, with financial support, training, and some monitoring
Shared house	A private home shared by several young adults who take full responsibility for house maintenance and their own personal affairs
Shelter	A congregate facility that provides short-term emergency housing
Single-room occupancy	A room for rent that typically has on-site access to kitchen facilities
Specialized family foster home	A situation in which a young person is placed with a community family specially licensed to provide care and sometimes specifically trained to provide independent living services
Specialized group home	A facility that is usually staffed as a group home; the focus is on developing the young person's self-sufficiency skills

(continued)

Table 1. *(continued)*

Subsidized housing	Government-supported low-income housing in which monthly rent is based on a percentage of the person's income
Subsidy program	A situation in which a young adult receives a monthly stipend from either a government source or an agency; stipend contributes to paying for a self-chosen living arrangement, food, and personal supplies; adherence to certain guidelines for participation is usually required
Supervised apartments	An apartment building that is rented or owned by an agency; numerous individuals live with a live-in supervisor, who typically occupies one of the units
Transitional living group home	A home typically affiliated with a treatment agency from which individuals may move after meeting certain goals

Robert continued:

> *The staff in the program had to be able to perform different roles. Sometimes they were therapists. There are times we are going through things and don't know how to handle it. They have to deal with people with histories of abusing themselves by cutting on their bodies or using drugs or alcohol. They need to help us to understand our feelings and even why it is important to have clean clothes or keep a clean house. They need to help us get and keep jobs, learn how to pay bills, and understand the value of hard work or the importance of being independent.*

Typical Housing Options for Young People

Housing options available for most individuals in the mental health system of care are usually defined by age. For individuals younger than 18, out-of-home placement would typically be in institutions, residential treatment centers, group homes, or foster homes. In each of these, there is a hierarchy of authority and a fairly rigid set of rules and guidelines for young people to follow. Typically, youth in any of these programs have limited control over their environment, movement, and finances; adults charged with residents' care make decisions for them. And yet, when they reach the age of 18, young people are expected to magically identify their own needs, wants, and desires and to make the appropriate choices to attain them or to have a system or network of providers make those choices for them.

Supports that Facilitate Success

Some ways of managing risk while helping a young adult succeed in independent housing include the following:

- Regular visits to the housing site by support staff
- Daily telephone contact with high-risk individuals
- A 24-hour on-call system to guide someone through a crisis
- Easy access by both tenant and landlord to support staff on a round-the-clock basis
- Regular contact with landlords or resident managers by support staff
- Weekly support or "problem-solving" groups for young adults living independently

GUIDELINES FOR MATCHING
YOUNG PEOPLE TO EXISTING HOUSING OPTIONS

Finding the most appropriate housing model for a particular young person is not a simple or easy task. A driving feature of a successful housing placement is that it is desired by the young person and that the appropriate, individually tailored supports are in place. A thorough assessment, including a complete review of whatever historical information is available about each young adult, may be the best predictor of success in any housing model.

Other Factors to Consider in Matching

In-depth assessments of an individual's interests, strengths, and potential for high-risk behavior is critical. Someone with a chemical-dependency problem, recent suicide attempts, severe depression, chronic criminal activities, or a high degree of promiscuity might not do well in a scattered-site setting unless appropriate support and supervision can be provided. Conversely, for some individuals it is proximity to other consumers that triggers high-risk behavior, and a scattered-site approach to housing is the only model that makes sense. It might be necessary to move a young person several times before the right fit is identified.

Making Expectations Clear

Regardless of the housing model used, policies that make basic rules and expectations clear to young people and that let them know the consequences of specific problems must be in place. A policy manual should include the following:

- Agreements about telephone use, utility use, and billing
- Agreements regarding who pays for property damage

- Visitor welcomes and restrictions
- Expectations regarding site cleanliness
- Move-out procedures
- Safety orientation
- Information regarding upkeep of property, furniture, smoke detectors, and fire extinguishers
- Guidelines about respect for other tenants and their privacy and property
- Clearly stated grounds for termination or transfer to another setting

PLANNING COMMUNITY HOUSING OPTIONS

It is important that planning for any type of housing, from the initial idea through implementation, operation, and ongoing refinement, include the young person. Even more important can be the belief that young adults should be involved in the planning stage to help identify the pluses and minuses of various aspects of a continuum of services that can address a broader range of needs. This is the only way to develop a program with any integrity and longevity.

Assessing Community Housing Needs for Young People

In planning a housing program, it is important to understand the community, including other services that are available to consumers with mental health issues and how these services are viewed by young people.

Partnerships in Planning Housing Options Including young adults in the planning and development of housing options sets the stage for the creation of partnerships between providers and young people that can improve the desirability and effectiveness of any program.

A task force of young people, family members, and service providers can provide the best analysis of existing services and gaps in services. Most are eager to participate, particularly if doing so results in their vision becoming reality. Young adults can provide a valuable vision of what their hopes, dreams, and fears are. As they gain experience, young adults can explain what worked or did not work for them. Families can provide information about both as well as information about how to obtain family support for a new project, an important piece of the planning process that can actually get a new program off the ground. Many members of family groups such as the National Alliance for the Mentally Ill and the Federation of Families for Children's Mental Health are highly motivated and well connected politically. They can provide tremendous support for a project that will meet the needs of family members.

Surveying the Community Surveys and interviews of young adults with mental illness, family members, and providers in San Mateo

County, California, yielded results that formed the basis for the development of housing programs and related support services specifically for young adults. Several items were agreed to by the majority of participants:

- Most young people believe that, on turning 18 years of age, they will get jobs, find girlfriends or boyfriends, rent apartments, and buy cars and that most of their problems will disappear.
- Young adults do not want to be housed with older adults.
- Young adults' needs are different from those of older adults.
- Fear is integral to the transition process.
- Young people in the mental health system experiment with drugs, alcohol, and sex as often as the rest of the population at this age.
- Staff working with youth must maintain an extremely flexible approach to providing services.
- Staff working with youth should also work with the families of those youth.
- Young adults maintain the hope that they will be able to move out of the mental health system of care. It is important to foster that hope and provide tangible opportunities to fulfill it through completion of school and productive work activities.
- Youth want to have a strong voice in how services are provided to them.
- Young adults want and need physical space that offers privacy.
- Outreach is successful only if there is something tangible and of value to offer the young adults.
- Support services must be practical in nature and tailored to the needs of young people.
- Young adults are frequently nocturnal beings. Be prepared with overnight support.

ESTABLISHING COMMUNITY HOUSING OPTIONS

Each community needs to develop a range of housing options. A particular agency must consider many things before deciding which role it will play in the process.

Agency Considerations

When looking at developing housing, there is a need to face the practical and unattractive issues that surface. Can the agency afford to be a landlord? This question relates to the financial aspects of being a landlord as well as the emotional aspects—can one maintain a good working relationship with someone who is one's tenant as well as a consumer? On the surface, this seems easy. In reality, being a "landlord" and a "therapist" simultaneously can put tremendous strain on all concerned.

Agency as a Landlord   Are your expectations of your tenants reasonable? Are you expecting more than a landlord on the open market would expect? Are you getting less? Are you spending time being upset over something related to the property at the expense of focusing on the young people's goals? You have worked long and hard to buy, rehabilitate, and furnish a wonderful place and "they're trashing it." "More money is being spent unplugging the toilets than in providing services." "Why don't they appreciate what we're providing?" These all are very real and common problems encountered by service providers who manage housing. In reality, because so much of the housing we provide is attached to program services, expectations for our residents are frequently significantly higher than what an average landlord would expect. Before going into the housing business, providers must be clear about their expectations and must master the logistics of being a landlord, including how to evict someone and what can happen during the process before the individual moves out.

However frightening it may be to purchase property, it can also improve the provision of services on a long-term basis. First, a piece of property is a financial asset. Barring unforeseen downturns in the market, a piece of property can actually stabilize an agency. Second, once a property is owned, the rents can be stabilized so that services do not revolve around always seeking new "affordable" housing for the tenants.

Realistically, most of the residents will be earning close to minimum wage while they are in the program. In some areas this may pay the rent on an apartment, but in most areas it will not. For example, in San Mateo County, California, just south of San Francisco, a typical one-bedroom apartment in 1998 rented for $900–$1,000 per month. Two-bedroom units rented for $1,500 and up. Minimum-wage earnings will not pay for this, nor will Supplemental Security Income or general assistance. The only way to make housing affordable is to subsidize it.

Alternatives to Being Landlords   Many providers have examined these issues and decided that they would rather work with landlords than become one. This is typically achieved by developing scattered-site models of housing, which involves becoming expert in leases and rental agreements. Again, studying the lease for what is required of tenants can save hours of frustration. Review each lease thoroughly, including the fine print. If possible, meet with the landlord. Form with the landlord a partnership that is designed to keep the young adult in housing (e.g., inform the landlord that she may call the agency if the young adult is having problems). This type of active partnership can provide these young people with the "second chance" they need to adjust to independent housing. This partnership will make it more likely that landlords will rent more units to other young adults represented by the agency because they will feel that there is a network of support available when problems occur. Lighthouse Youth Services finds landlords willing to terminate leases early when a person leaves unexpectedly for whatever reason. Landlords are also asked to allow different young adults to move in during a leasing period.

Scattered-Site Apartments The scattered-site model works best in regions where rents are affordable and vacancies are frequent. With a vacancy rate of less than 2%, it might not be possible to develop or sustain this model in metropolitan areas such as the San Francisco Bay area. Apartment rents in the Midwest are typically much more affordable, in the $300–$400 range and sometimes even lower. It might be difficult to develop scattered-site apartments in rural areas because of the lack of apartment stock and poor public transportation.

Young Adult Preferences The scattered-site model is close to a real-life situation, which is preferred by most young people, is future oriented, and avoids the time- and capital-consuming practice of finding and developing new properties. It is a model that builds on some important assumptions, listed below, regarding young people and their transition experiences.

- *Assumption 1:* Young adults learn best by doing, when experiencing directly the consequences of their actions.
- *Assumption 2:* Young adults learn best when they have no other choice but to take action on their own behalf.
- *Assumption 3:* In an independent apartment, a young adult is forced to develop an internal locus of control to succeed without constant supervision.
- *Assumption 4:* The transition from supervised living to self-reliant living will be smoother if the current living arrangement resembles the future situation for the young adult.
- *Assumption 5:* The young adult will develop coping skills to contend with issues such as loneliness, control of visitors, fellow tenants, and landlords.

Supports to Maximize Success Lighthouse Youth Services has found it useful for the agency to sign the lease for minors living in single apartments. By doing this, the agency can remove a young person immediately and not have to wait out a lengthy eviction process. Landlords often ask for troublesome youth to be removed but are open to other young adults from the program taking over the lease.

Agency Management: Advantages and Limitations in Scattered-Site Housing For a program to be successful with a scattered-site apartment plan, it must locate landlords and suitable, affordable apartments. The advantages of this housing alternative can be significant. An organization does not have to purchase and maintain a piece of property, a potentially costly venture at best, and there is no wait for residents to move in. Individuals can also choose locations that are convenient for them, close to work, school, and social support. Group and crowd control problems are no longer the agency's primary issue in working with an individual. (Most problems reported by supervised apartment programs are problems between residents.) The scattered-site model can be tailored to the types of supports required by young people. It can accommodate various levels of support, from a live-in monitor to a non–live-in support coordinator.

The program is not limited by size. The entire community provides possible housing sites. A scattered-site model can be an ideal public–private partnership, making the best use of available resources. Many landlords may also become "ad hoc social workers," helping to reinforce expectations of young adults that are necessary for successful apartment living. For many young adults, especially those who are without a family home, the central issue is having some type of control over their lives. Giving a young adult personal space can be a significant form of empowerment.

Lighthouse Youth Services is an example of a scattered-site housing program. It has a daily population of 50 youth in county custody living in their own apartments rented from private landlords and an additional 60 young adults and their children living in various supervised settings in agency-owned property. Lighthouse Youth Services staff feel it is a plus that one agency is able to provide a continuum of housing options and is able to assist young people both during and after custody by children's services. The county understands that many of the youth discharged from care at 18 will need help for the rest of their lives.

Making Choices in Housing Options

Providing housing and related support services to young people with emotional or behavioral problems can be a risky business, whether the agency owns or leases a facility or is using a scattered-site housing model. Although all tenants, not just young adults, can cause problems for other residents, damage property, and create public relations problems for a landlord regardless of the type of housing, young adults may pose a higher risk simply because of their lack of experience combined with their high energy. Friends and relatives of the resident can also cause problems and damage or may actually take over the place and create safety issues for program and/or support staff. In scattered-site situations, loneliness can cause individuals to stray from their goals and violate rules by having endless gatherings of friends or overnight visitors.

The boards of directors of many agencies have hindered program development as a result of liability concerns, and local service providers might not want to place young adults in a program due to their perception of the risks involved because the program does not provide the degree of supervision they are accustomed to having for the young adults in their care.

Developing and operating any of the housing models described here takes time, patience, and openness on the part of everyone involved. It helps to learn from the experience of other programs (e.g., by visiting homeless, runaway, or adult mental health programs) before deciding which model is appropriate for an area and before starting to develop new housing options. Call other providers, visit transition programs, and read as much as possible so that the experience of both the agency and the young people can be as positive as possible.

Agency Funding and Liability Issues

When staffing a program for young people, it is important to have personnel with a great deal of field experience with youth. Staff intuition has sometimes proved more precise in predicting success than any empirical testing.

Agency Liability under Different Housing Options   A major concern for agency boards is liability. Renting from private landlords puts an agency at risk in a different way from when the property is owned outright by the agency. Programs around the country have dealt with this issue through policy development, renter's insurance, honest communication with landlords, and the existence of short-term backup housing in case it becomes too risky to keep a resident in existing housing.

Capital Expenditure Issues   A number of nonprofit agencies have purchased single-family homes and rental properties for use by their clients. These purchases have been funded through government funding, bank loans, private foundations, and funds saved by the local county mental health division as a result of the success of community-based programs, which are less costly than institutional care. Between 1995 and 1998, the San Mateo County Mental Health Services Division provided more than $500,000 in funding for the purchase of housing properties. This was matched by more than $500,000 in funding from the local housing division through Community Development Block

Grants (funded by the U.S. Department of Housing and Urban Development [HUD]). One of the first projects funded through this joint effort was the purchase by the Mental Health Association of San Mateo County of a fourplex specifically to house young adults in transition. The Mental Health Association formed a collaboration with Caminar, another nonprofit agency, to establish the YAIL program. Since that time, the Mental Health Association, Caminar, and other nonprofit organizations have purchased new housing to serve a range of needs, including young adults in transition. By 1998, more than 35 rental units had become affordable for young adults.

Shelter Plus Care   A second program for funding is through the HUD-funded Shelter Plus Care program. One of the largest segments of HUD funds earmarked to serve the homeless or individuals at risk for homelessness has been McKinney Homeless Assistance Act funds. (The young people with mental illness served meet the second criterion in that they are frequently at risk of becoming homeless.) This program was initially funded through local housing authority applications to HUD. Shelter Plus Care is designed to provide housing and supportive services on a long-term basis for homeless people with disabilities (U.S. Department of Housing and Urban Development, 1998). In many communities, this funding has allowed for the purchase and rehabilitation of rental properties and has provided federal housing subsidies for rental units. This program allows participants to pay 30% of their income for rent, regardless of the total amount of rent. The subsidy pays the balance. The unique aspect of this program is that, in exchange for agreeing to receive support services, a participant receives a housing subsidy that can be used in any housing option.

HUD Continuum of Care   HUD funds may be used for the purchase or rehabilitation of community properties and for related support services. In 1996, five separate McKinney Act funding streams were combined into a single formula grant designed to enable communities to develop a coordinated continuum of care system (U.S. Department of Housing and Urban Development, 1998). The overall funding is known as "the continuum of care." Each community or county receives a designated amount of money, based on a HUD formula that determines need, for the establishment and continuation of programs designed to "break the cycle of homelessness." These funds are administered through local government agencies (e.g., local housing authorities, county departments or divisions of housing) and require consumer, provider, and community input to identify needs and develop services to meet those needs. Once a community group makes these decisions and sets proposed programs in a priority list, funding is guaranteed up to the maximum allowed by the formula.

Participation in this process can result in significant funding. Young adults are a "hot topic," so the timing for making them a priority in a community's continuum of care application and receiving funding to support housing for them is good. However, putting together a multisource funding package is time consuming and involves complex record keeping and reporting. Nevertheless, housing options tailored to the preferences and needs of these young adults must be created to facilitate their transition to adulthood.

CONCLUSIONS

This chapter concludes with some final thoughts from Robert:

> *In closing, I would like to say that the most important thing in wanting to change is hope ... hope that a new life and new way of being is possible. ... We will build upon that hope. Show us how to solve our own troubles. We will make mistakes, but please let us learn from them ... don't take the mistakes away from us. The chance to change can come at 16, 19, or at 45. Hope is the most vital and most important factor. Hope is change and lives being used productively.*

REFERENCES

Bryson, K., & Casper, L.M. (1997). *Household and family characteristics: March 1997.* Washington, DC: U.S. Bureau of the Census.

U.S. Department of Housing and Urban Development (HUD). (1998). *Connecting with communities: A user's guide to HUD programs and the SuperNOFA process* (pp. 33–55). Washington, DC: Author.

SUGGESTED READINGS

Barth, R.P. (1986, May/June). Emancipation services for children in foster care. *Social Work,* 165–171.

Barth, R.P. (1990). On their own: The experiences of youth after foster care. *Child and Adolescent Social Work, 7*(5), 419–440.

Brinkman, A.S., Day, S., & Cuthbert, P. (1991). A supervised independent-living orientation program for adolescents. *Child Welfare, 70*(1), 69–80.

Cook, R. (1988). Trends and needs in programming for independent living. *Child Welfare, 67,* 497–514.

Cook, R. (1991). *A national evaluation of Title IV-E foster care independent living program for youth, phase 2: Final report.* Rockville, MD: Westat.

Courtney, M., Piliavin, I., & Grogan-Taylor, A. (1995). *The Wisconsin study of youth aging out of out-of-home care: A portrait of children about to leave care.* Madison, WI: Institute for Research on Poverty.

Courtney, M.E., & Barth, R.P. (1996). Pathways of older adolescents out of foster care: Implications for independent living services. *Social Work, 41*(1), 75–83.

English, D.J., Kouidou-Giles, S., & Plocke, M. (1994). Readiness for independence: A study of youth in foster care. *Child and Youth Services Review, 16,* 147–158.

Festinger, T. (1983). *No one ever asked us: A postscript to foster care.* New York: Columbia University Press.

Kroner, M.J. (1988). Living arrangement options for young people preparing for independent living. *Child Welfare, 67,* 547–562.

Kroner, M.J. (1999). *Housing options for independent living programs.* Washington, DC: Child Welfare League of America.

Mangine, S.J., Royse, D., Wiehe, V.R., & Nietzel, M.T. (1990). Homelessness among adults raised as foster children: A survey of drop-in center users. *Psychological Reports, 67,* 739–745.

Mech, E.V. (1994). Foster youths in transition: Research perspectives on preparation for independent living. *Child Welfare, 73*(5), 603–623.

Modrein, M.J. (1989). Emotionally handicapped youth in transition: Issues and principles for program development. *Community Mental Health Journal, 25*(3), 219–227.

Pettiford, P.M. (1981). *Foster care and welfare dependency: A research note.* New York: City of New York, Human Resources Administration.

Shaffer, D., & Caton, C.L. (1984). *Runaway and homeless youth in New York City.* New York: Division of Child Psychiatry, New York State Psychiatric Institute and Columbia University College of Physicians and Surgeons.

Stone, J.D. (1987). *Ready, set, go: An agency guide to independent living.* Washington, DC: Child Welfare League of America.

6

Teaching and Developing Improved Community Life Competencies

Michael Bullis,
Chad J. Tehan, and Hewitt B. Clark

I look at transition programs as a system of networking in employment, education, independent living, and social relationships. My transition facilitator helped me to access and secure services and supports within this system so that I could achieve success on my own.
—Chad J. Tehan

The transition from adolescence to adulthood presents new and often bewildering challenges to young people. Opening a checking account, finding an apartment to rent, managing a monthly budget, and dealing with neighbors are just a few of the many skills required to live independently in the community. These activities are difficult for most young people to perform, but they are especially hard for young people with emotional or behavioral difficulties. As was discussed in Chapter 1, this population exhibits the poorest community adjustment outcomes of any disability group (Marder, 1992; Wagner, Blackorby, Cameto, & Newman, 1993). These adjustment issues are complicated by two factors: 1) ineffective and inappropriate instruction offered in the public schools that generally does not address instruction in the skills needed to make the transition successfully to the community (Dryfoos, 1993; Knitzer, Steinberg, & Fleisch, 1990) and 2) the virtual absence of a community-based, integrated system of services and supports (Kortering & Edgar, 1988; Marder, Wechsler, & Valdes, 1993; see also Chapters 2 and 8). In short, a population that presents extreme service needs is not being prepared in the existing educational and social services structure to enter work, living, and social environments successfully, nor are services available in the community to provide the support and instruction necessary for these young people to succeed in these areas of community and adult life.

Moreover, there is no one intervention that, when implemented, will affect all other aspects of these young people's lives dramatically. Instead, the great majority of these young people require comprehensive, multifaceted interventions focusing on all transition outcome domains (see Chapter 2), involving various other agencies and staff. To address the varied needs of this population during the transition to the community, it is important to provide individualized, intensive interventions in the public schools and during the transition to work, living, and social settings in the community (Clark, Unger, & Stewart, 1993; Walker & Bullis, 1995).

Such an array of integrated services is rare, and there seems to be both reluctance and lack of awareness on the part of many educators and social service practitioners regarding the way in which such services should be offered (Fredericks, 1995). This void is particularly unfortunate because adolescence is a time when 1) young people with emotional or behavioral difficulties generally have developed at least some of the basic cognitive capabilities necessary to learn applied tasks (e.g., balancing a checkbook), 2) they are beginning to realize that emancipation to adult roles is the next step of their lives, and 3) they are preparing to leave or are being forced to leave their home or residential setting to enter the "real world." Thus, the capabilities of these young people to learn community-relevant skills have increased, and many important and demanding issues (e.g., employment, independent living) are beginning to assume a primary place in their thoughts.

At the same time, the durability of the types of emotional or behavioral difficulties presented by this population must be recognized. Studies have demonstrated positive effects for this population only while interventions and supports are in place, with limited maintenance and generalization of these effects once the interventions have ended (Kazdin, 1987b; Wolf, Braukmann, & Ramp, 1987). So, although the secondary grades can be a fertile time to provide interventions and supports that address pragmatic skills and transition goals (Albee, 1982; Hobbs & Robinson, 1982), it is essential to acknowledge that these skills must be taught in an efficient and effective manner if these young people are to learn the competencies necessary to achieve their own goals and succeed in their transition to community and adult life.

Moreover, there is a delicate balance that must be struck on the part of instructional and service delivery personnel to teach and support the individual and, at the same time, allow these young people to explore their own goals and at times experience the natural consequences of failure, which is also a powerful aspect of the learning process. When effective teaching encompasses generalization strategies (e.g., concurrent parent training, practice in natural environments, booster sessions), the acquisition of new skills occurs and the use of these over time is enhanced (Kazdin, Bass, Siegel, & Thomas, 1989; Lochman, 1992).

The purpose of this chapter is to address the development and training of the skills necessary for youth and young adults with emotional or behavioral difficulties to succeed in community life settings. These community life competencies are those that have been shown to be germane to success in employment, postsecondary education, and independent living in housing and the community and that are needed specifically by young people to improve the likelihood of success in their endeavors.

TEACHING: AN ESSENTIAL ROLE FOR
ALL TRANSITION-RELATED PERSONNEL

The teaching of relevant community life skills should be assumed by practitioners and educators across the child- and adult-serving systems and can be greatly enhanced by the involvement of a person specifically assigned to serve, teach, and support these young people in the formulation and pursuit of their transition-related goals. Such a practitioner, sometimes called a *transition facilitator*, might be employed by the school system or by the children's mental health, adult mental health, or other service systems. The transition facilitator works collaboratively across all of the relevant natural support systems and the child- and adult-serving systems to secure the necessary supports and services, including the teaching of improved competencies to maximize the person's likelihood of success (Bullis & Paris, 1995; Bullis et al., 1994; Clark et al., 1993; see also Chapter 2). However, the teaching of community-relevant skills is not the exclusive role of the facilitator; rather, it is a function that parents, foster parents, teachers at all grade levels, group home personnel, and mental health, rehabilitation, and guidance counselors can and should assume.

The four major sets of responsibilities for transition facilitators are 1) intake and functional assessment, 2) transition planning and service coordination, 3) social and life skills instruction, and 4) placement and support in community employment and living situations (Bullis &

Paris, 1995; Clark, 1998; see also Chapters 2 and 8). These responsibility sets are interdependent and often are conducted simultaneously, with teaching of skills being integral across these four sets. Volumes have been written on these areas, so this chapter summarizes and highlights only the key components of each topic. Where possible, we identify some other references that can be reviewed for more detail and guidance. Along this line, readers may also find the following transition World Wide Web site to be of interest regarding the roles and responsibilities of transition facilitators, staff-to-participant ratios, and other program descriptions: http://www.fmhi.usf.edu/cfs/policy/tip/tiphp.htm.

Intake and Functional Assessment

In our experience, many of the young people who are referred to a transition program have 1) minimal work experiences, 2) ill-defined goals and aspirations, and 3) undeveloped work, education, and community life skills. Moreover, youth with emotional or behavioral difficulties tend to come to transition programs either with numerous assessments conducted over a long period of time or with virtually no completed assessments and little background information. Frankly, neither alternative is optimal, but surprisingly both share a common problem. For young people with numerous assessments, it is difficult to organize and integrate the results into a coherent package, and often, many of the assessments may focus on abstract cognitive or psychological traits that have only a tangential relationship to transition-related skills and activities for these young people. For young people with minimal assessment data, it is necessary to conduct assessments related to the transition process. The question, then, is what kind of assessment should be conducted?

We believe that intake is crucial, because accurate and comprehensive information on the individual—her emotional or behavioral characteristics, vocational and life goals, strengths and interests, and available supports—must be considered in service planning and delivery. Intake should be conducted as quickly as possible, because delays may cause a young person to abandon the transition program. At the same time, we must caution against providing services to an individual in the absence of complete background information, because safety for the participant, co-workers, and others in the community is paramount and this background information must be considered carefully in making work, living, or academic placements. As a general rule, this information can be obtained from the referral source (e.g., schools, social services agencies) and in many cases can be used to secure services for community agencies (e.g., mental health, vocational rehabilitation). However, we must caution against overreacting to information in agency records. Sometimes we find "carryover baggage" from one report to subsequent reports. For example, the label of *firesetter* persists across psychiatric reports for a 15-year-old boy, but the only incident was playing with matches at age 5. Another example might be a report of a 17-year-old girl who "strips her clothing and frequently tries to run away," but these events occurred only in one particular residential facility in which she was placed from age 12 to age 14.

Because agencies outside of the public schools may use eligibility criteria that are different from those used by the schools, it is important to contact these programs to ensure that the young people fulfill these criteria and obtain services with as few obstacles as possible (Rutherford, Bullis, Wheeler-Anderson, & Griller, in press). Having a relationship and/or interagency agreement established with these agencies can be extremely helpful in securing needed services in a timely fashion (see Chapters 2, 8, and 12).

As part of the transition facilitator's initial contact with each young person, we recommend conducting a brief interview to ascertain the individual's vocational experiences, goals, interests, strengths, and concerns (Corbitt & Paris, in press). Questions also should be asked about the young person's daily schedule to focus efforts on realistic and workable placement alternatives. For young people with limited work experiences, hobbies can be a great source of ideas for types of employment to target when job development begins. Often, youth have specific ideas about where they would like to work and—equally important—firm notions about where they would not like to work. We generally discourage using career interest inventories with this population, particularly early in the program, because these measures have not been developed or standardized for these young people and many youth simply have not had enough experiences to make valid responses regarding their career goals and aspirations.

In a similar vein, it is important not to give too much credence to the results of traditional academic, cognitive, and psychological assessments in planning transition interventions, because the results of these instruments have not been proved to be related to transition skills and success for these young people (Cohen & Anthony, 1984). Hursh and Kerns (1988) reached a similar conclusion regarding the use of traditional assessments for adolescents with emotional or behavioral difficulties and recommend ongoing assessments in the placement settings that can be used flexibly and over time to profile behavioral growth and change. Moreover, the vocational evaluation or assessment process (Pruitt, 1976), which typically is implemented within a rehabilitation facility or vocational evaluation center during a specific period of time (e.g., 4–6 weeks), also should be avoided—even those that include commercially available work samples or locally developed work samples that represent jobs available in the community. The psychometric properties of these instruments generally are poor (DeStefano, 1987; Frey, 1984), and the results of these assessments tend to provide only "static" data on the individual's skills. In addition, the procedures are difficult to use in a longitudinal manner to document growth and/or maturation (Sitlington, Brolin, Clark, & Vacanti, 1985). Indeed, several studies demonstrate that results from these types of measures have little relationship to eventual rehabilitation outcomes (e.g., Cook, 1978; Cook & Brookings, 1980).

In recognition of these shortcomings, "functional assessment" of actual work, living, social, and educational skills has been recommended for use in transition and rehabilitation (Halpern & Fuhrer, 1984). (*Note: Functional assessment* also is used in the Individuals with Disabilities Education Act [IDEA] Amendments of 1997 [PL 105-17], the federal law governing special education programs. In IDEA, *functional assessment* refers to analyzing the behavioral contingencies that may influence negative, or antisocial, behaviors exhibited in the school setting. This assessment process can be particularly useful in understanding environmental factors that may be controlling the challenging behaviors that an individual is exhibiting, allowing for the formulation of an intervention that is tailored to the needs of that individual [Horner, Sprague, & Flannery, 1993]. These two usages of the term *functional assessment* are not synonymous.)

Functional assessment, as used in this chapter, is characterized by several features:

1. It addresses the unique work, education, and community adjustment strengths, needs, and preferences of the individual.
2. It appraises the characteristics of target employment, education, and community settings.
3. It allows for the ongoing appraisal of a participant's skill acquisition and progress.
4. It involves the collection of data from multiple sources (e.g., the individual, teacher, counselor, direct observation).
5. It uses direct observation, behavioral rating scales, and assessment instruments that meet generally accepted standards of psychometric reliability and validity (Halpern & Fuhrer, 1984).

These results should profile an individual's unique strengths, needs, and goals that result in "tailored" interventions for that person and should be used over time to profile her progress.

In line with these guidelines, we believe it important for this type of assessment process to rely heavily on checklists, rating scales, and interviews that can be administered quickly and at multiple times to chart the individual's growth and changes. An excellent book by Hursh and Kerns (1988) provides an overview of assessment procedures with applicability to transition programs for young people with emotional or behavioral difficulties. Bullis and Davis (1999) presented a model of functional assessment for use in organizing existing assessment data as well as assessments for making initial transition and rehabilitation plans.

Once transition services begin and placements are made, the assessment process focuses on the relationship of the individual to the demands of each transition setting. Waintrup and Kelley (1999) offered new ways to assess and identify setting demands, accommodations, and supports, information with critical implications for maximizing the person–setting "fit." Nishioka (in press-a) describes ways to monitor and document transition achievement and problems in a coherent and practical manner, data that should serve to alter and focus interventions for individuals to address their specific and pressing needs.

Transition Planning and Service Coordination

Transition planning and service coordination are closely related. As a young person and the transition facilitator develop a plan to guide the transition process, the supports and services necessary to facilitate that plan should become apparent. Conversely, as service/support requirements are defined and altered as the young person progresses in the transition process, the transition plan should be changed to reflect these new needs and goals. In this section, we discuss some aspects of transition planning, particularly the necessity of skill development related to this function. For a description of the service coordination role, see Chapter 8.

As these youth begin to address transition issues, they are faced with a number of critical life decisions (e.g., What kind of work should I do? Should I go to college? Should I live in another town?) that can involve a bewildering array of community agencies and staff. Both IDEA and the Rehabilitation Act Amendments of 1992 emphasize the importance of "self-determination" in the provision of services to people with disabilities and specifically with regard to the way in which services and plans are developed to address these personal life goals. Self-determination, or "informed decision making," relates to the ability to plan and direct one's own life course in different settings, including those situations that constitute the transition domains of employment, educational opportunities, living situations, and community-life adjustment. Furthermore, this informed decision-making ability may be the most important aspect of human functioning (Bandura, 1982, 1986) and is a key element of transition success (Halpern, 1993; Szymanski, 1994). Accordingly, young people should be involved centrally in planning their service program by 1) identifying their own strengths, interests, and needs, 2) making informed decisions regarding their desires and future goals, and 3) being responsible to the maximum extent possible for securing vocational, educational, and living situation placements and opportunities, along with relevant supports and services.

Of course, simply saying that young people with emotional or behavioral difficulties should be involved in planning and deciding their own futures does not ensure that it will happen, because self-determination is an abstract and underaddressed piece of the transition process. Halpern (1996, cited by Bullis & Benz, 1996) identified several core principles, presented in Table 1, that should be incorporated into self-directed planning efforts.

Table 1.   Principles for preparing young people for self-directed planning

- *Students must be taught how to do transition planning.* Planning is not something that comes naturally to adolescents. For most youth, the future is something far away and perhaps even somewhat overwhelming. It may even be unrealistic to think that adolescents 16–18 years of age can plan thoughtfully about the future. If we are to expect youth to engage in self-directed transition-planning activities, then we must be intentional and explicit about teaching them how to do so.

- *Self-evaluation is an essential foundation for engaging in transition planning.* Youth must gain an understanding of who they are to explore meaningfully who they want to become. This approach runs counter to traditional assessment practices in schools. In most circumstances, students experience assessment as something that is done *to them*. Using self-evaluation as a foundation can provide a powerful motivation for young people to engage in transition planning. Self-evaluation should help youth understand their strengths, weaknesses, needs, and preferences in four general areas: personal life, jobs, continuing education, and living in the community.

- *Self-directed transition planning should be taught as a problem-solving process that students can use throughout their lives.* Some goals that youth set are accomplished, and other goals need to be developed. Other goals are not accomplished and need to be revised, or different goals will need to be developed. In either case, goals change over time. Moreover, in adulthood these individuals encounter new life transitions that must be addressed.

- *Youth must be taught how to implement their goals.* The purpose of transition planning is not to *develop* plans. The purpose is to *accomplish* plans. Again, this does not come naturally for many adolescents, especially for many youth with emotional or behavioral difficulties. Youth must be taught how to implement their plans in a practical, concrete manner. They must be taught how to self-monitor their activities and progress and how to make adjustments based on experience.

From Halpern, A. (1996). *Some reflections about self-directed transition planning: Keynote address.* Vancouver, WA: Annual Washington State Transition Conference.

The principles outlined in Table 1 provide clear service delivery guidelines that should be adhered to for all youth and young adults. However, young people with emotional or behavioral difficulties present complicating service delivery issues, because their thinking and planning skills may not be at the level of those of their peers without emotional or behavioral difficulties and these deficits may negatively influence their behavior and ability to make informed decisions. For example, in a study of the school-to-community transition of youth with disabilities conducted at the University of Oregon, 47% of participants with emotional or behavioral difficulties reported that they "sometimes" or "hardly ever" exhibited appropriate problem solving in response to typical social problems (Doren, 1992). The great majority of these individuals also reported being arrested at least once while in school. Furthermore, many had neither the number nor the richness of work and life experiences necessary to make informed choices based on prerequisite skills or awareness. For example, approximately 50% of youth with emotional or behavioral difficulties dropped out of school by age 16 and many more exhibited a pattern of sporadic school attendance (Dryfoos, 1990), and the great majority of them had few successful work placements at the time of transition (Marder, 1992; Valdes, Williamson, & Wagner, 1990).

Thus, the task of assisting these young people in developing their own transition and life plans, while at the same time providing the appropriate level of support and guidance to them in their efforts, represents a thorny service delivery issue. On the one hand, it is critical to offer a service framework that allows these young people to recognize and pursue their own goals, activities that involve self-direction and motivation, responsibilities, and risks for success and failure. On the other hand, merely allowing these young people to seek and pursue their goals without structure does not do justice to the magnitude of their difficulties, nor does such an approach provide the structure necessary to acquire the types of successful experiences these youth need to make informed life choices and to gain the skills necessary to succeed as adults in our society. And, because each young person presents different interests, needs, and skills, no single service delivery approach fits everyone. Accordingly, we believe that it is important to follow two basic rules.

First, young people should be afforded continuing opportunities to present their goals and desires and to pursue ways to achieve these ends. No one should be forced to take a job, enter a program, or pursue a line of training merely because the option exists. Instead, the individual's stated goals should be respected and used to form the basis of the service delivery plan. Support should then be offered in a manner that is reassuring and helpful, not rigid and authoritarian.

It should be recognized that as young people amass different experiences, their goals and desires may change. For example, a young person without a work history may believe that she wants to work in food processing until actually being placed in such a position and realizing that the job is not to her liking. As a rule, these types of experiences are typical during adolescence, and we do not believe that such events are bad, provided that the young person is facilitated and supported in the appropriate way to leave the particular situation. Such experiences may be difficult for some individuals, but these events provide a necessary foundation on which young people can make other, better-informed choices regarding their work goals and allow them to learn other important life skills.

Second, we believe it important for young people to be taught how to make informed choices regarding their life goals in a logical and effective manner. There are essentially two complementary ways to address this issue for individuals with emotional or behavioral difficulties. Initially and at various times during service delivery, it is possible to conduct a person-centered planning process to operationalize the individual's transition goals, either while in school through the individualized education program or while in vocational rehabilitation through the individualized work readiness plan, or in a less formal way within the mental health system or in foster care. Person-centered planning emphasizes the central role of the individual in setting personal goals and transition activities that foster self-empowerment and self-determination. Table 2 presents an overview of these procedures.

Coupled with this individualized planning and instructional approach are formal instructional curricula that can be offered to groups of young people to teach them life-planning skills. An excellent example of such programs is the Next STEP (Student Transition and Educational Planning) curriculum (Halpern et al., 1998), which takes young people through the process of planning their transition from school to the next logical placement setting. Structured exercises are used to guide youth in how to make decisions and to provide a "hard" product of the decision-making process (i.e., results that can be referred to and altered as the need arises). Other such curricula are available and may be well suited to working with these youth (e.g., Kincaid, 1996; *The Real Game Series*, 1996; Webb et al., 1999). We should caution, however, that research data on the efficacy of these programs for this population are not available, so scientific evidence to substantiate the effect of these interventions on young people with emotional or behavioral difficulties has not yet been established.

Table 2.   Agenda for a person-centered planning meeting

1. Introductions/overview of meeting
    Why we are here: We each share a vision for the young person and are willing to explore ideas and options to assist him in reaching his goals and to provide support and help along the way.
    Each person explains her relationship to the young man.
    Everyone is equal and has an equal say; however, the young person has the right of final approval of all suggestions.
    Define *map*: A way of locating a destination and direction by exploring a variety of routes.
    Explain the "brainstorming" process: All comments and questions must be positive, all ideas are valid, and no judgment of others' ideas is permitted. Be creative!

2. Who is (*young person's name*)?
    Everyone lists words that describe the young man. What are his strengths, gifts, abilities, interests?

3. Hopes and dreams
    What are the young person's hopes and dreams? How does he want his life to turn out (long- and short-term goals)?
    What are the hopes and dreams of other meeting participants for the young person?

4. Nightmares
    If there is no plan and no support, what is the worst-case scenario? (If you do what you've always done, you'll get what you've always gotten. Some people have things *happen* to them, some *watch* things happen, others *make things* happen.)

5. Target and prioritize goals
    Prioritize a goal list and target two or three goals to begin to work toward.

6. Fears and obstacles with regard to achieving targeted goals
    What could keep some of these goals from being achieved?

7. Identify strategies to overcome obstacles
    What must be done to achieve the goals? How can fears and obstacles be overcome?

8. Action plan
    What to do?
    Who can help?
    By when?

9. Closure
    Recognition of the young person
    Recognition of each participant's contribution
    Challenge young person and participants to work toward goals
    Plan follow-up activities and set meeting date

Community Life and Social Skills Training

Almost by definition, young people with emotional or behavioral difficulties present some level of social and life skills impairments, as indicated by a generalized propensity to interact with peers, family members, adults, and others in a manner that is not consistent with social mores and that is not effective. This generic characteristic is crucial to note and to address because social skills have been related to work success, peer acceptance, and general life adjustment as well as to transition success (Bullis & Davis, 1996, 1997; Chadsey-Rusch, 1990; D'Zurilla, 1986; Kelly, 1982; Parker & Asher, 1987; Spivack, Platt, & Shure, 1976). Moreover, because transition programs focus on preparing young people for placement in community work, living, and educational environments, it is highly likely for youth in these programs to face interactions with unfamiliar people in unfamiliar settings with unfamiliar rules and expectations. For example, we have mentioned several times that these young people generally do not have extensive work histories. It follows that they may not have the necessary experiences to know how to behave appropriately or a clear understanding of what is expected behavior in a work setting. This lack of awareness and skills can have dire consequences.

We strongly believe that transition programs for youth and young adults should include social skills training germane to the work, living, and educational demands of the environments in which the young people exist or are placed. This instruction can be offered formally in a group or classroom format or more informally on an individualized basis in home, school, work, and/or community settings. In any case, the instruction should be based on contemporary social learning models as applied to social and life skills training. Figure 1 presents an overview of this conceptualization of social skills, which borrows heavily from McFall's (1982) classic discussion of social behavior from a social learning perspective. In this section, we discuss this orientation briefly and then describe its application to individualized and group interventions.

Social Skills Training Framework Social behavior is regulated through both cognitive and behavioral processes. It is important to recognize this duality of systems because it is widely believed that young people with emotional or behavioral difficulties tend to possess thinking errors that contribute greatly to their inappropriate behaviors (Henggeler, 1989; Kazdin, 1987a). With an understanding that there are different levels at which the social skills deficit could be based, it should be possible to pinpoint the areas of strengths and weaknesses and focus subsequent intervention efforts.

We call the first step of the social skills training process *situation/ problem recognition*. In this step, the individual involved in the interaction interprets the context in which the interaction occurs and then discerns subtle nuances surrounding that exchange, whether by reading nonverbal cues from the other person in the interaction or by interpreting the prevailing mood of that individual. Of specific relevance to these young people is the way in which they interpret a social interaction—

Social Skills Training: Conceptual Framework

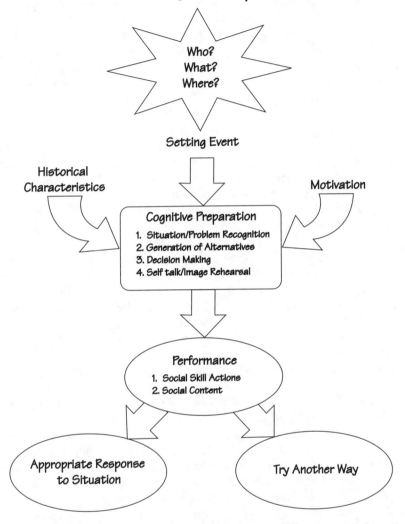

Figure 1.   Conceptual overview of the social skills training process. (Adapted from McFall, R. [1982]. A review and reformulation of the concept of social skills. *Behavioral Assessment, 4,* 25; copyright © 1982, with permission from Elsevier Science.)

an interpretation that is based, in large part, on their histories and personal characteristics. Thus, a person who has a history of being treated harshly or of acting aggressively in other social interactions is more likely than her peers without such histories to impute negative connotations to a benign event (Dodge, Price, Bachorowski, & Newman,

1990). After this initial "sizing up" of the situation, it is important for the individual to generate a number of possible solutions or behavioral responses to the presenting interaction, a process called *generation of alternatives*. From this array of alternatives, the individual then chooses what he believes to be the best possible response to the situation, a step called *decision making*. In the final cognitive step, the individual performs *self-talk/self-image rehearsal* of what he will do to implement and perform that response alternative.

After this cognitive preparation to behave, the individual performs the selected alternative behavioral response to the presenting situation. The behavioral response consists of two observable components. *Social skills actions* are the means by which the individual expresses the content of the interaction (e.g., smiles, gestures, body movements) and represent subtle nuances of social interactions that can greatly influence the other person's interpretation of the behavioral response (Spence, 1981). The *social content* of the response is what is actually said or performed in relation to the presenting situation.

The effectiveness of the response—*appropriate* or *try another way*—is a judgment predicated in large part on the impressions or reactions of some third party. For example, in a job setting such a judge might be a supervisor; and in a living situation, it might be a roommate, spouse, or landlord. These judgments may vary according to who the judge is (e.g., supervisors may view the same behavior very differently from co-workers) and where the behavior occurs (e.g., behaviors in a production setting may be judged differently from behaviors in a break or eating area).

After the behavior is performed, the young person performing the behavior should *analyze the consequences* of her initial behavioral response and, if necessary, reformulate another response to the presenting interaction. It is possible for the response to the presenting situation to produce a variation of the situation—essentially creating another situation—to which the young person also must respond.

Social Skills Training: Individualized or Group Although social skills classes involving small groups of 6–10 young people can be convened on a regular (e.g., weekly) basis to review transition (i.e., job, living, school, social) problems, numerous instances are available to teach the individuals in a one-to-one situation within relevant community settings or in simulated community situations. The conceptual framework for either individual or group training is the same as that described previously. Also, the same behavioral principles for effective teaching of social skills are applicable to individual or group interactions and involve the behavioral principles described in Table 3. In this section, we describe a small-group approach to training that is readily

Table 3. Behavioral principles for social skills training

Provide a rationale for the training.

Use modeling of target behaviors within the training.
   Trainer as model
   Videotape models
   Trainees as models
   Combination of models

Verbalize behavioral examples.

Use structured role-playing.

Use semistructured interactions.

Use unstructured interactions.

Use corrective feedback and reinforcement after interactions.
   Trainers/trainees
   Trainees/trainees

Train for generalization of behavior.
   Present novel stimuli in training
   Focus attention on natural settings
   Require social skills homework in natural settings
   Critique and reinforce performance on homework

adaptable to teaching an individual in an informal manner to resolve a particular issue.

In a weekly meeting overseen by the social skills instructor (e.g., teacher, transition facilitator, school or mental health counselor), a group of youth may convene to address and discuss their experiences in their work placements. To encourage attendance and meaningful participation in the instructional process, social skills instructors should monitor attendance carefully to remind young people of the meeting and should ensure that food and refreshments are available during the session. The meeting should begin with a general discussion of the types of experiences encountered since the last meeting. It may be possible to identify a common theme that is prevalent across the group or, if no theme is evident, to ask individuals to describe a situation that has caused them discomfort or a problem. After disclosure, the social skills instructor asks other members of the group to volunteer brief examples of similar types of problems or interactions they have experienced. The importance of these interactions and their direct relevance to the youth should be stressed. The social skills instructor, in conjunction with the young person describing the initial problem, could then role-play the event to present the content of the social situation.

After this presentation, the other youth should critique the situation to identify the specific roles and positions of the people in the interaction (situation/problem recognition). Once the situation/problem is defined, possible response alternatives to the situation should be generated by the group (generation of alternatives). From this list of response alternatives, a response or a group of responses that seems to be most appropriate to the situation should be identified (decision making). After this step is completed, the effective and ineffective responses to the situation should be presented and discussed to identify why one type of response could be effective but another may not be effective (analysis of consequences). Once the generally agreed-on response is selected, the response should be role-played with the young person modeling that behavioral response to the situation. Care should be taken to have the youth critique both the content of what is said or performed (social content) and the way in which the content is presented (social skill actions). This last process also reflects the analysis of consequences, which was addressed earlier in the selection of the response alternatives.

Social Skills Instructors Every citizen should be supporting appropriate social skills repertoires in children, adolescents, and young adults through recognition and reinforcement of these developing repertoires. Transition facilitators often develop close working relationships with the young people with whom they work, and thus they are uniquely suited to conduct social skills and life skills training. First, in their ongoing contact with the young people, facilitators have great awareness of the types of social problems these youth encounter. Second, because the facilitator does or should have regular contact with the young people, they have more opportunities to intervene with them on an individualized basis to teach them about social behavior in a variety of community settings.

However, social skills instruction cannot be achieved fully by the transition facilitator. Parents, teachers, foster parents, school guidance counselors, and mental health therapists all can learn to apply the social skills training model and assume responsibility to support and teach socially relevant skills. Translation facilitators often conduct social skills groups with young people and simultaneously guide other individuals relevant to the young people (e.g., teachers, co-worker mentors, school guidance counselors, foster parents) in the roles that they can play in supporting and/or teaching social skills with these young people. These strategies help facilitate the generalization and application of appropriate skills by young people in community-relevant settings (Baum, Clark, McCarthy, Sandler, & Carpenter, 1986; Clark, Striefel, Bedlington, & Naiman, 1989; Kazdin, Bass, Siegel, & Thomas, 1989; Lochman, 1992).

Space limitations do not allow us to present a lengthy treatment of social skills and other life skills training and development. For readers who are interested in learning more about social skills training, books by D'Zurilla (1986) and Kelly (1982) and an article by Sheridan, Hungelmann, and Maughan (1999) provided clear and comprehensive overviews of the social skills training process. *Teaching Social Skills to Youth* by Dowd and Tierney (1992), *The Prepare Curriculum* by Goldstein (1999), and the Adolescent Social Skills Effectiveness Training (ASSET) curriculum by Hazel, Schumaker, Sherman, and Sheldon-Wildgen (1981, 1982) are excellent social skills training programs focused specifically on the needs of at-risk adolescents and for which there is empirical evidence to support the relevance and effectiveness in positively affecting the social repertoires of this specific population.

Placement and Support in Community Employment and Living Situations

There is no substitute for the experiences that older youth and young adults gain through placement in independent living scattered-site apartments and in competitive work environments. Institutional facilities and simulated or "make-work" jobs in sheltered settings simply do not provide the same quality of demands and experiences. Independent living and competitive job settings hold certain expectations for social and productivity behaviors and provide models for these repertoires. At the same time, the problems involved in offering such placements should be recognized. Many young people are difficult enough to monitor within the confines of the school building, and that difficulty increases in relatively unrestricted living situations and jobs in the community. This difficulty is further compounded by the fact that these young people should be afforded multiple job placements to explore their own vocational interests and to formulate their likes and desires. Securing competitive job opportunities for young people is an important part of a comprehensive transition program—it is not an end in itself, however.

At first, it may seem that securing a job for an individual and keeping that person employed is easy. Typically, however, it is not (see also Chapter 4). A common mistake that is made is thinking that if young people could get jobs—any jobs—their lives would be changed. To the contrary, the vocational maturity that one develops from these experiences is critical and typically is not gained through a haphazard approach. Such development must be fostered through careful service provision. However, we are often delighted with the extent to which a young person learns and displays an array of appropriate behaviors in natural settings (e.g., a competitive job) in which typical adults model relevant behaviors and expectations. The likelihood of this type of learning taking place in natural settings is increased through the use of co-worker mentors and/or effective on-site training and supervision.

The criterion of employment should be viewed as only one indicator of transition success, not as the sole criterion. Using such an index of success, a job that is menial, low paying, and without benefits and that has little intrinsic reward (i.e., the worker does not like the job) is viewed no differently from a high-paying job with a career path and fringe benefits that the worker finds very rewarding. We need to reconsider the idea that any type of employment is a suitable goal for these young people and adopt a standard similar to one we would have for our own children.

Competitive work placements for these youth fulfill three major roles; they should 1) provide actual work production skills, 2) foster job-related social skills, and 3) be structured in such a way to allow experiences across a number of different job placements that aid the individual in deciding about long-term vocational goals—goals that focus service delivery efforts and lead to the greater probability of long-term job success. Too often in transition programs, young people are placed in jobs merely because the jobs are available and not because they are of any interest. It should be no surprise, then, when youth act out or sabotage such placements, because the work holds no interest or reward for them. A compelling study (Lofquist & Dawis, 1969) dramatically demonstrates that people are more likely to continue to work and to do their jobs well if they enjoy those jobs. Moreover, the primary means by which people gain the awareness necessary to make these judgments is through various work experiences. Clearly, a balance must be struck between the individual's work interests and the availability of job placements. This exercise should centrally involve the young person and, as appropriate, family members and other relevant individuals (e.g., teacher, therapist, natural support network representative). The realistic sharing of ideas and job possibilities can be a rewarding experience for all and can serve to shape a vocational plan that will be meaningful for the student and his future.

Most jobs that are found by people in the general public are located through an individual's personal contacts, such as relatives or friends (Azrin & Besalel, 1980)—what has been termed "the self/family/friend network" (Edgar & Levine, 1987). In a real sense, the transition facilitator acts in this role to introduce young people to different jobs. It is important that the facilitator and the young person work together to develop and secure employment consistent with the participant's career goals and interests. Because these interests may change as varied vocational and academic experiences accrue, it should be acceptable for a young person to be placed in multiple jobs.

General preemployment training should be provided to each participant on an individual basis by the facilitator and—if feasible and acceptable to the young person—through ongoing educational and vocational classes. A specific set of skills to be learned is job interviewing. Interviews afford the employer the opportunity to review and approve of the individual before hiring, shifting the responsibility for the hiring decision from the facilitator and offering the young person the experience of interviewing for a position. Because most young people change jobs and career aspirations numerous times, these skills have generalized applications and are important to them in seeking future jobs. Consequently, a fair portion of the preemployment training should involve job search skills, résumé writing, interview techniques and practice, and other skills related to the demands typical of worksites (e.g., following multiple-component instructions). The exact amount of this type of training is, of course, predicated on the needs of the individual and his work history and capabilities.

Of course, some jobs may not fit a particular young person for different reasons. It may be that an individual's unique set of behaviors cannot be accommodated in a job setting or that a job placement either exacerbates these conditions or creates a dangerous situation for the young person or for others. Nishioka (in press-b) presents a summary of behavioral issues that may relate to the job setting and concomitant safeguards that can be taken.

Although allowances should be made for young people to have multiple job placements, it is best if these job changes are not made in a random or noncontingent manner. Instead, job placements should be planned carefully, and youth should earn the privilege of entering progressively more demanding and more rewarding placements through appropriate behaviors and successes. Exactly how such a progression should be structured is a major issue to be addressed.

Table 4 presents five phases of responsibilities and supports for integrating young people into competitive job placements. There is between phases a developmental progression that reflects the level of work responsibility, the level of reward from the job, and the way in which the youth is monitored and supported. In our experience, some young people may spend weeks in one phase, whereas others may be placed in a phase for only a few days before they demonstrate suitable competence to be moved ahead. Some young people show a level of competence that demonstrates their ability to function with minimal monitoring and supports, so they may be able to start at or progress rapidly to a rather advanced phase. Also, the role of the transition facilitator often is modified to accommodate the young person (e.g., she does not want the stigma of a "job coach" at the worksite, so the facilitator works with her and the employer behind the scenes). The facilitator's role may shift when arrangements are made for a young person

Table 4. Five phases that young people go through in competitive employment

Learning phase

The worker is supervised and trained regarding all tasks and duties by the transition facilitator (TF).

The worker learns various job duties required at the jobsite.

The worker learns and follows all rules and regulations as posted at the jobsite.

The worker begins to identify and work on skills and behaviors exhibited at the jobsite.

The TF collects and records all data from skill and behavior programs.

The TF, in conjunction with the worker, begins to explore transportation options such as city buses, bicycling, and walking.

The worker may begin bus training if appropriate and available.

The worker maintains a minimum of 3 working hours per week.

The TF delivers all consequences to and makes all contacts with the worker.

Responsibility phase

The TF makes intermittent quality checks while at the jobsite.

The worker begins to maintain various job duties independently.

The worker begins to follow all rules and regulations independently at the jobsite.

The worker begins to set his own goals with the TF and watches his own behaviors.

The TF collects and records all data from skill and behavior programs.

The worker begins transporting herself by public transportation, if available, with the TF's guidance and supervision.

The worker uses vocational time wisely and maintains satisfactory work rate and quality.

The worker maintains at least 5 working hours per week.

The worker begins to receive and respond to occasional feedback from employer.

The TF delivers all consequences to and makes the majority of contacts with the worker.

Transition phase

The TF is not at the jobsite but makes intermittent quality checks.

The worker is independent in all job duties and tasks.

The worker follows all rules and regulations independently at the jobsite.

The worker works toward vocational goals and maintains her own behaviors.

The worker's skill and behavior data are monitored with a travel card.

The worker transports herself independently to and from work.

The worker maintains work quality equal to that of a typical employee.

The worker maintains at least 10 working hours per week.

The worker responds to the employer in all job-related matters.

The employer delivers the majority of consequences to the worker.

Independent phase

The TF makes intermittent quality checks by telephone.

The worker is independent in all job duties and tasks.

The worker follows all rules and regulations independently at the jobsite.

The worker continues to work toward vocational goals and monitors his own behaviors.

The worker has no formal behavior programs.

The worker transports himself independently to and from the worksite.

The worker maintains work quality equal to that of a typical employee.

The worker maintains at least 10 working hours per week.

The worker responds to the employer in all job-related matters.

The employer delivers all consequences to the worker.

The worker is eligible for placement in paid employment with TF support.

(continued)

Table 4. (*continued*)

Employable phase

The TF assists with administrative issues.
The employer trains and manages the worker.
The worker reaches vocational goals.
The worker transports herself independently to and from work.
The worker maintains at least 20 working hours per week for 1 year.
The worker is able to secure paid employment on her own.

to be mentored on the job by a co-worker, who assists the young person in learning job tasks and, more important, the performance and social expectations of the workplace. In any case, this system provides the facilitator with a framework for the level of competencies that young people need within the workplace and the concomitant monitoring and supports that may be needed by them for success. This system benefits the students through the teaching of the requisite skills necessary for success in the current placement and in future placements that may be more demanding.

We are always attempting to maximize the opportunities for young people to secure job experiences that match their interests, needs, and goals. Although we have focused much of our discussion in this chapter on employment, similar teaching/supports/services strategies apply to the other transition domains of educational opportunities, living situation, and community-life adjustment.

CONCLUSIONS

Young people with emotional or behavioral difficulties can learn to become productive citizens and workers provided that they receive focused and effective instruction and support to learn and practice the skills needed to become successful. Perhaps the best way for them to learn these skills is through a close relationship with a caring and skilled transition facilitator or other mentor/caregiver/teacher/counselor and through opportunities to explore different job, living, educational, social, and community situations. There is no denying that these young people can present unique and demanding challenges to the social services, vocational, and educational arenas. At the same time, the role of the transition facilitator is uniquely suited to addressing these issues in a direct manner. By offering these young people tangible, real-world skills training and experiences that are based on their interests, the facilitator and others can powerfully affect these individuals' transition skills and ultimate success. We are hopeful that the suggestions offered in this chapter will prove applicable and that they will in some way affect the lives of these young people positively in their transition pursuits.

REFERENCES

Albee, G. (1982). Preventing psychopathology and promoting human potential. *American Psychologist, 37,* 1043–1050.

Azrin, N., & Besalel, V. (1980). *Job club counselor's manual.* Baltimore: University Park Press.

Bandura, A. (1982). The psychology of chance encounters and life paths. *American Psychologist, 37,* 747–755.

Bandura, A. (1986). *Social foundations of thought and action: A social cognitive theory.* Upper Saddle River, NJ: Prentice-Hall.

Baum, J.G., Clark, H.B., McCarthy, W., Sandler, J., & Carpenter, R. (1986). An analysis of the acquisition and generalization of social skills in troubled youth: Combining social skills training, cognitive self-talk, and relaxation procedures. *Journal of Child and Family Behavior Therapy, 8*(4), 1–27.

Bullis, M., & Benz, M. (1996). *Effective secondary/transition programs for adolescents with behavioral disorders.* Arden Hills, MN: Behavioral Institute for Children and Adolescents.

Bullis, M., & Davis, C. (1996). Further examination of job-related social skills measures for adolescents and young adults with emotional and behavioral disorders. *Behavioral Disorders, 21,* 161–172.

Bullis, M., & Davis, C. (1997). Further examination of community-based social skills measures for adolescents and young adults with emotional and behavioral disorders. *Behavioral Disorders, 23,* 231–241.

Bullis, M., & Davis, C. (Eds.). (1999). *Functional assessment procedures in transition and rehabilitation for adolescents and adults with learning disorders.* Austin, TX: PRO-ED.

Bullis, M., Fredericks, H.D.B., Lehman, C., Paris, K., Corbitt, J., & Johnson, B. (1994). Description and evaluation of the Job Designs program for adolescents with emotional or behavioral disorders. *Behavioral Disorders, 19,* 254–268.

Bullis, M., & Paris, K. (1995). Competitive employment and service management for adolescents and young adults with emotional and behavioral disorders. *Special Services in the Schools, 10,* 77–96.

Chadsey-Rusch, J. (1990). Teaching social skills on the job. In F.R. Rusch (Ed.), *Supported employment: Models, methods, and issues* (pp. 161–180). Sycamore, IL: Sycamore Publishing Co.

Clark, H.B. (1998). *Transition to Independence Process (TIP): TIP system development and operations manual.* Tampa: University of South Florida, Louis de la Parte Florida Mental Health Institute.

Clark, H.B., Striefel, S., Bedlington, M., & Naiman, D. (1989). A social skills development model: Coping strategy for children with chronic illness. *Journal of Children's Health Care, 18,* 19–29.

Clark, H.B., Unger, K.V., & Stewart, E.S. (1993). Transition of youth and young adults with emotional/behavioral disorders into employment, education, and independent living. *Community Alternatives: International Journal of Family Care, 5*(2), 19–46.

Cohen, B., & Anthony, W. (1984). Functional assessment in psychiatric rehabilitation. In A.S. Halpern & M.J. Fuhrer (Eds.), *Functional assessment in rehabilitation* (pp. 79–100). Baltimore: Paul H. Brookes Publishing Co.

Cook, D. (1978). Effectiveness of vocational evaluation training recommendations. *Vocational Evaluation and Work Adjustment Bulletin, 11*(3), 8–13.

Cook, D., & Brookings, J. (1980). The relationship of rehabilitation client vocational appraisal to training outcomes and employment. *Journal of Applied Rehabilitation Counseling, 11,* 32–35.

Corbitt, J., & Paris, K. (in press). Intake and pre-placement. In M. Bullis & H.D.B. Fredericks (Eds.), *Providing effective vocational/transition services to adolescents with emotional and behavioral disorders.* Arden Hills, MN: Behavioral Institute for Children and Adolescents.

DeStefano, L. (1987). The use of standardized assessment in supported employment. In L. DeStefano & F. Rusch (Eds.), *Supported employment in Illinois: Assessment methodology and research issues* (pp. 55–98). Champaign, IL: Transition Institute.

Dodge, K., Price, J., Bachorowski, J., & Newman, J. (1990). Hostile attributional biases in severely aggressive adolescents. *Journal of Abnormal Psychology, 99,* 385–392.

Doren, B. (1992). *Social problems of adolescents with disabilities in transition.* Eugene: University of Oregon, Secondary and Transition Programs.

Dowd, T., & Tierney, J. (1992). *Teaching social skills to youth: A curriculum for child-care providers.* Boys Town, NE: Boys Town Press.

Dryfoos, J. (1990). *Adolescents at risk.* New York: Oxford University Press.

Dryfoos, J. (1993). Schools as places for health, mental health, and social services. In R. Takanishi (Ed.), *Adolescence in the 90's: Risk and opportunity* (pp. 82–109). New York: Teachers College Press.

D'Zurilla, T.J. (1986). *Problem solving therapy: A social competence approach to clinical intervention.* New York: Springer-Verlag New York.

Edgar, E., & Levine, P. (1987). *Special education students in transition: Washington state data 1976–1986.* Seattle: University of Washington, Experimental Education Unit.

Fredericks, H.D.B. (1995). An education perspective. In C.M. Nelson, B. Wolford, & R. Rutherford (Eds.), *Comprehensive and collaborative systems that work for troubled youth: A national agenda* (pp. 68–89). Richmond: Eastern Kentucky University, National Coalition for Juvenile Justice Services, Training Resource Center.

Frey, W. (1984). Functional assessment in the '80s. In A.S. Halpern & M.J. Fuhrer (Eds.), *Functional assessment in rehabilitation* (pp. 11–44). Baltimore: Paul H. Brookes Publishing Co.

Goldstein, A.P. (1999). *The Prepare Curriculum: Teaching prosocial competencies* (Rev. ed.). Champaign, IL: Research Press Co.

Halpern, A.S. (1993). Quality of life as a conceptual framework for evaluating transition outcomes. *Exceptional Children, 59,* 486–498.

Halpern, A.S. (1996). *Some reflections about self-directed transition planning.* Keynote address presented at the annual meeting of the Washington State Transition Conference, Vancouver, WA.

Halpern, A.S., & Fuhrer, M.J. (Eds.). (1984). *Functional assessment in rehabilitation.* Baltimore: Paul H. Brookes Publishing Co.

Halpern, A.S., Herr, C., Wolf, N., Lawson, J., Doren, B., & Johnson, M. (1998). *The Next S.T.E.P. (Student Transition and Educational Planning) curriculum.* Austin, TX: PRO-ED.

Hazel, J.S., Schumaker, J.B., Sherman, J., & Sheldon-Wildgen, J. (1981). The development and evaluation of a group skills training program for court-adjudicated youth. In D. Upper & S. Ross (Eds.), *Behavioral group therapy* (pp. 113–152). Champaign, IL: Research Press Co.

Hazel, J.S., Schumaker, J.B., Sherman, J.A., & Sheldon-Wildgen, J. (1982). Group social skills training: A program for court-adjudicated probationary youth. *Criminal Justice and Behavior, 9*, 35–53.

Henggeler, S. (1989). *Delinquency in adolescence.* Thousand Oaks, CA: Sage Publications.

Hobbs, N., & Robinson, S. (1982). Adolescent development and public policy. *American Psychologist, 37*, 212–223.

Horner, R.H., Sprague, J.R., & Flannery, K.B. (1993). Building functional curricula for students with severe intellectual disabilities. In R. Van Houten & S. Axelrod (Eds.), *Behavior analysis and treatment* (pp. 47–71). New York: Plenum Press.

Hursh, N., & Kerns, A. (1988). *Vocational evaluation in special education.* San Diego: College-Hill Press.

Kazdin, A.E. (1987a). *Conduct disorders in childhood and adolescence.* Thousand Oaks, CA: Sage Publications.

Kazdin, A.E. (1987b). Treatment of antisocial behavior in children: Current status and future directions. *Psychological Bulletin, 102*, 187–203.

Kazdin, A.E., Bass, D., Siegel, T., & Thomas, C. (1989). Cognitive-behavioral therapy and relationship therapy in the treatment of children referred for antisocial behavior. *Journal of Consulting and Clinical Psychology, 57*(4), 522–535.

Kelly, J. (1982). *Social skills training.* New York: Springer-Verlag New York.

Kincaid, D. (1996). Person-centered planning. In L.K. Koegel, R.L. Koegel, & G. Dunlap (Eds.), *Positive behavioral support: Including people with difficult behavior in the community* (pp. 439–465). Baltimore: Paul H. Brookes Publishing Co.

Knitzer, J., Steinberg, Z., & Fleisch, B. (1990). *At the schoolhouse door.* New York: Bank Street College of Education.

Kortering, L.J., & Edgar, E.B. (1988). Vocational rehabilitation and special education: A need for cooperation. *Rehabilitation Counseling Bulletin, 31*, 178–184.

Lochman, J.E. (1992). Cognitive-behavioral intervention with aggressive boys: Three-year follow-up and preventive effects. *Journal of Consulting and Clinical Psychology, 60*(3), 426–432.

Lofquist, L., & Dawis, R. (1969). *Adjustment to work: A psychological view of man's problems in a work-oriented society.* Stamford, CT: Appleton-Century-Crofts.

Marder, C. (1992). *Secondary students classified as seriously emotionally disturbed: How are they being served?* Menlo Park, CA: SRI International.

Marder, C., Wechsler, M., & Valdes, K. (1993). *Services for youth with disabilities after secondary school.* Menlo Park, CA: SRI International.

McFall, R. (1982). A review and reformulation of the concept of social skills. *Behavioral Assessment, 4*, 1–33.

Nishioka, V. (in press-a). Job training and support. In M. Bullis & H.D.B. Fredericks (Eds.), *Providing effective vocational/transition services to adolescents with emotional and behavioral disorders.* Arden Hills, MN: Behavioral Institute for Children and Adolescents.

Nishioka, V. (in press-b). Tracking student progress. In M. Bullis & H.D.B. Fredericks (Eds.), *Providing effective vocational/transition services to adolescents with emotional and behavioral disorders.* Arden Hills, MN: Behavioral Institute for Children and Adolescents.

Parker, J., & Asher, S. (1987). Peer relations and later personal adjustment: Are low-accepted children at risk? *Psychological Bulletin, 102*, 357–389.

Pruitt, W. (1976). Vocational evaluation: Yesterday, today, and tomorrow. *Vocational Evaluation and Work Adjustment Bulletin, 9*, 8–16.

Rutherford, R., Bullis, M., Wheeler-Anderson, C., & Griller, H. (in press). *Youth with special education disabilities in the correctional system: Prevalence rates and identification issues.* Washington, DC: Office of Juvenile Justice and Prevention and U.S. Department of Education, Office of Special Education Programs and Rehabilitative Services.

Sheridan, S.M., Hungelmann, A., & Maughan, D.P. (1999). A contextualized framework for social skills assessment, intervention, and generalization. *School Psychology Review, 28,* 84–103.

Sitlington, P., Brolin, D., Clark, G., & Vacanti, J. (1985). Career/vocational assessment in the public school setting: The position of the Division on Career Development. *Career Development for Exceptional Individuals, 8,* 3–6.

Spence, S.H. (1981). Validation of social skills of adolescent males in an interview conversation with a previously unknown adult. *Journal of Applied Behavior Analysis, 14,* 159–168.

Spivack, G., Platt, J., & Shure, M. (1976). *The problem solving approach to adjustment.* San Francisco: Jossey-Bass.

Szymanski, E. (1994). Transition: Life-span and life-space considerations for empowerment. *Exceptional Children, 60,* 402–410.

The Real Game Series. (1996). St. Joseph, New Brunswick, Canada: Robinson and Blackmore Publishing.

Valdes, K., Williamson, C., & Wagner, M. (1990). *The National Longitudinal Transition Study of special education students: Vol. 3. Youth categorized as emotionally disturbed.* Menlo Park, CA: SRI International.

Wagner, M., Blackorby, J., Cameto, R., & Newman, L. (1993). *What makes a difference? Influences on postschool outcomes of youth with disabilities.* Menlo Park, CA: SRI International.

Waintrup, M., & Kelley, P. (1999). Situational assessment. In M. Bullis & C. Davis (Eds.), *Functional assessment procedures in transition and rehabilitation for adolescents and adults with learning disorders* (pp. 47–66). Austin, TX: PRO-ED.

Walker, H., & Bullis, M. (1995). A comprehensive services model for troubled youth. In C.M. Nelson, B. Wolford, & R. Rutherford (Eds.), *Comprehensive and collaborative systems that work for troubled youth: A national agenda* (pp. 122–148). Richmond: Eastern Kentucky University, National Coalition for Juvenile Justice Services, Training Resource Center.

Webb, K., Repetto, J., Beutel, A., Perkins, D., Bailey, M., Schwartz, S.E., Perry, L.J., & Tucker, V.L. (1999). *Dare to dream: A guide to planning your future.* Tallahassee: Transition Center, Florida Department of Education.

Wolf, M., Braukmann, C., & Ramp, K. (1987). Serious delinquent behavior as a part of a significantly handicapping condition: Cures and supportive environments. *Journal of Applied Behavior Analysis, 20,* 347–359.

7

Clinical and Substance Abuse Treatment

Applications in the Trenches

*Maria A. Brucculeri, Tali Gogol-Ostrowski,
David Stewart, Justin Sloan, and Maryann Davis*

Young adulthood is a confusing time even under the best of circumstances. Is the person an adolescent or an adult? Is he independent or the responsibility of parents and other authorities, and to what degree? Successful young adults find ways to develop an interactive autonomy. That is, they achieve independent status through interactions with peers and adults within a variety of contexts, including school, work, and family. Young adults with emotional or behavioral difficulties who receive public services have often experienced a good deal of failure. This experience leads many to develop "stories" about themselves that define both past and future as destined for failure. Instead of interacting within normative contexts, they have engaged with state agencies. These systems teach young people and their families to question their decision-making abilities and promote dependence on professional "authorities." Young people need to find a way to recognize the difficulties of the past while actively seeking positive opportunities in the future. This is a tremendous challenge for young people and their families and the transition facilitators in their lives.

This chapter describes a clinical stance that is particularly helpful in working with young adults with emotional or behavioral difficulties. Many traditional clinical approaches emphasize problems, pathology, and individuals out of their natural context. The stance described herein is consistent with the values of the Transition to Independence Process (TIP) system (see Chapter 2) and emphasizes strengths, possibilities, and natural context. Mental health and substance abuse treatment can occur in a variety of settings (e.g., individual therapy, group therapy, residential treatment, supported living). A therapeutic relationship can develop in an ever broader spectrum of situations (e.g., service coordination, teacher–student relationships, spiritual guidance, mentorships). The clinical stance described herein can be applied in any of these situations and settings and by individuals doing this kind of work, who are referred to as *transition facilitators*. This approach requires access to clinical supervision that is consistent with the approach, the support of colleagues, and sufficient time with each young person to form and maintain a trusting relationship. Additional considerations in working with young people with co-occurring problems with substance use are offered as well. The chapter is written with the help of several young adults, one of whom, the fourth author, is quoted throughout the chapter.

The clinical stance presented herein is drawn from some 40 cumulative years of applications in the trenches. A single chapter cannot do justice to a complete consideration of clinical and substance abuse issues among young people. Thus, we encourage those who work with youth in transition to read and secure training and field supervision in the intervention strategies described in mutisystemic therapy (Henggeler, Schoenwald, Broduin Rowland, & Cunningham, 1998) and other strategies tailored to resolving impasses between adolescents and parents (e.g., Diamond & Liddle, 1996) and substance abuse treatment (e.g., Azrin et al., 1996; Henggeler, 1997; Liddle, 1999).

NECESSARY PHILOSOPHY AND THERAPEUTIC STANCE

When working with adolescents and young adults, even the most experienced and proficient clinicians can find themselves ignored, working without a customer (Berg, 1994), or just plain stuck. The first major section of this chapter frames a clinical stance that helps overcome these challenges. As described in Chapter 1, these youth and young adults are at a developmental level where they are demonstrating separation and choice making and are doing so in the context of natural settings where adults have minimal influence and peers dominate. In order for a transition facilitator to assist a young person, a relationship needs to be developed with her on her terrain. Effective problem solving, social skills training, and anger management training can be accomplished only when the young person will approach the transition facilitator. This coming together can be assisted through the use of good clinical skills (e.g., listening), mediation of reinforcers (e.g., after our session, I'll drop you off at the recreation center), establishment of clear ground rules and related consequences (e.g., physical aggression will result in the police being called), and the use of relationship development skills (e.g., showing interest in her topics, being available). This clinical stance sets the occasion for the young person to explore future possibilities and the behavioral, attitudinal, and ecological changes that she may need to achieve her goals. Transition facilitators can assist young people in exploring possibilities and changes through their continuing demonstration of the following four values: 1) encourage hope, 2) see problems within context, 3) allow flexible boundaries between transition facilitators and young people, and 4) encourage natural supports.

Encourage Hope

The field abounds with support for models of therapeutic intervention that emphasize highlighting and building on strengths and noting and exploring exceptions to problem behaviors. One such approach, Possibility Thinking (O'Hanlon, 1993), goes beyond Positive Thinking. Briefly, Possibility Thinking allows for the recognition of the severity of the situation and the possibility that circumstances can change. Typically, young people arrive at a transition facilitator's door with ample evidence of failure in their lives and extensive histories of treatments that have proved ineffective. Inevitably, blame creeps in. The young person is often seen as unmotivated or resistant to change and "earns" increasingly more pathological labels. Such histories can become quite powerful as the young people and their facilitators begin to adopt the unavoidable pessimism of bulky case files, numerous ineffective interventions, and failed attempts to change. Positive Thinking alone cannot erase brutal histories of trauma, years of separation and losses, discrimination, or poverty and their lasting impact. However, because Positive Thinking includes recognition of the severity of past and current situations while emphasizing the possibility of change, positive change can occur.

Adopting the stance that life offers more opportunities than have already been presented affects the nature and dialogue of the helping relationship. The facilitator is expectant of and vigilant for change. A sense of urgency is generated even in long-standing situations. The facilitator explores everything related to change: exceptions to problems, small changes, who and what is helpful, and even why things are not worse. Goals for therapy are more easily generated when change remains in the forefront and the goals are defined in terms of the presence of behaviors rather than the absence of them. For example, rather than the goal of decreasing anxiety, one would look for sufficient confidence to attend three job interviews this week. In this way, both the transition facilitator and the young person can monitor successes.

It is important to highlight the young person's and the family's expertise because systems have often communicated, even unintentionally, that the young person and the young person's family do not have the knowledge or the ability to effect positive change. Youth can be helped to see the merits of their efforts and small successes even in poor overall outcomes. Following standard solution-focused strategies, the transition facilitator can explore exceptions to the problem behavior, contexts in which the problem behavior does not occur, and how it is defeated. All of these areas exemplify the young person's strengths and can be framed as such. Similarly, parents' attempts to change generally exemplify certain strengths, even if the overall effort is unsuccessful. The skillful facilitator sees myriad strengths once he begins to look. Issues of reempowering parents in their parental authority should be emphasized because parents have often moved or been moved into more distant positions regarding their children. This is particularly true in out-of-home placements. Given the nature of such settings, facilitators must actively seek antidotes to the almost unavoidable message to parents that they are not in charge. One method of accomplishing this involves doing away with points and level systems. Rather, facilitators ask parents to define limits and consequences for their adolescents even when they are out of the home. For example, if the young person engages in seriously inappropriate behavior, the parents can be called and asked what to do about it. This can be somewhat disorienting for parents and young people alike at first; however, because it more accurately reflects the rules of the natural setting (to which it is hoped that the young person will return), it more easily transfers to enduring change.

This type of therapeutic approach can be difficult for transition facilitators. Being open to more favorable possibilities despite concrete evidence to the contrary can result in the facilitator's being labeled "clinically naive," "unsophisticated," and even "arrogant" by other professionals and systems. Young adults who have experienced the positive thinking of transition facilitators, however, have noted that the facilitator's belief that their lives could be different was contagious:

> Other professionals and paraprofessionals believe too much of what they read in the files and in their books! I would do anything to avoid talking to people like that. It's like you are already condemned and they don't think you're going to do anything with your life anyway. Sometimes you think that yourself; you don't need a therapist to think that.

Hopelessness about success can also lead to waxing and waning motivation for change. Enhancing motivation, then, also encourages hope. Inspirational writer Anthony Robbins (Robbins & Covan, 1993) proposed that change occurs either because a problem is so painful that it is avoided at any cost or because a dream is so big that it actually pulls for change. Enhancing motivation, then, can be thought of as stoking either of these fires. It may be useful, for example, to send people on dream-building excursions on which they collect data and fill in the imaginary pictures of the success they seek. Visiting college campuses and talking with students, test-driving new cars, viewing nice apartments, and shadowing a worker in a chosen profession are all examples of dream-building excursions. Reluctant young people may be more likely to go on such excursions with a family member or a transition facilitator along. On the opposite pole, drawing attention to the pain suffered can also enhance motivation. Rather than propose or encourage any solution, the facilitator continuously notes the dilemmas, sacrifices, and obstacles that the problem creates for the young person. When change is suggested by the young person, the facilitator cautions that it may be hasty and that there may be some benefits to the problem that have not yet manifested themselves. The angrier and more forceful the young person's statements about wanting change, the better. Concrete, small change steps should be goals at this point.

View Problems in Context

Although there are many areas for intervention (e.g., biological, internal, unconscious), one recommended bias is to focus on social context. Young adults are moving between many new relationships as they position themselves and are positioned more autonomously and/or responsibly. Difficulties that arise during this life stage exist in the context of these new relationships, as do their solutions. In this approach, the transition facilitator focuses on the patterns of communication between the young adult and others with whom she has significant relationships. The facilitator is interested in what is going on between people and who is available to be helpful.

When problems are interactionally defined, therapy includes as many others involved with the problem as possible. Directive family therapists have termed this working with the *problem-defined system* (Haley, 1987). Therapy should also include those who could be helpful. This serves to strengthen youth's natural support systems (see Chapter 11). Young adults often identify a short list but can broaden it with encouragement from a trusted other. Such encouragement generally involves paring down the idea of "helpful" so that small contributions are visible. For example, a father who has an embattled relationship with his young adult son may be seen as a resource if he is willing to provide monthly transportation to a training program. It should also be noted that success with small contributions from unlikely sources has a way of generalizing into less disappointment, improved relationships, and larger contributions. Furthermore, this process self-generates in that more and more individuals are willing to serve as resources if they have to make only small contributions. Conversely, excluding someone can be determined. A distraught mother brought her suicidal daughter from the emergency room to an interview and tearfully volunteered that she should not participate because she had been told that she had a "toxic relationship" with her child. Working with young adults and their families for any length of time can easily convince a facilitator that parents and their growing children often bring out the worst in each other, yet it is a tremendously arrogant notion that one can sever the relationship by excluding it from therapeutic dialogue. It also sends a clear message that there is no possibility for change. Difficulty between people is one of the more compelling reasons for inclusion. More subtle examples of exclusion occur frequently with collateral professionals (e.g., school personnel, probation officers, psychiatrists), particularly if they are in disagreement. Opportunities to help focus change efforts through collaboration among those in the natural and formal support systems are too easily lost.

Allow Flexible Boundaries

Helping professionals are usually cautioned about allowing their personal selves to enter into therapeutic relationships (i.e., countertransference). If a young person asks whether you have children, you are instructed to respond, "My, you are curious about me." When this scenario was described to a group of young adults who were being interviewed during the writing of this book, a massive groan resounded through the group. Not one of them would work with a transition facilitator who would not answer questions about herself. Indeed, young adults were clear in their position that facilitators need to present themselves honestly and fully. Young people require an element of relevance in their relationships, and the facilitator should be exposed sufficiently to be assessed along the following line: Is this someone who has the capacity to understand me and the context that is my life? Note that the issue is about the capacity to comprehend rather than about shared experience. Qualification certainly exists along lines of similar journeys; however, the transition facilitator does not have to be an ex-gang member to understand that survival and success in a context of violence is different from that in middle-class America: "Don't tell me to just walk away from a fight because then you show me that you understand nothing." The type of relationship that results from this stance is clearly more intimate than that allowed by the typical boundaries that exist between professional and young person: "If you want someone to talk to you, you have to talk to them first. You've got to show yourself as a person." It is difficult to learn these broader boundaries. However, success is manifested in the young person's willingness to disclose and discharge emotion. Successful transition facilitators get fired and rehired by young people all the time because they are perceived as being able to take it and to care enough to come back. These transition facilitators do not demand respect, but they seem to earn it naturally. Moreover, the relationship that is formed can withstand a good deal of confrontation on both sides: "There's a serious no-bullshit clause, and you both get called on it."

Flexibility in where, when, and how therapy occurs also facilitates work with young people. A community-based approach that allows for flexibility in where therapy takes place is helpful. A number of simultaneous messages, even if not intended, are sent to young adults who are required to meet weekly in a facilitator's office. A certain hierarchy is assumed, with the facilitator established as expert. The young person understands that he should present himself in certain ways. Moreover, many young adults who have had ample childhood and adolescent therapy experience expect that they will be required to talk about their feelings, take responsibility for themselves, and become insightful about their lives. With these aspects given, therapy is avoided like the dentist's drill: "Why would I go somewhere where the guy says, 'Tell me more about that,' to everything I say?" In contrast, a community-based approach corrects the hierarchy, making the transition facilitator a guest in the young person's territory. The facilitator more easily and genuinely adopts a stance of ignorance with regard to the young person's context and asks to be taught what is important and what is in the way of getting there. Home-based work can allow the facilitator to penetrate the understandable reluctance of someone whose therapy has failed before: "If I am supposed to come to your office, I might say no or I might just not show. If you come to me, I'll probably be there and give you a chance. I figure you might be different."

Young adults find it easier to talk in a casual setting. Doing something practical together, such as driving to pick up a job application, is also a good way to engage a young person and communicate the desire to be helpful. Young adults often appreciate facilitators' abilities to see concrete goals as worthy of their attention, particularly when such issues can wreak havoc on young people's lives. They have learned that all the talking in the world does not remedy certain things: "Don't make me tell you how frustrated I am that I don't have a job. It is much better to figure out how to fill out applications and go drop them off. Anyway,

I have talked about more important stuff in the car than anyplace else." There are times, of course, when it is best to meet in an office or a neutral space, particularly if safety issues are involved (see, e.g., Peters & Hills, 1999). Again, flexibility is the key.

Putting into practice these recommended boundaries and stances for engagement with young adults can be extremely difficult. In addition to going against much of what is learned during training, using oneself in this way can make work more difficult. It has been these authors' experiences that colleagues working in traditional settings generally do not understand the approach and do not support it. This work seems less "professional" and less important. Because transition facilitators develop a deeper understanding of young people's difficulties, they express those difficulties in terms of life experiences rather than diagnoses. Of course, exceptions are made, such as when helping a young person to evaluate her medication, but thinking in terms of life rather than diagnostic terms is emphasized. Accommodating young people's needs makes schedules less predictable. Driving through communities in all kinds of weather, finding parking, getting lost, feeling unsafe, and being stood up are common occurrences. Relationships with young people are as unique as the individuals themselves. One young person is seen on a twice-weekly basis and another once a month, and still another fits into the facilitator's schedule on little notice. Secondhand smoke is inhaled from time to time, and eating in fast-food restaurants is common. Young people curse and scream when they are angry, and family members call with no regard for boundaries or confidentiality. All of this is expected as the facilitator becomes relevant, just a typical person who is determined to be helpful: "My worker deals with the bullshit. She doesn't always like it, but she always hangs in."

Encourage Natural Supports: The Family Resource

Commonly, young adults come to transition facilitators as if they have no family: "The parents are out of the picture." "No one wants anything to do with this kid anymore." "The father is out of the country, and the mother doesn't speak English and doesn't believe in therapy." "The family is abusive." "The young person doesn't want them involved." These statements often lead transition facilitators to discount the young adult's most immediate and powerful resource: the family. Formerly, family therapists wanted to include the family because they were seen as the source of the problem. The recommendation here to include family members is based on the fact that they are viewed as holding the most potent solutions. This is not to say that inclusion of the family is easy, given the statements quoted previously. Family involvement, however, can be the key to shorter treatment and more lasting change.

Obtaining Permission to Involve Family One of the most vexing hurdles in working with young adults is obtaining access to their families. This hurdle is poignantly exemplified by the following story. There was a time when Dean used drugs extensively. During this time he received multiple diagnoses, medications and hospitalizations. During one hospitalization the staff determined that his primary problem was drug use. Upon hearing this, his parents offered to buy him the stereo equipment that he wanted so badly if he would just quit drugs. The therapist told Dean that he didn't think this was a good solution to his problems, so Dean wouldn't allow the therapist to speak with his parents. Dean was soon listening to music and abusing drugs dangerously. Dean later related that he felt that his parents were in the most powerful position to help with his drug problem, and that they were well intentioned, but they had been eliminated from the conversation because of his legal ability to withhold permission for therapists to include them.

Because young adults have the legal right to deny family and significant-other involvement in the therapeutic process and because these relationships are often very strained, it can be difficult to obtain permission from young adults to include their families and to communicate openly with them. Emphatic refusals for permission, multiple conditions for communication, and denials that the family is interested or even exists are common. Transition facilitators must obey the laws regarding confidentiality; however, the issue of family involvement should not be abandoned during therapy. As the relationship between the transition facilitator and young person deepens and trust is built, the young person may agree to family involvement. A caring facilitator's knowledge that family relationships are important and enthusiasm regarding the possibility that positive change will occur can be contagious over time.

With Whom to Ally Many transition facilitators feel conflicted in their alliances to the young person versus the family. This is particularly so when the situation calls for parents to take a hard line or to withhold something, as in the example above. It is important that facilitators remember that their primary alliances are with the young people, secondarily with their families, and thus against the problem. Experience has clearly demonstrated that lack of family involvement most often delays positive change and, unfortunately, too often obstructs it. Therefore, in their alliance with the young person, the transition facilitator must be a strong advocate of family participation. However, the facilitator must be cautious about overidentification with other family members. If the transition facilitator's focus on the young person is lost, the intervention is likely to fail.

Barriers to Family Involvement Families of young adults involved in the various helping systems tend to share characteristics with regard to their willingness or ability to participate in therapeutic dialogue (see Chapter 11). They are often fatigued. Typically, they have participated in a number of therapies and are weary of more talk and hopeless about any power they have to effect change. Service providers have promised and failed in the past, and there is little motivation to invest with new ones. Shame, blame, and guilt exist. Sometimes there is fear of what will happen if the transition to independence fails. Sometimes the family has been wronged by the systems that have attempted to help them and they believe they now must protect themselves. Family members might believe that it is best to back away from the young adult. They may simply be angry as a result of any one of a number of common frustrations during this life phase. After diligent, if not stubborn, pursuit, however, it is unusual to find a family that cannot help significantly.

An example can be seen in the case of a family referred for compulsory treatment by the state child protective agency because the 17-year-old daughter disclosed ongoing sexual abuse by her father. The parents had driven their daughter to the hospital on her return home after being missing for more than a week. The young woman made her disclosure upon admission, and the parents were unable to visit her or to get any information from the hospital regarding her condition. The state protective agency took emergency custody of the girl. The referral information was vivid and graphic. The state worker reported that the father was missing two fingers on one hand, which he had cut off during an occult ritual, and that his abuse of his daughter was likely part of such practices. The facilitator's first telephone contacts with the family were terminated as soon as the facilitator identified herself. Later, the parents told the facilitator that they would rather disappear during the middle of the night than meet for "forced therapy." Ultimately, the transition facilitator was able to schedule a meeting by suggesting that the agenda be to "kick the state out of the family's life." As the facilitator arrived at the home, she learned that the family's pet snake was lost in the home and panicked. The family's assistance in calming the facilitator set the stage for an open dialogue. The family revealed that the young woman had been involved with a gang for a number of years. The young woman corroborated that during her frequent disappearances she was with her friends. She was involved in a number of criminal activities but had yet to be caught. Her parents had surprised her by driving her to the hospital, and she and her "mates" had invented the sexual abuse story. A falling out with a friend in whose family she had been protectively placed resulted in her going back home without the state knowing about it. The family had already started to negotiate new rules for their relationships. Incidentally, the father had lost his fingers in Vietnam.

Resurrecting Family Hope   Given the experiences of this and other families, the first task for the transition facilitator is to resurrect hope. It is useful to assume that the family wants the young person to succeed and is willing under the right circumstances to invest some effort toward this end. It is the facilitator's job to arrange the "right circumstances." A nice way to begin is to acknowledge the ordeal that everyone has been through and to note that they deserve a break before anything else. Madannes (1984) described a strategy of inviting the family to make a memory. The family has ample memories of the awful problems, and it would be nice to have something with which to counter these in the years to come. The family is then helped to arrange to make a good memory and sent off to do it. For those transition facilitators who have flexible funds available, sponsoring such activities is a strong way to encourage change and simply to help people feel better. Programs can elaborate on this idea by scheduling a series of "family fun days" throughout the year and inviting all young people to partake as needed. One can imagine the changes that occur between people as they laugh and enjoy each other in a context apart from the problems that have divided them. Fishing trips, dance parties, barbecues, chair massages, and other activities all are relatively inexpensive vehicles for alleviating the effects of numerous years of stress at least long enough to notice that other possibilities exist. Have a photographer along to take family pictures that can provide a concrete example that things can be different.

Resurrecting hope in situations previously believed to be hopeless can be especially difficult. It may be a challenge even to set the first appointment. One transition facilitator described a father who chose to spend a half hour chatting at the door with proselytizers rather than return to the kitchen table for a family interview. For these reasons, any and every contact with the young person's family becomes a precious opportunity to invite hope. Milton Erikson (cited in Haley, 1973) recommended that the facilitator talk about change as if it would necessarily occur. For example, the facilitator can phrase questions in a particular manner: "When your son grows up and is able to hold a job, do you think you will be able to enjoy each other more? Would that be something you would be interested in? Enjoying each other more?" The dialogue that occurs as a result of this type of questioning facilitates hope and goal setting for therapy.

After such an interview, the transition facilitator can concretely negotiate the terms for involvement. Be realistic about the commitment required and the nature of the involvement that is likely to produce change. Reminding the family that the problems took some time to get to the current level of intensity and that overcoming these problems is going to require considerable effort demonstrates the transition facilitator to be realistic yet confident that change will occur and that it is dependent on the family's influence. Family members may negotiate for the minimal effort required to produce change by saying what they are unwilling to do (e.g., take time off from work, sacrifice another relationship). If family members remain reluctant, they can be asked what circumstances would be required for them to reconsider, what they would have to see to change their minds, and who else in the extended natural support system might feel differently. It can be helpful to point out that other providers have failed in the past and that the process will likely continue to fail without the power and deep emotional connection and commitment of the family.

Additional useful interview techniques can be borrowed from other schools of therapy (see Berg, 1994; de Shazer, 1985; Haley, 1987; White, 1986). In particular, the solution-focused model offers goal-setting strategies that maintain positive momentum and clarity in the therapy (Berg, 1994). The narrative school describes the powerful process of externalization (White, 1986), which allows facilitators, young people, and family members to unite against the problem. The strategic or directive therapy approach is especially helpful in framing the problem in workable ways and providing techniques to inspire change. In *Leaving Home*, Haley (1980) tackled some of the more chronic and incapacitating difficulties of this life stage. The pragmatism common to all of these approaches remains at the core of recommended practices for working with young adults: "The bottom line is that something different has to happen that's good—no matter what it takes!"

It can also be helpful to frame presenting difficulties in terms of problems related to growing up. Although this sounds simplistic, it provides a much more approachable set of tasks for both parents and young people than much of the diagnostic jargon to which they are accustomed. Young adult failure in school, for example, can be framed as a fear of growing up, and other adults in the natural network can be recruited to calm, encourage, and even desensitize the young adult. Similarly, a young adult's difficulty in maintaining employment can be addressed as trouble with leaving home. Parents can then identify what skills need to be learned for the young person's ultimate independence and how best to teach those skills. Young people can find this theme particularly annoying ("I think that's pretty ridiculous!"), yet this frustration can also be a motivator to prove the transition facilitator and parents wrong. The strategic school offers an array of "annoying" yet motivating themes, such as suggesting that young people are sacrificing themselves for their parents' benefit or that they have somehow gotten the idea that their parents need them to stay home (Haley, 1980; Madannes, 1981, 1984).

Encourage Natural Supports: Connecting with Others

Young people and their families who experience difficulty around transition often isolate themselves in shame and guilt (see Chapters 9 and 11). Parents stop talking to other parents, and young people tend to avoid others whom they perceive as more successful, which can isolate them from valuable resources and solutions. It is important for transition facilitators to introduce and arrange opportunities for connection. This can be accomplished within the context of extended family and friends and/or within larger community institutions. Drawing an extended family tree can help to identify potential resources. Also, it is essential to know what the community offers. This includes the tenacious ability to solicit community churches, groups, and organizations to recruit "natural" mentors. There are many individuals who attend Rotary meetings, fraternity organizations, and the like for just these purposes. When young people connect to others, there is a normalizing and calming feeling of shared experience. Virtually every adult has some story about the difficulties involved in transition. Although they may seem unlikely sources of help, successful adults can lend surprisingly wonderful perspectives on the common obstacles to growing up. Sharing stories in a comfortable forum can enlighten and inspire many changes and recruit many supports. Once reconnected, young adults and their families may also be inspired to broaden their circles further and even reach out to others in need. There is nothing more curative than the experience of helping another (see Chapter 10).

RECOMMENDED STRATEGIES FOR TREATING CO-OCCURRING PROBLEMATIC SUBSTANCE USE

Within the framework of the clinical stance described previously, additional considerations for helping those with co-occurring substance use difficulties are described in this section. The following case study illustrates key elements for treatment consideration.

Susan was an 18-year-old woman who spent 6 months in a juvenile corrections facility for assault. Susan did well in detention, earning her general equivalency diploma and participating in anger management and substance abuse groups. She was treated for depression and posttraumatic stress disorder before and during her incarceration. Her transition from the juvenile corrections facility to the community was smooth. Her probation officer found her a job, and she was willing to pay rent to her grandmother. Susan continued to see her mental health therapist each week for support and management of her depression. She talked with her therapist about feeling lonely and bored. She explained that her grandmother lived across town from her old neighborhood and that she missed her friends. She knew, however, that to stay out of trouble she needed to stay away from her old friends and her "old ways."

For more than 2 months, Susan met all of her probation requirements: She had a job, attended therapy, abstained from drugs and alcohol, and lived with her grandmother. She felt good about how well she was doing, although her loneliness and boredom continued. She had not gone to the parties to which her co-workers had invited her because she guessed that people would be getting high and drunk. Her probation officer, therapist, and grandmother praised her. When Susan recalled that she felt more relaxed and had more fun when she was drinking and using marijuana, her therapist helped her make a list of other activities she could do for fun.

Three months after her release, Susan and her grandmother had an argument. She stormed out of the house and went to work. This time, when her co-workers invited her to go out with them, she said yes. She did not return home until the next afternoon. Her grandmother was worried and upset and threatened to call her probation officer. Susan was more concerned about failing the urinalysis because of her use of marijuana the night before. She went out with her new friends the next night, and this time she was afraid to go back home. A month later, Susan's probation officer issued a warrant for her arrest. She had missed her scheduled urinalysis, dropped out of counseling, and been absent from her grandmother's house for 2 weeks. When Susan was picked up by the police in her old neighborhood, she was also charged with riding in a stolen car and possession of marijuana. Now jailed, she has also lost her job.

According to the National Household Survey of Drug Abuse (Substance Abuse and Mental Health Services Administration [SAMHSA], 1997), young people between 16 and 25 years of age are the heaviest users of illicit drugs (Figure 1). Nearly one in five members of this age group uses an illicit drug each month, and an equal number are binge drinkers. Clearly, drugs and alcohol are a constant presence for this age group. With a prevalence of almost 50%, substance use

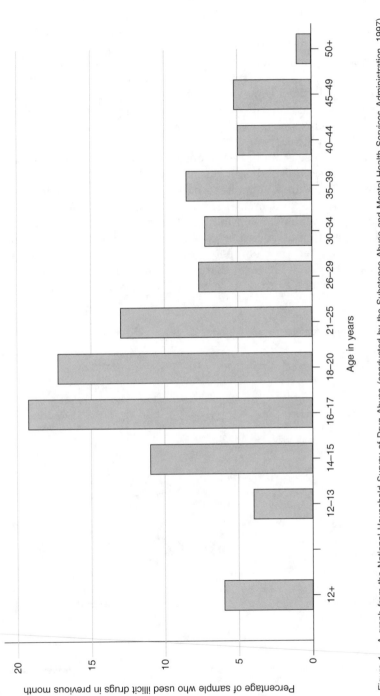

Figure 1. A graph from the National Household Survey of Drug Abuse (conducted by the Substance Abuse and Mental Health Services Administration, 1997) demonstrating the significant increase in drug involvement during adolescence and young adulthood. (From Substance Abuse and Mental Health Services Administration. [1997]. *National household survey of drug abuse* [Online]. Available http://www.health.org/pubs/97hhs/nhsda976.gif.)

147

disorders are the single most common group of diagnoses among 17- to 25-year-olds with emotional or behavioral difficulties (Davis & Vander Stoep, 1997). For youth in transition such as Susan, any substance use poses a significant problem. Susan's case illustrates one of the ways that young people with emotional or behavioral difficulties may become "ensnared" (Moffitt, 1993) by corrections systems because of their substance use. Ethnic minority youth are also at higher risk for negative legal consequences as a result of substance use (Stewart, Brown, & Myers, 1997; Welte & Barnes, 1987).

Substance use is implicated in poor outcomes at each stage of transition for adolescents and young adults (Brook, Cohen, & Brook, 1998; Moffitt, 1993). Figure 2 illustrates a proposed pathway from adolescent problem behavior and mental health problems to young adult outcomes based on the work of Moffitt (1993) and Brook et al. (1998). This model suggests that adolescent snares mediate the relationship between adolescent problem behavior and young adult outcomes. "Snares comprise experiences that rule out lucrative jobs, higher education, or attracting a prosocial spouse.... The concept of snares includes

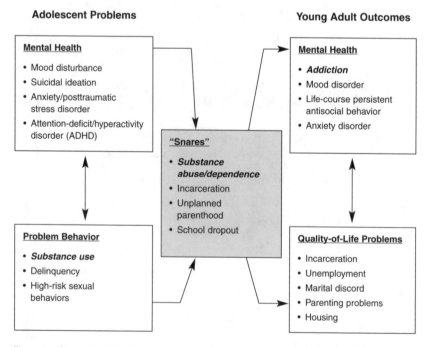

Figure 2.   The pathway from adolescent problem behavior and mental health symptoms to persistent impairment in adulthood is mediated by adolescent "snares."

things such as unplanned parenthood, addiction to drugs or alcohol, school dropout ... and time lost to normal development while incarcerated for crime" (Moffitt, Caspi, Dickson, Silva, & Stanton, 1996, p. 404).

Treating substance use problems among youth with emotional or behavioral difficulties is particularly difficult because of the interrelations between substance use and mental health problems, the prevalence of substance use in this age group, and the role of peer relationships in maintaining these difficulties. Adolescent substance use (Bentler, 1992) and antisocial behavior (Gottfredson, 1990) are consistently found to be strongly related to peer substance use and antisocial behavior (Hawkins, Catalan, & Milner, 1992; Henggeler, 1989). Peers often choose each other on the basis of shared values and mutual reinforcement of problem behaviors (Dishion, Patterson, & Reid, 1988), and social learning theory holds that the modeling of problem behaviors by peers reinforces and maintains problem behaviors.

Substance use, then, has a multifaceted connection to emotional and behavioral difficulties and to social relationships. Therefore, interventions to reduce the negative consequences of substance use on young people in transition must be as multifaceted and contextually oriented as the problem itself.

Multimodal Substance Abuse Treatment

The case of Susan describes a typical young person who is in transition and has clearly identified mental health symptoms (depression, anxiety, antisocial behavior) but whose substance use problems are less clearly defined. It is unlikely that Susan has a diagnosable substance dependence disorder, and her substance abuse problem would be difficult to distinguish from the heavy substance use pattern exhibited by many 18-year-olds. Susan could enroll in a leading college and fail to reduce her exposure to the problematic substance use of her peers. For Susan, the consequences of substance use are amplified by her probation status and her mental health symptoms. Despite a marked improvement in her emotional or behavioral functioning after being released from juvenile detention, a relapse to substance use led her back to increased antisocial activities and ultimately back to jail. Had Susan been identified as chemically dependent, she might have received treatment that focused more on her ability to abstain from drugs and alcohol, although this would have depended on her willingness to acknowledge her addiction and adhere to 12-step treatment models. Youth with co-occurring mental health and substance abuse problems are often turned away from inpatient chemical dependency services that require motivation, behavioral self-control, and the goal of abstinence. Trends in behaviorally based substance abuse treatment interventions offer hope for youth who are in the mental health and juvenile justice systems and do not meet eligibility requirements for substance abuse treatment and for youth who have failed to comply with the traditional model of services (e.g., 12-step programs). Three of those interventions, motivational enhancement (Miller & Rollnick, 1991), relapse prevention (Marlatt & Gordon, 1985), and community reinforcement training (Baer, 1993; Carroll, 1997) have demonstrated efficacy with substance users and abusers. These approaches are also appropriate for substance abuse aftercare. The following description is based on the application of these treatment approaches to young people who have emotional or behavioral difficulties and substance use problems or disorders.

Motivational Enhancement The motivational enhancement approach to changing addictive behavior (Miller & Rollnick, 1991) promotes engagement and motivation in youth and families. This approach assesses readiness to change and provides intervention strategies to match. Clinicians and transition facilitators use motivational approaches to create or strengthen the desire to change. Denial is not "confronted" in young people; rather, young people are encouraged to explore the ways that substance use interferes with life goals through objective feedback from facilitators. By frankly acknowledging the positive reasons young people have for using substances, facilitators gain credibility and are better able to provide objective feedback about substance use.

Relapse Prevention Relapse prevention principles (Marlatt & Gordon, 1985) anticipate relapse from the beginning of treatment and are designed to prevent relapse to substance use and delinquent behavior, to reduce the harm of relapse by limiting its length and severity, and to prevent treatment dropout after relapse. The transition facilitator and the young person identify high-risk situations continuously during treatment. Adolescents have been found to be most vulnerable to substance use relapse in social situations (Brown, Mott, & Myers, 1990) as well as in situations involving conflict and negative affect. Facilitators ask young people and families to plan for these high-risk situations and to practice these plans. In weekly group or individual sessions, young people review the situations in which they found themselves and the coping strategies they used. Probation officers, primary care physicians, and/or mental health therapists may find it useful to conduct regular urinalyses. This can be mandated by probation or agreed to by the young person when entering treatment. Regular urinalysis allows the treatment team to build a stepwise response to substance use that is not dependent on self-report or parent report.

When relapse occurs, facilitators coach young people and their families to implement a relapse plan that minimizes the harm of the relapse and retains the family in treatment. The young person is encouraged to describe her likely actions before, during, and after relapse, and the family and the facilitator are given permission to intervene at each of these points.

Community Reinforcement Training Clinicians and transition facilitators also help parents and the community team or "concerned others" to implement a community reinforcement plan. This involves providing clear rewards for sobriety and clear consequences for use. For example, a young person may receive monetary reinforcement for a clean urinalysis each week, whereas substance use may result in a probation violation and a weekend in detention. These contingencies are outlined for the young person in a family contract.

These models are focused on integrating substance use reduction interventions into mental health treatment. Had Susan received this type of intervention, there are several points at which outcomes might have been improved. Her ongoing sense that her loneliness and boredom might be alleviated by substance use could have been addressed in the motivational enhancement phase. She would have been encouraged to describe the negative and positive effects of substance use and might have developed self-correcting strategies to her positive memories of substance use. Also, a proactive effort to engage Susan in activities of interest (e.g., volleyball at the YWCA) might have set the occasion for her developing relationships with a peer group that was motivated to maintain good social and productive engagement (e.g., attending school, achieving at work). A relapse prevention plan not only would have praised Susan for "just saying no" but also would have rehearsed her behavior in the multiple high-risk situations in which she found herself, including being tempted to use after interpersonal conflict. Susan would have benefited from a relapse plan that outlined what she could do after a slip. She may have been invited to call her transition facilitator, a sober support person, or even her grandmother to help her get herself out of the relapse situation. A community reinforcement plan would have allowed Susan to make informed decisions about the consequences of her relapse. She was able to catastrophize her situation because no one had described for her what would happen if she used drugs and alcohol. If Susan had known that her grandmother and her probation officer would have a specific and proportional response to her relapse, she might have been better able to return to her positive functioning. Youth who have persistent and diagnosable substance use disorders may need to be enrolled in substance abuse treatment services. The transition facilitator may still be a primary agent of change in these situations and can serve to motivate young people to seek treatment (Miller & Rollnick, 1991). The therapist can also provide concurrent mental health treatment that includes relapse prevention and community reinforcement strategies and very likely will be a source of ongoing mental health treatment after discharge from time-limited chemical dependency services.

CONCLUSIONS

Working with transition-age youth and their families provides many challenges for transition facilitators. This chapter advocates for helping strategies that invite hope, enhance motivation, and are sufficiently flexible to accommodate the various needs and characteristics of young people in transition and their families. Facilitators are encouraged to focus on strengths and possibilities and to respect and use the powerful resources of the family. It is hoped that these recommendations will provide transition facilitators with additional resources and encouragement to serve this important and often neglected population.

REFERENCES

Azrin, N.H., Acierno, R., Kogan, E.S., Donohue, B., Desalel, V.A., & McMahon, P.T. (1996). Follow-up results of supportive versus behavioral therapy for illicit drug use. *Behaviour Research and Therapy, 34*(1), 41–46.

Baer, J.S. (1993). Etiology and secondary prevention of alcohol problems with young adults. In J.S. Baer & G.A. Marlatt (Eds.), *Addictive behaviors across the life span: Prevention, treatment, and policy issues.* Thousand Oaks, CA: Sage Publications.

Bentler, P.M. (1992). Etiologies and consequences of adolescent drug use: Implications for prevention. *Journal of Addictive Diseases, 11*, 47–61.

Berg, I.K. (1994). *Family based services: A solution focused approach.* New York: W.W. Norton.

Brook, J.S., Cohen, D., & Brook, D.W. (1998). Longitudinal study of co-occurring disorders, psychiatric disorders, and substance use. *Journal of the American Academy of Child and Adolescent Psychiatry, 37*, 322–330.

Brown, F.A., Mott, N.A., & Myers, M.G. (1990). Adolescent alcohol and drug treatment outcomes. In R.R. Watson (Ed.), *Drug and alcohol abuse reviews: Drug and alcohol abuse treatment prevention* (pp. 373–403). Clifton, NJ: Humana Press.

Carroll, K.M. (1997). Relapse prevention as a psychosocial treatment: A review of controlled clinical trials. In G.A. Marlatt & G.R. VandenBos (Eds.), *Addictive behaviors: Readings on etiology, prevention and treatment.* Washington, DC: American Psychological Association.

Davis, M., & Vander Stoep, A. (1997). The transition to adulthood for youth who have serious emotional disturbance: Developmental transition and young adult outcomes. *Journal of Mental Health Administration, 24*, 400–427.

de Shazer, S. (1985). *Keys to solution in brief therapy.* New York: W.W. Norton.

Diamond, G., & Liddle, H.A. (1996). Resolving a therapeutic impasse between parents and adolescents in multidimensional family therapy. *Journal of Consulting and Clinical Psychology, 64*(3), 481–488.

Dishion, T.J., Patterson, G.R., & Reid, J.R. (1988). Parent and peer factors associated with drug sampling in early adolescence: Implications for treatment.

National Institute on Drug Abuse Research Monograph Series, 77, 69–93.

Gottfredson, D.C. (1990). Changing school structure to benefit high-risk youth. In P.E. Leone (Ed.), *Understanding troubled and troubling youth* (Sage Focused Editions: Vol. 116, pp. 246–271). Thousand Oaks, CA: Sage Publications.

Haley, J. (1973). *Uncommon therapy*. New York: W.W. Norton.

Haley, J. (1980). *Leaving home: The therapy of disturbed young people*. New York: McGraw-Hill.

Haley, J. (1987). *Problem-solving therapy* (2nd ed.). San Francisco: Jossey-Bass.

Hawkins, J.D., Catalano, R.F., & Miller, J.Y. (1992). Risk and protective factors for alcohol and other drug problems in adolescence and early adulthood: Implications for substance abuse prevention. *Psychological Bulletin, 112*, 64–105.

Henggeler, S.W. (1997). The development of effective drug abuse services for youth. In J.A. Egertson, D.M. Fox, & A.I. Leshner (Eds.), *Treating drug abusers effectively* (pp. 253–279). New York: Blackwell.

Henggeler, S.W., Schoenwald, S.K., Borduin, C.M., Rowland, M.D., & Cunningham, P.B. (Eds.) (1998). *Multisystem treatment of antisocial behavior in children and adolescents: Treatment manuals for practitioners*. New York: Guilford Press.

Liddle, H.A. (1999). Theory development in a family-based therapy for adolescent drug abuse. *Journal of Clinical Child Psychology, 28*(4), 521–532.

Madannes, C. (1981). *Strategic family therapy*. San Francisco: Jossey-Bass.

Madannes, C. (1984). *Behind the one-way mirror: Advances in the practice of strategic therapy*. San Francisco: Jossey-Bass.

Marlatt, G.A., & Gordon, J.R. (Eds.). (1985). *Relapse prevention*. New York: Guilford Press.

Miller, W.R., & Rollnick, S. (1991). *Motivational interviewing: Preparing people to change addictive behavior*. New York: Guilford Press.

Moffitt, T.E. (1993). Adolescence-limited and life-course persistent antisocial behavior: A developmental taxonomy. *Psychological Review, 100*, 674–701.

Moffitt, T.E., Caspi, A., Dickson, N., Silva, P., & Stanton, W. (1996). Childhood-onset versus adolescent-onset antisocial conduct problems in males: Natural history from ages 3 to 18 years. *Development and Psychopathology, 8*, 399–424.

O'Hanlon, W. (1993). Possibility therapy: From iatrogenic injury to iatrogenic healing. In S. Gilligan & P. Reese (Eds.), *Therapeutic conversations* (pp. 3–21). New York: W.W. Norton.

Peters, R.H., & Hills, H.A. (1999). Community treatment and supervision strategies for offenders with co-occurring disorders: What works? In E. Latessa (Ed.), *Strategic solutions: The International Community Corrections Association examines substance abuse* (pp. 81–137). Lanham, MD: American Correctional Association.

Robbins, A., & Covan, F. (1993). *Awaken the giant within: How to take immediate control of your mental, emotional, physical, and financial destiny*. New York: Simon & Schuster.

Stewart, D.G., Brown, S.A., & Myers, M.G. (1997). Antisocial behavior and psychoactive substance involvement among non-Hispanic Caucasian adolescents in substance abuse treatment. *Journal of Child and Adolescent Substance Abuse, 6*, 1–22.

Substance Abuse and Mental Health Services Administration (SAMHSA). (1997). *National Household Survey of Drug Abuse* [Online]. Available http://www.health.org/pubs/97hhs/nhsda976.gif.

Welte, J.W., & Barnes, G.M. (1987). Alcohol use among adolescent minority groups. *Journal of Studies on Alcohol, 48,* 329–336.

White, M. (1986). Ritual of inclusion: An approach to extreme uncontrolled behaviors in children and adolescents: The externalizing of the problem. *Dulwich Centre Review,* 20–27.

8

Transition Coordination

Helping Young People Pull it All Together

Dan Bridgeo, Maryann Davis, and Yati Florida

Thomas just turned 18. He has posttraumatic stress and major depressive disorder. He doesn't take his medication. Repeated violent outbursts resulted in his expulsion from residential school. He can obtain his diploma in a year, but his high school is unable to find a school that will accept him. His mother has moved back to Jamaica and he lives with his aunt. He has nothing to do during the day and usually gets into trouble when he has free time. He is verbally abusive at home, and doesn't contribute to performing any chores. His aunt wants him to move out. Social services and children's mental health have provided services to Thomas in the past, however, he doesn't qualify for adult mental health services, and wants nothing to do with social services. On his 18th birthday, there was no lead agency to provide assistance. He and his aunt both want him to finish school. His aunt felt that no one was helping her and Thomas, and she felt desperate.

Thomas is typical of many young people who have emotional or behavioral difficulties and need assistance in making the transition into adult functioning. He is not prepared to enter the adult world and needs someone to help him identify his goals for becoming prepared and to link him to individualized supports that can help him achieve

This chapter was supported by a grant from the van Ameringen Foundation to the second author.

155

those goals. *Supports* refers to both formal services and informal resources that can assist young people. This has been called *service coordination* or *case management,* but as applied to youth in transition is referred to as *transition coordination* hereinafter. Providing transition coordination for young people such as Thomas is tremendously challenging because of the unique developmental stage of transition and the many system problems that exist (see Chapter 1).

System deficits have a particular impact on transition coordination because they limit the supports to which transition coordinators can link young people. The major system challenge facing young people with emotional or behavioral difficulties, their families, and transition coordinators is that there are few appropriate services that young people in transition can obtain once they cross the age threshold into adulthood (see Chapter 1). Thus, the best practices described in this book are mostly unavailable. In these circumstances, transition coordinators must help plan and coordinate many supports that can be created from the natural support system (family, social network, and community resources such as churches or recreation departments) and formal supports to which anyone can gain access (e.g., a therapist who accepts Medicaid). Thus, the greatest challenge for transition coordinators is finding or creating appropriate, appealing supports that address the unique strengths and needs of young people with emotional or behavioral difficulties (see Chapters 1 and 2).

This chapter focuses on the process of transition coordination that transcends system problems and describes two specific approaches (Project Nexus and the Transitional Community Treatment Team [TCTT]). Processes shared by both approaches are described first, followed by the defining characteristics of each.

ONE TO ONE: TRANSITION COORDINATORS AND YOUNG ADULTS

As with all good practices, good transition coordination must fit with each individual's path along the developmental curve of transition (Davis & Vander Stoep, 1997; see also Chapters 1 and 2). The relationship between the transition coordinator and the young person, the role of the transition coordinator, and the processes of transition planning, coordination, and implementation described herein are powerfully shaped by these developmental characteristics. Particularly important characteristics are 1) a general distrust of and rebellion toward authority, 2) the need to experiment with different lifestyle options, 3) developmental changes in family relationships, and 4) the need to develop the skills of identifying and setting goals, making plans, identifying resources, and pursuing plans.

Engagement

Service coordination for young people relies on a successful engagement process. This section examines barriers to engagement, strategies for engaging young people, and strategies for engaging families.

Barriers to Engagement Transition coordination begins with transition coordinators' establishing a relationship with the young person and engaging him in transition planning. There are several general barriers to engagement. Young people's mistrust of authority figures and adults in general is pervasive. The ambivalence that many young people feel about developing independence often results in inconsistent engagement. Transition coordinators' negative reactions to young people's experimentation, although often understandable, impede engagement. Coordinators' disrespect or insensitivity toward young people and their desires, goals, and culture also get in the way.

Strategies for Engaging Young People The therapeutic stance that Brucculeri, Gogol-Ostrowski, Stewart, and Sloan (see Chapter 7) describe and the philosophy and guidelines that Clark, Deschênes, and Jones (see Chapter 2) operationalize encourage engagement. Adopting this therapeutic stance requires transition coordinators to have some clinical sophistication and agencies to provide clinical supervision. Coordinators use their clinical skills to form a therapeutic relationship with each young person, to help young people address intra- and interpersonal issues, and to identify clinical issues (which may originate with the young person, the family, or systems) that interfere with young people's pursuing their goals. The nature of the relationship between the transition coordinator and the young person described here can be achieved only when coordinators serve a small number of young people at a time (fewer than 15). The exact number is influenced by the availability of other helpers and resources. Project Nexus (described in this chapter) transition coordinators serve 6–8 individuals at a time, distributed evenly across individuals who need multiple face-to-face meetings and intensive behind-the-scenes support each week, those who need less intensive assistance, and those who need minimal supports. The Transitional Community Treatment Team (TCTT) (also described in this chapter) has 7 transition coordinators and 10 other professionals on the team. The team serves 97 young people.

Respect for Individuals and Adolescent Culture Respect for individuals and adolescent culture is essential for working with young people (see Table 1). Respect is more important than having knowledge of specific cultural details. Trust can be enhanced by the transition coordinator's being honest about her ignorance and asking young people to teach her about the music, movies, language, or other things that are important to them. Young people require honesty and genuineness.

Table 1. Guidelines for engagement with transition-age youth and young adults

---

Respect individuality and choices.
Be aware of significant, unique cultural aspects of adolescence.
Understand the adolescent developmental stage.
Be flexible.
Foster autonomy and responsibility.
Become an advocate and teach self-advocacy.
Work with young people at their convenience and on their turf.
Promote family involvement while respecting young adults' choices.
Keep a positive attitude and a sense of humor.

Most young people abhor traditional therapeutic distance. Young people are more engaged by transition coordinators who say and act as if the young person and his unique goals, dreams, and actions drive the transition coordination process.

Understand Typical Adolescent Development and Be Flexible Typical adolescent experimentation and trying on of different identities (Marcia, 1980) means that young adults sometimes make mistakes and poor decisions. Transition coordinators, using a nonjudgmental stance, can help young people consider the pros and cons of their choices and learn from the consequences. In this context, an unconditional commitment philosophy requires flexible responses to acting-out behaviors and open-door eligibility retention policies. The safety net of transition services must remain in place.

Transition Coordinators Work in the Field Coordinators meet with young people and their families in their homes, their schools, their places of work, and in settings such as donut or coffee shops rather than the coordinator's office. Young people and their families have had too many negative experiences with the generally hierarchical culture of office-based services and need to hear the message that their convenience is important and their turf is fine. Some of the best meetings occur in cars as coordinators give young people rides to work, job interviews, or other such places.

Coordinators must be patient because engagement can take a long time. The more familiar coordinators are with adolescents, the more respectful and patient they tend to be.

Strategies for Engaging Families For youth with family ties, the family remains an important resource, although relationships are often complex during the transition period. Baker and Intagliata (1992) described six service coordination functions in which family members can and do make a difference:

1. Assessing young people's needs
2. Linking young people to supports
3. Monitoring the quality of provided supports
4. Assisting young people in daily living
5. Intervening in crises
6. Advocacy

These functions parallel many of the most critical functions of transition coordinators.

Maximizing family and extended family supports while respecting the young person's growing autonomy enhances engagement and success (see Chapter 11). Emphasizing the young person's choices while respecting the role of the family in the young person's life achieves this goal. This balance is challenging when conflict emerges between family members. Good communication practices, supportive counseling, and educational information help to mediate such conflicts (see Chapter 7). It is especially important to link families to education and support groups. Referring families to the Families-in-Touch program of the National Alliance for the Mentally Ill or to the Parent-to-Parent program of the Federation of Families, convening a support group that emphasizes young adults, or encouraging other existing family support groups to do so are excellent options. When families are supported and informed, particularly by other experienced and knowledgeable families, they are more able to assist their young adults and face the challenges of transition. This helps achieve the major transition coordination goal of facilitating and sustaining lifelong natural family and community-based supports.

Transition Coordinator's Role
The role of the transition coordinator is to *help* the young person to

1. Identify short- and long-term goals
2. Develop a plan for pursuing those goals
3. Identify resources that will assist and support her
4. Emphasize family and other natural supports
5. Coordinate formal "helpers"
6. Communicate her goals and plans
7. Oversee implementation of changes to the plan
8. Track her progress across goals

Teacher The transition coordinator teaches the skills of goal setting, planning, resource identification, engagement, and enactment that will help young people lead planful adult lives (i.e., lives in which they can identify goals, find and engage resources to help them pursue their goals) and master the elements of independent living (see Chapter 6). Transition coordinators teach skills directly (e.g., by teaching how to find resources), through mentoring (e.g., by sharing their own choice processes), and through group settings (e.g., by conducting classes on budgeting). Nonjudgmentally reviewing the choice process involved in goal setting and pursuing is a tremendously powerful teaching tool. Encouraging young adults to do for themselves what is required to pursue a goal, such as making appointments to see apartments and getting directions, rather than doing it for them allows them to develop skills and to take ownership of their progress. Teaching self-advocacy is also part of the process and is achieved by assertiveness training, coaching, modeling, and respectfully including the young person in every aspect of transition planning and coordination.

Counselor Transition coordinators can also be therapists or mentors, helping young people with social, relationship, and interpersonal skills, using their relationship and modeling as a basis. Coordinators may lead psychoeducational or support groups that are of interest to youth in transition (see discussion under "Mental Health/Substance Abuse" heading in this chapter.) Transition coordinators are cheerleaders, encouraging young people in the exciting and arduous process of entering adulthood and helping them see their strengths rather than focus on their difficulties.

Coordinator and Advocate The transition coordinator is the system coordinator. It is his goal to make systems work for young people, to know child and adult systems and community resources, to forge crucial relationships within systems to facilitate service access, to deal with intersystem conflict, and to make programs more helpful to young adults. One of the most important roles of the transition coordinator is that of advocate. Given the dearth of system supports, it falls to transition coordinators to push systems on behalf of young adults. Coordinators, who straddle youth and adult systems and develop a unique understanding of the different systems, can prevent people from falling through the cracks. They gain credibility as advocates when they base their decisions on the most appropriate developmental service or option that exists in each situation.

Conducting training for schools and human services agencies on adolescent development and effective treatment strategies for young adults is a way to advocate for all young adults in a community. This increases the sensitivity and awareness of individuals working with young adults and can increase system competency. Transition coordinators can also facilitate system change by providing consultation to child and adult services that work more marginally with the population.

Young Adults' Role

Young adults should feel empowered in every aspect of planning and implementation. In other words, they should feel that it is their goals, dreams, and choices that energize the transition plan and subsequent activities. They should be asked what their goals are, how they wish to prioritize them, and how they can be assisted in achieving them. Coordinators can assist young adults in considering goals, priorities, and supports that they may not have considered previously. Coordinators can point out possible consequences of an individual's choices that they feel are not optimal, but the choice and the driving force must be the young person's. If the young person does not genuinely embrace a plan, she is unlikely to be successful in it.

TRANSITION PLANNING AND SUPPORT COORDINATION

Life Domains Transition Planning

Life Domain Assessments Transition planning must be comprehensive so that any area of functioning that can support or impede young adult functioning is addressed. Life domains, not service domains, define areas of functioning. Service domains have artificial boundaries that impede comprehensive planning. Life domains are most relevant to young people. Transition coordination begins with a comprehensive, individualized life domains assessment. This is the foundation for planning and implementing specific services and supports for young people. The strengths of the young person are assessed, and needs in each life domain are addressed by building on those strengths. Strengths extend across life domains, whereas needs are organized by domains. Thus, one strength can provide the foundation for addressing needs in several domains. Life domains include the following:

1. Vocation/education
2. Residence/independent living
3. Mental health/substance abuse
4. Social support, recreation, and community membership
5. Legal assistance
6. Family relationships and parenting
7. Finances
8. Medical health
9. Safety planning

Bullis, Tehan, and Clark (see Chapter 6) present an outline for conducting functional assessments.

Setting Goals   Based on the assessment, specific short- and long-term goals should be developed with the young adult. Often, only one or two prioritized domains are addressed at one time. These priorities may reflect critical challenges, such as imminent homelessness, or areas that the young person is willing to "test out" on the transition coordinator, such as buying a car. Because life domains are interrelated, discussion of all domains usually occurs eventually. Goals should be life goals, not service goals. For example, therapy is not a goal. A goal may be controlling inappropriate social responses toward family members, and therapy is a means by which to achieve that goal. Goals may be embraced and discarded repeatedly. Long-term goals usually represent what must be accomplished for successful emancipation and transition to adulthood (see Table 2).

Support Plan   Details of the planning and implementation process that differ between Project News and TCTT are described in a later section of this chapter. Generally, support plans build on young people's strengths and identify sources of support (e.g., a cousin, a counselor), procedures (e.g., give driving lessons, explore feelings toward abusive father), and payment source.

Support Planning Team   The team that works with each young person to help construct, support, and modify the transition plan is individualized. Young people work with coordinators to construct a team that consists of the young person, individuals close to the young person, the transition coordinator, and involved professionals (e.g., therapists, vocational rehabilitation counselors). In the Nexus approach, the ideal team membership is half nonprofessional. As young people "age out" of children's services, the professional portion of the team decreases.

Table 2.   Examples of goals and plans in transition planning

Long-term goals	Short-term goals	Plan
Full-time employment	Determine vocational strengths and interests	Participate in a vocational assessment
Obtain own apartment	Increase responsibility for independent living	Reduce structure in current foster home
Develop a supportive peer group	Participate in a social recreation activity	Meet with a clubhouse peer mentor for support
Assume responsibility for care of one's child	Know healthy parenting practices	Complete a referral to a teen parenting class
Budget funds to meet all monthly bills	Assume responsibility for the telephone bill	Review telephone bill with foster parents and pay share of bill

Many young people are uninterested in participating in any kind of team meeting. They usually have extensive experience with team meetings and believe that the adults in those meetings see and treat them as children. They also do not like being the focus of attention. Team meetings are not held in the absence of the young person. Thus, team meetings are often more virtual than real. Once the young person and the transition coordinator develop a plan, the coordinator often leads a meeting of the young person and his natural support system to develop support for the plan and determine each person's role. The transition coordinator then talks with involved professionals about the plan and obtains their input, establishes their roles, and shares the young person's perspective. All team members come to agreement on priorities and actions and work together to find creative ways to address needs. Much of the "system work" is done at this level, with the coordinator advocating for the young person's goals and plans, presenting him in a positive light, and encouraging professionals to be supportive and strength based. Coordinators encourage young people to speak with involved professionals about their own decisions as their sense of self-advocacy grows. The team reconvenes to reconsider major changes to a plan.

Flexible Funds Transition supports are greatly enhanced by the availability of a flexible fund. A *flexible fund* is a pool of money that can be used to pay for anything that will aid an individual's progress. A sufficient flexible fund minimizes the necessity for categorical programs and promotes creative and individualized services and supports. This is particularly critical for this population because there are few appropriate services available. Flexible funds should be used as a last resort after other sources of payment are exhausted. Young people—and their families, as appropriate—should be asked to contribute something, even if it is just $5, toward most costs addressed by flexible funds. This request communicates the belief that they have the capacity to contribute. Nexus flexible funds have been used to pay for such things as flowers for prom dates, a mother's overnight stay in a hotel to give her a much-needed respite, prescription eyeglasses, cab fare out of a dangerous situation, and a therapist who was no longer covered by a young person's insurance. Flexible funds are also used to pay for expenses such as non-professional mentors, assist with rental deposits or rent, match savings to encourage savings, provide emergency funds, and purchase building tools necessary for a new job.

Plan Implementation and Maintenance The young person and the coordinator are partners in the oversight of plan implementation and maintenance. Short-term goals should be measurable and clear so that coordinators and young people can easily monitor progress and identify problems. Celebrating the achievement of short-term goals along the way helps to reinforce and consolidate small gains. Coordinators have young adults' permission to interact with all other involved parties, such as school counselors, probation officers, or parents, to determine how things are going from their perspective or to help the young person express concerns. Advocacy often occurs at this level.

Life Domain Services and Supports

The following sections describe service coordination issues in each life domain. Each domain section begins with excerpts from a paper written by Yati Florida, our young adult co-author.

Vocation/Education

I was encouraged continuously to further my education and to get my [general equivalency diploma].... I now have a nurse's aide certification and I'm taking two classes for college credit.

Obtaining a high school diploma is critical for future success (Asche, 1993) and is a high priority for most young adults. Transition coordinators often assist individuals to maintain or reengage in an educational program. Young people and their families often do not know their rights with regard to obtaining a high school education. Coordinators can help advocate for school enrollment, appropriate placement, and, for special education students, the timely development of individualized education programs. Alternative educational settings that are new to young people can reengage those who have quit school. Coordinators should encourage young people who have dropped out of school or fallen behind in grade level and want to move on to employment to earn their diplomas or general equivalency diplomas either before or while pursuing employment (see Chapter 3).

Transition coordinators are critical in facilitating the transition from school to work (see Chapter 6). Most young adults with emotional or behavioral difficulties do not attend college, and they are often expected to find jobs and become self-supporting before they are ready. Establishing occupational stability may involve providing additional supports to public vocational rehabilitation programs to make them more palatable to young people. For example, accompanying a young person to meet with a vocational rehabilitation counselor can make the difference between receiving vocational rehabilitation services or not. Natural supports or mentors can help encourage and sustain young people through trials in school, training, and employment experiences (see Chapter 4).

Individuals who receive Social Security benefits and wish to attempt employment are at risk of job loss without immediate benefit reinstatement. The most practical approach may be for the young person to work part time while sustaining a reduced benefit until it is clear that employment is of interest and sustainable. An emergency fund, supported by the young person and the transition coordination agency, can help overcome gaps in Social Security support.

Residence/Independent Living

> *I was raised in the system from the age of 8.... At 18 I went to the supervised apartment program and the team provided female wraparound staff to help me.... After 1 year I was able to move to my own apartment.*

Many young adults emerging from the child mental health, child welfare, and juvenile justice systems are forced to live independently because their previous residential situations are no longer available to them. Others may feel pressure from family members or have their own desires to move into their own homes. Housing and treatment plans should emphasize the least restrictive community setting with appropriate supports (see Chapter 5). However, finding affordable, appropriate housing is often one of the most difficult tasks of transition coordination.

Youth should be incrementally prepared for independent living while still in a supported environment by reducing rules and structure and increasing responsibilities and autonomy. For example, it is appropriate to gradually phase individuals out of level systems, drop curfews, and expect them to perform their own daily living tasks and assume increasing financial responsibility.

Young adults should make the transition to new living situations gradually. Basic supports during the transition to apartment living should include readily available natural supports or in-home staff, access to 24-hour telephone supports, access to transportation, a safety plan, and access to peer supports. Already emancipated peers can provide consultation to those who are just entering the process.

Mental Health/Substance Abuse

> *I was first diagnosed with bipolar disorder when I was 14 years old.... My transition coordinator got me into an outpatient dual-diagnosis treatment program.... I grew to understand how to cope with other emotional issues I had been dealing with in my life.*

The stresses of the transition period can exacerbate existing emotional or behavioral difficulties, increase or initiate substance use problems, and mark the onset of major mental illnesses (Kaplan & Sadock, 1997). Young adults can benefit from continued or renewed treatment that is sensitive to this developmental stage. Aggressive and comprehensive treatment at the onset of major mental illness reduces the severity and risks of a more chronic course of illness (Keshaven, Vaulx-Smith, & Anderson, 1995). However, young people are often unreceptive to treatment. It can be more effective to suggest treatment in the context of their other goals. For example, if a young woman needs roommates to afford the apartment that she likes yet keeps losing roommates because of arguments, she might be motivated to seek treatment that will help her avoid arguments and keep her apartment.

Young people often benefit from group treatment modalities such as psychoeducational and support groups (Azima, 1996). Psychoeducational groups on assertiveness training, anger management, parenting, psychiatric medication, psychiatric disorders, and independent living are relevant to young people. Common support groups include those concerned with drug/alcohol abuse, survivors of physical/sexual abuse or neglect, children of alcoholics, parenting, sexual orientation, and gender.

Family involvement in treatment issues is important to consider (Goldscheider, 1997). Transition can be a stressful time for families, and the support and structured engagement of families can help reduce stress by enhancing their availability to young adults. Transition coordinators can identify providers who address family involvement and family support groups and can provide educational material for family members.

Social Support, Recreation, and Community Involvement

> *I gained weight due to my medications.... The staff took me to the health club to help me with my goal of losing weight.... Sometimes I went to parties with the other clients.*

Improving social supports and enhancing the recreational and community involvement of young people contribute greatly to their overall quality of life, are normalizing, and are more enduring than formal supports. Many youth in transition experience social isolation and have missed out on experiences such as team sports, concerts, and dating. Facilitating peer forums, such as recreation activities, can help improve social and communication skills and meet the need of exposure to a positive peer culture, which every age group shares.

Most of these young people have limited funds for recreation. Transition coordinators can teach them how to use inexpensive community resources such as community recreation centers. Agencies can help coordinate economical recreation activities, such as weekend hikes or trips to the local beach, or offer a place where young people can get together and fix a spaghetti dinner. Transition agencies may take advantage of local resources, such as church recreation halls or grants from local organizations such as Lions or women's clubs, to expand their capacity for inexpensive recreation.

Legal Assistance

> *I was put in jail for 2 weeks, and I received 2 years' probation for disorderly conduct.... The judge ordered me to take my medication and to work with my transition coordinator.*

Young people may be involved in a variety of legal situations, including the resolution of child welfare custody arrangements for themselves or their children, juvenile or adult criminal court, and involuntary or outpatient commitment hearings. Transition coordinators can be called on to testify about custody recommendations, which can create conflict-of-interest dilemmas. They may participate in criminal or civil court proceedings to ensure accountability, find representation, and advocate for the most appropriate treatment. Thorough knowledge regarding systems and community resources can make the difference between appropriate and inappropriate court decisions. Unconditional commitment may mean working with young people while they are incarcerated or involuntarily committed.

Family Relationships and Parenting

> *We talked about my family and some of the problems that we had.... I see them more often now and I'm trying to be a role model for my cousins.*

The importance of family involvement has already been discussed. A disproportionate number of young people with emotional or behavioral difficulties are parents. Parenting can be particularly difficult for this group because they are often struggling with their own developmental issues and limitations. Prenatal and child care are often needed by pregnant women and new parents. Some of these supports can be found in existing community resources, such as those to coordinate support groups, find a young parent mentor, or provide hands-on assistance and instruction to the family.

Financial Supports

> *My bills were paid with the assistance of my transition coordinator, Kim, until I felt comfortable enough handling the finances myself.... I occasionally needed some financial help and Kim would give me money from the emergency fund.*

Establishing financial independence is difficult for young people in transition. Individuals as young as age 16 who are exiting children's systems may need to provide for themselves completely. Young people working full time often join the working poor, with minimum-wage income and no health insurance. There is no fiscal safety net. Any major expense, including medical bills, can put young people into great debt. Transition coordinators can anticipate changes in insurance coverage and find other coverage whenever possible. Coordinators can provide budget guidance and tips on stretching an income and can help young people establish and maintain an emergency fund. Flexible funds can be used to supplement the emergency fund.

Payeeship programs for individuals receiving Social Security benefits can be very effective. The payee is a combination banker and guardian of funds. Housing stability is usually improved because rent and utilities are paid jointly by the young person and the payee representative before other expenditures are negotiated. Ideally, the payee provides budgeting instruction, which eventually results in the young person's assuming financial responsibility.

Medical Health

> *My transition coordinator took me to see the psychiatrist every month.... We talked about how my medications were working.... I don't have health insurance right now.*

Problems with health coverage form a basic barrier to adequate health care. For young people covered by either Medicaid or their parents' health insurance policies, coverage often ends at a particular age or is tied to school attendance, and adult eligibility must be established. Eligibility loss can result in medical bills that are not covered by medical insurance. Young adults may also face their first state hospital admission during a psychiatric crisis because there is no coverage for private care. Transition coordinators can anticipate changes in health care coverage, prepare young people for the likelihood of hospital admission, and help them obtain care at free clinics or medical centers that do not turn away low-income and indigent individuals.

Health education for young adults is essential to reduce the incidence of sexually transmitted diseases, human immunodeficiency virus (HIV) infection, acquired immunodeficiency syndrome (AIDS), and unwanted pregnancies. Providing linkages to adult public health services and educational programs can reduce risk factors, but peer-teaching models represent the most effective strategy for reducing high-risk behaviors (Woods et al., 1998; Wright, Gonzalez, Werner, Laugher, & Wallace, 1998).

Safety Planning

There were times when I needed some additional assistance because I felt alone and unsafe.... It made me feel better just to know that someone was there any hour of the day.

The impulsiveness, substance abuse, onset of major mental illnesses, and emergence of gender identity issues in adolescence all are potential contributing factors to higher-risk behaviors in crisis situations. Adult and child systems differ in their crisis resource networks and access rules. Once they are 18 years old, young adults, not parents or guardians, must admit themselves into treatment. This also means that they can walk away from care unless they have met the legal criterion of danger to themselves or others. This shift in legal standing can be very disturbing to parents.

Detailed safety plans should anticipate a range of scenarios and delineate procedures and available resources. Plans should be disseminated to all involved parties, such as families, after-hours on-call staff, crisis centers, and young people. Development of individualized and creative resources may fill gaps in existing crisis services. Use of a safe house, emergency apartment, specialized home-based worker, or therapeutic foster home can divert or deescalate crisis situations.

TRANSITION COORDINATION MODELS

Both approaches described in this section share the processes just described; what follows are descriptions of the values and procedures that distinguish the two. West, Fetzer, Graham, and Keller (see Chapter 10) describe another transition coordination approach involving consumers as peer advocates.

Project Nexus

Project Nexus is an intensive clinical transition coordination model that serves five suburban Boston communities. The model embraces many values and practices of the wraparound process (VanDenBerg & Grealish, 1996), but its developmentally appropriate approach for transition-age youth is significantly different from that of the wrap-around model. The wraparound process has been described and studied extensively (Cauce et al., 1994; Clark, Lee, Prange, & McDonald, 1996; Clark, Schaefer, Burchard, & Welkowicz, 1992; Evans, Armstrong, & Kuppinger, 1996; Hyde, Burchard, & Woodworth, 1996; VanDenBerg & Grealish, 1996; Yoe, Santarcangelo, Atkins, & Burchard, 1996). Briefly, wraparound processes are shaped by a set of philosophical elements that emphasize community-based efforts that are individualized to build on children's and families' strengths to address their needs, are unconditional, and involve parents as partners. Wraparound processes are implemented on an interagency basis and are owned by the larger community. There must also be access to flexible noncategorical funding.

Values

Natural and Individualized Supports Nexus places particular emphasis on natural and creative supports. Nexus espouses that the goal of formal supports, including transition coordination, is to make themselves unnecessary for the young person over time. This can best be achieved through building the young person's natural support system and teaching her how to maintain that support system and to obtain resources in the community. Furthermore, Nexus holds that truly individualized supports must be created because few formal categorical supports are good matches for young people's strengths and needs. Like many locations, the community in which Nexus is offered has few formal, appropriate supports available for the young people served. Creative, individualized supports that emphasize existing resources of family and community are both ideal and necessary in the Nexus approach.

Interagency and Community Ownership Nexus emphasizes the importance of transition coordination as an interagency effort and of community ownership. Young people entering Nexus have been involved with various child and adult agencies. These agencies' ownership of and coordination through Nexus is critical to working together to help youth in transition and in increasing system awareness of transition issues; that is, they have ownership of the Nexus process and thus feel a responsibility for its success and have an investment in helping to solve the problems that face young people whom they serve as well as the systemic issues. Community ownership is key to obtaining community-based supports. The more the community is aware of the challenges faced by youth in transition and makes itself available to these young people, the more the young people will feel a part of the community and work to maintain community membership.

Family Involvement Appropriate family involvement differentiates Nexus from wraparound processes. Wraparound approaches involve a partnership with parents and family members to help them and their children. Nexus strongly emphasizes family involvement in transition planning and coordination, but its primary partnership is with the young people; families are involved at the level that is appropriate for each young person's degree of individuation and separation.

Who Is Served Nexus serves individuals ages 17–23 years who have received services from the children's mental health, child welfare, juvenile justice, or special education systems as adolescents and who are exiting these systems or who have only special education involvement. All individuals receiving Nexus services have significant emotional or behavioral difficulties and need assistance with young adult functioning.

Organizational Structure Project Nexus is an interagency effort among the University of Massachusetts Medical School, the Massachusetts departments of mental health, child welfare, juvenile justice, and vocational rehabilitation, and the special education departments of the towns served. A grant from the van Ameringen Foundation to the second author provides most of the funding for Nexus, supplemented mostly by in-kind support from the entities listed previously. The transition team consists of the transition coordinators and their supervisors. Transition coordinators have specialty areas of expertise, such as housing or vocational resources, special education services and systems, and specific ethnic group cultures. The transition team is part of the University of Massachusetts, which also oversees the flexible fund. A community advisory committee consisting of parent and consumer advocates, representatives from each of the human services agencies and local special education programs, and local business leaders provides guidance on appropriate referrals and flexible fund expenditures and addresses system barriers. Community advisory committee involvement helps build community and system awareness, ownership, and knowledge (see Chapter 2).

Unique Strategies and Procedures

Transition Coordinators' Clinical Stance Nexus coordinators are guided by the clinical approach described by Brucculeri and colleagues (see Chapter 7). Nexus coordinators are distinctive in their use of nonjargonistic language and nonpathologizing conceptualizations of young people's actions and feelings. This approach helps young people see that their feelings and behaviors are not so different from those of everyone else and that changing behaviors or feelings to be more "normal" or "accepted" is a matter of degree, not of type. Feeling less different from others also promotes a sense of belonging. Coordinators also encourage others providing supports to use a similar approach.

Community Emphasis in Transition Planning Nexus transition planning enacts the value of building young people's natural supports by supporting, creating, coordinating, and teaching young people how to use existing resources. Nexus offers no more support than transition coordinators and the flexible fund. All other supports for young people come from the community and any appropriate formal supports that can be obtained. Nexus coordinators are extremely adept at identifying potential resources and making them appropriate for young people. They are also skilled at tapping the best creativity in the support-planning team. A young person's move to independent housing offers a good example of the use of creative supports. The flexible fund can be used to "match" the young person's savings, to progressively diminishing rent support, or to provide loans to help support the financial move to independent living. Landlords have been befriended and provided with certain guarantees about tenancy to open doors for housing. A young person can be supported in her initial move to independent living by housing "mentors," such as older siblings, cousins, friends, or other Nexus young people living independently, who can spend evenings or stay overnight to ease the adjustment to independent status. All of these situations build a young person's capacity to use his natural support system by providing teaching opportunities in areas such as budgeting, maintaining supportive relationships, and being responsible to landlords. It also enhances their feelings of membership in their community.

The ideal transition support plan focuses more on informal than formal supports. The plan shown in Table 3 built on the young man's strong motivation to finish high school, his enjoyment of positive adult attention, and his and his mother's love for each other. His team included his aunt, grandmother, transition coordinator, school principal, and school social worker.

Evaluation Young people receiving Nexus services undergo baseline and semiannual assessments with standardized instruments. They also participate in monthly telephone interviews to assess concrete indicators of functioning. Although the results are preliminary and no adequate comparison group is yet available, evaluation data are tentatively encouraging. While enrolled in Nexus, youth do better in their community adjustment than youth in national longitudinal studies identified as having serious emotional disturbance who are receiving "services as usual" (reviewed by Davis & Vander Stoep, 1997). Sufficient data regarding community functioning after leaving Nexus services are not yet available. The point-in-time rates of community adjustment in national studies were compared with community adjustment rates reported by Nexus

Table 3. Typical Nexus support plan

Long-term goal	Short-term goal	Plan	Payor
Complete high school	Control anger at school	See "Increase positive interactions at home" below. T. will also see school social worker whenever he feels he is about to do something to get in trouble.	School
	Encourage school completion	All team members will ask T. at least weekly about how school is going, what he is enjoying, and whether they can help in any way. Transition coordinator (TC) will work with T. to find within 1 month a mentor who will do recreation activities with him and encourage his efforts at school completion within 8–10 hours per week.	Flexible fund
	Identify family support needs	See "Increase positive interactions at home" below.	Flexible fund
Move into own apartment	Do own laundry	Do laundry once each week starting next week. T.'s aunt will teach how laundry is done by accompanying T. the first time, then by being available when he does laundry each Friday. T.'s aunt will not pick up T.'s clothes or assist in any other manner. TC will check with T. and his aunt on progress.	Aunt buys detergent
	Cook one dinner per week	T. will cook one meal per week, starting next week. T. will schedule the meal on Mondays at either home or his grandmother's house for either his family or his grandmother. Aunt or grandmother will help by taking T. shopping for ingredients of meal T. chooses and by helping minimally in the actual preparation. TC will check with T., aunt, and grandmother on progress.	Aunt or grandmother buys food
	Increase positive interactions at home	TC will hold family meetings within 2 weeks to explore with T. and aunt the possibility of an in-home family therapist, develop a set of home social rules and consequences and rewards, find a family activity to do together, and check with both on progress in reducing conflict. Aunt wants some time to herself; TC will find respite worker to stay with children periodically while aunt has blocks of time to herself beginning in 2 weeks. T. will see a psychotherapist to talk about where his anger comes from and other ways to express it. TC will help find psychotherapist, and first visit will be within 3 weeks. See psychiatrist for more appealing medications. TC will find psychiatrist and take T. to first visit within 2 weeks.	Aunt's insurance and flexible fund

youth during the month with the largest number of young participants. Nexus youth experienced less school dropout (14% versus 28%–64%; reviewed by Davis & Vander Stoep, 1997), unemployment (36% versus 48%–52%; see Chapter 1), adult arrests (5% versus 45%; Davis & Cooper, 1998), and homelessness (16% versus 30%; Davis & Vander Stoep, 1997).

Transitional Community Treatment Team

The Transitional Community Treatment Team (TCTT) program operating in Columbus, Ohio, is grounded in the Program in Assertive Community Treatment (PACT) model (Stein & Santos, 1998). Research findings on PACT have confirmed its effectiveness (Stein & Santos, 1998).

Values   TCTT has several defining characteristics. These include the presence of an interdisciplinary team, assertive work, and a focus on the nature of severe mental illness and family work, which are described next.

The Interdisciplinary Team   The TCTT model emphasizes the values outlined in Table 4 (Stein & Santos, 1998). An interdisciplinary professional team is used for the clinical core of transition planning and services because it can directly provide comprehensive, flexible services

---

Table 4.   Treatment principles of the Transitional Community Treatment Team

Structural principles of teamwork: A team approach to accomplish indicated tasks, share responsibility, share governance, cross-train team members, integrate services

Principles of working with young people: Use an assertive approach, do a careful clinical assessment, capitalize on young person's strength, tailor programming to individual's needs, deliver services in person, titrate support, relate to young people as responsible citizens, make crisis stabilization services available 24 hours per day

Principles of working with the community: Use an assertive approach, use a wide variety of community resources, provide support and education to community members, retain responsibility for young person's care

Principles of working with families: The assertive community treatment team works closely with the family using problem-solving and psychoeducational approaches. The basic assumptions about the nature of mental illness presented to families include the following:

- Severe mental illnesses have clear and demonstrable causative biological components.
- Severe mental illnesses are lifelong conditions characterized by episodes of symptom intensity, which can diminish slowly in the absence of stress.
- One of the impairments resulting from severe mental illness involves attention and arousal, impairing a person's ability to gauge stimuli adequately.
- Families can have an influence on this biological process so that they either are able to protect the individual from episodes of symptom intensity or exacerbate them inadvertently.
- Living with a relative with a mental illness has consequences for the family in that the stigma associated with mental illness negatively affects the social support networks of the family.

From Stein, L.I., & Santos, A.B. (1998). *Assertive community treatment of persons with severe mental illness* (p. 70). New York: W.W. Norton; reprinted by permission.

to achieve ongoing stability and promote rehabilitation. The services and treatment approaches are integrated and complementary because they are offered by a single team. The team approach is also advantageous in that cross-training within the team provides broad expertise among team members, and the contributions of different team members based on their different perspectives promote creative problem solving. Finally, because engagement is such a difficult task with young people, once engagement occurs the whole team has a foot in the door. This is a tremendous advantage because it simultaneously increases the probability that a young person will accept needed psychotherapy, psychopharmacology, rehabilitation, medical treatment, and independent living supports. In other approaches, the willingness to engage with providers offering these services is often achieved one at a time.

Assertive Work Assertive work means active outreach, an emphasis on community-based care, and, most important, advocacy. The TCTT advocates for young adults through work at many levels. Encouraging empowerment, as described previously, forms the basis of individual advocacy work. Advocacy activities described as the transition coordinator's role (see the "One-to-One: Transition Coordinators and Young Adults" heading) are emphasized by TCTT. Also, at the system level, TCTT staff participate in interagency children's forums and coordinate a transition forum that gathers child and adult workers to address the needs of this population.

Nature of Severe Mental Illness and Family Work The TCTT primarily serves young people who have developed severe mental illness. The belief that severe mental illnesses are biological in nature and of lifelong duration guides TCTT work. Symptoms of severe mental illnesses can diminish slowly in the absence of stress. Significant emotional or behavioral difficulties can also stem from trauma or other experiences. Family members can affect these difficulties through their purposeful or inadvertent influences on the young person's stress. Family members often need to work to maintain an adequate social support network. Psychoeducational and problem-solving approaches work best to support families.

Who Is Served The TCTT serves individuals ages 16–22 who are diagnosed with mental illness and evaluated to be at the highest risk for institutional placement, suicide, or homelessness. Most of these young people have multiple system involvement and histories of hospitalizations, and many of them have dual diagnoses of mental retardation and/or substance abuse. The TCTT serves young people who are expected to experience the greatest difficulty making the transition to adulthood. The average length of stay with the TCTT is approximately 4 years.

Organizational Structure   The TCTT has been operated by North Central Mental Health Services in Columbus, Ohio, since 1990. The team consists of a team leader, seven transition coordinators, a psychiatrist, a nurse, a therapist, two vocational specialists, three case aides, and the resident manager of the TCTT-supervised apartment program. Transition coordinators broker services, and all team members provide individual and group treatment. The team operates a supervised and an unsupervised apartment program.

The TCTT is funded by a contract with the county's department of mental health and substance abuse services. The contract provides some money for a flexible fund, and flexible funds are also obtained from a fund for children and adolescents served by multiple agencies and from a fund for individuals in the mental health system.

Unique Strategies and Procedures   The TCTT conducts daily team meetings and offers predominantly direct provision of services and an individualized planning team approach.

Daily Team Meetings   Each day begins with a multidisciplinary team meeting for planning and service coordination. Team meetings are efficient vehicles to ensure service and clinical coordination. For example, if a young woman was suicidal overnight but not at the point of going to an emergency room, her therapist, transition coordinator, psychiatrist, and supervised apartment staff would be quickly informed about the precipitating events, safety contract (i.e., an interim safety plan that is developed between the young person and staff), and clinical intervention. Group clinical supervision is achieved during this meeting to keep all involved professionals informed and in agreement.

Direct Provision of Services   As can be seen from this description, the TCTT directly provides the majority of each young person's formal services. All staff but the psychiatrist and the therapist offer services in the young person's natural environment. Services that are needed beyond what the team can provide directly are brokered.

Transition-Planning Team   As with the Nexus approach, each young person also has a "personal" planning team that consists of her natural support system, the transition coordinator, and involved professionals. The transition coordinator represents the TCTT in this forum and coordinates its efforts with other system workers and the natural support system. This personal team, led by the transition coordinator, works with each young person to develop and modify the transition support plan.

Evaluation   Characteristics of the first 100 young adults referred for services were examined during the 4 years prior to and the 4 years after their admission to the TCTT. Results of this study show promise in several areas (Bridgeo, 1997). Compared to the pre-TCTT enrollment period, psychiatric hospitalization was reduced dramatically (81%). At the end of the post-TCTT enrollment period, more than 90% of the housing arrangements for these young people were in natural settings, predominantly in independent apartments. Young people served by the TCTT had good success in school enrollment or completion (65% had completed or were continuing in educational settings), and 78% were employed or participating in vocational training programs. At discharge, the typical young adult goes on, either without services (45%) or continues in office-based outpatient service coordination or treatment (31%) rather than to an adult community treatment team (20%). This supports the proposition that individuals require only a minimum dose of assertive community treatment before moving on to less intensive care (Scott & Dixon 1995), even among this youthful and challenged population.

CONCLUSIONS

Both Project Nexus and the Transitional Community Treatment Team coordinate and provide comprehensive supports to assist young people as they enter adulthood. Both have been shown to be effective. Each approach's practices are more similar than different because they are shaped primarily by the unique transition stage of development, the nature of emotional or behavioral difficulties, and the belief in the importance of families and communities.

REFERENCES

Asche, J.A. (1993). *Finish for the future: America's communities respond.* Alexandria, VA: National Association of Partners in Education.

Azima, F.J.C. (1996). Status of adolescent research. In P. Kymissis & D.A. Halperin (Eds.), *Group therapy with children and adolescents* (pp. 369–386). Washington, DC: American Psychiatric Press.

Baker, F., & Intagliata, J. (1992). Case management. In R.P. Liberman (Ed.), *Handbook of psychiatric rehabilitation* (pp. 213–243). New York: Macmillan.

Bridgeo, D. (1997). *The Transitional Community Treatment Team: The first one hundred clients.* Unpublished doctoral dissertation, Union Institute, Cincinnati, OH.

Cauce, A., Morgan, C., Wagner, V., Moore, E., Sy, J., Wurzbacher, K., Weede, K., Tomlin, S., & Blanchard, T. (1994). Effectiveness of intensive case management for homeless adolescents: Results of a 3-month follow-up. *Journal of Emotional and Behavioral Disorders, 2*, 219–227.

Clark, H.B., Lee, B., Prange, M.E., & McDonald, B.A. (1996). Children lost within the foster care system: Can wraparound service strategies improve placement outcomes? *Journal of Child and Family Studies, 5*, 39–54.

Clarke, R., Schaefer, M., Burchard, J., & Welkowicz, J. (1992) Wrapping community-based mental health services around children with a severe behavioral disorder: Evaluation of Project Wraparound. *Journal of Child and Family Studies, 1*, 241–261.

Davis, M., & Cooper, D.K. (1998). Adult arrest of youth with serious emotional disturbance. In C. Liberton, K. Kutash, & R.M. Friedman (Eds.), *Proceedings of the tenth annual research conference on a system of care for children's mental health: Expanding the research base* (pp. 335–338). Tampa: University of South Florida, Louis de la Parte Florida Mental Health Institute.

Davis, M., & Vander Stoep, A. (1997). The transition to adulthood among children and adolescents who have serious emotional disturbance: Part I. Developmental transitions. *Journal of Mental Health Administration, 24,* 400–427.

Evans, M.I., Armstrong, M.E., & Kuppinger, A.D. (1996). Family-centered intensive case management: A step toward understanding individualized care. *Journal of Child and Family Studies, 5,* 55–65.

Goldscheider, F. (1997). Recent changes in the U.S. young adult living arrangements in comparative perspective. *Journal of Family Issues, 18,* 708–724.

Hyde, K.L., Burchard, J.D., & Woodworth, K. (1996). Wrapping services in an urban setting. *Journal of Child and Family Studies, 5,* 67–82.

Kaplan, H.I., & Sadock, B.J. (1997). *Kaplan and Sadock's synopsis of psychiatry: Behavioral sciences, clinical psychiatry* (8th ed.). Philadelphia: Lippincott Williams & Wilkins.

Keshaven, M.S., Vaulx-Smith, P., & Anderson, S. (1995). Schizophrenia. In V.B. Van Hasselt & M. Hersen (Eds.), *Handbook of adolescent psychopathology: A guide to diagnosis and treatment* (pp. 465–496). Lanham, MD: Lexington Books.

Marcia, J. (1980). Identity in adolescence. In J. Adelson (Ed.), *Handbook of adolescent psychology* (pp. 159–187). New York: John Wiley & Sons.

Scott, J.E., & Dixon, L.B. (1995). Assertive community treatment and case management for schizophrenia. *Schizophrenia Bulletin, 21,* 657–668.

Stein, L.I., & Santos, A.B. (1998). *Assertive community treatment of persons with severe mental illness.* New York: W.W. Norton.

VanDenBerg, J., & Grealish, E.M. (1996). Individualized services and supports through the wraparound process: Philosophy and procedures. *Journal of Child and Family Studies, 5,* 7–21.

Woods, E.R., Samples, C.L., Melchiono, M.W., Keenan, P.M., Fox, D.J., Chase, L.H., Tierney, S., Price, V.A., Paradise, J.E., O'Brien, R.F., Mansfield, C.J., Brooke, R.A., Allen, D., & Goodman, E. (1998). Boston HAPPENS program: A model of health care for HIV-positive, homeless, and at-risk youth. *Journal of Adolescent Health, 23*(2), 37–48.

Wright, E.R., Gonzalez, C., Werner, J.N., Laugher, S.T., & Wallace, M. (1998). Indiana Youth Access Project: A model for responding to the HIV risk behaviors of gay, lesbian, and bisexual youth in the heartland. *Journal of Adolescent Health, 23*(2), 83–95.

Yoe, J.T., Santarcangelo, S., Atkins, M., & Burchard, J.D. (1996). Wraparound care in Vermont: Program development, implementation, and evaluation of a statewide system of individualized services. *Journal of Child and Family Studies, 5,* 23–39.

III

Young Adult
and Family Perspectives

9

Who Will
Hear Our Voices?

Jane Adams, Melissa Nolte, and Jill Schalansky

> When we don't know each other's stories, we substitute our own
> myth about who that person is. When we are operating with only a
> myth, none of that person's truth will ever be known to us, and we
> will injure them, mostly without ever meaning to. (Wehmiller, 1992,
> p. 380)

The following stories represent the youth-to-adult transition experience. The stories are from young adults who were and may still be
the consumers in special education, mental health, foster care, and
substance abuse systems. This chapter describes the perspectives of
their transition experiences and the beneficial or detrimental roles of
the service systems in their lives and the lives of their families.

These young adults come from all parts of the United States and
represent the diversity of young people being served, or not being
served, by the service systems. They have grown up in suburban and
urban areas and represent both genders and different ethnic populations, and they have experienced extensive out-of-home placements.

In addition to the three young adult narratives from New York
City, Albuquerque, and Topeka, we present perspectives from 60
Kansas youth who attended the 1998 Youth in Action Conference
(sponsored by Keys for Networking, Inc., and the Kansas Department
of Mental Health). Through processes involving drawing, sculpting,
talking, and other unstructured activities, these 60 youth developed a
statewide youth network for support and information sharing. At the
conference and through the network, they supported and encouraged
each other to participate in proceedings to influence state laws and

service provision, to create their own forum to speak publicly about services that worked or did not work for them, and to identify the characteristics of people whom they perceive as providing services that have helped them the most. Many of the issues raised by the 60 young people attending the conference drove the framework of this chapter.

As a starting place, let us visit the perspectives of Amin, Jill, and Sean. Each story presents the individual's perspective with regard to the following: 1) what worked for him or her in the system in which he or she grew up, 2) what was needed from that system, and 3) what is still needed. After the three testimonies, we examine common themes and suggest strategies that service personnel can use to ensure voice and ownership for young people seeking self-determination in their lives.

AMIN'S STORY (NEW YORK CITY)

The only thing that got me through all my problems was my mother. A single mother with three kids, she managed to attend school and earn two master's degrees. She saw me through the hard times. She was always behind me. She kept pushing me and kept picking me up, but she never tried to run my life. She never tried to rule me. Decisions were made in our household by compromise and by talking it out, not by, "I say you do it. This is my roof. You live by my rules."

My mother allowed me to express myself. For me, this proved that she supported me and listened to what I wanted and needed. She made her decisions after hearing my opinion, which made me feel as if my voice was heard. She made fair decisions. She listened to me.

For me, a lot of my problems in transition have to do with me not letting go of being a teenager but still wanting the freedom of being an adult. I currently work as a peer counselor with children who have emotional difficulties. My job is to take them out, play games with them, and listen to them. I can be a kid with them and still do my job. I still want to be a kid myself sometimes. This is good for me.

I know I've been through a lot. I was in a gang, in and out. I did drugs. I have dealt with a lot of mental problems. I'm still dealing with them today, and my mother is still behind me.

I'm in the process of moving to my own apartment. My mother doesn't want me to move out of her house to go away to school. I have a serious health condition. She doesn't think I can deal with it on my own. I suffer from seizures, so I need medical insurance. I can't afford the bills myself.

I just recently found out that my grandfather is a pedophile who abused my aunts and a lot of the children in my family. The man is 79 years old. His crimes have pretty much torn my family apart. What confuses me is that while my uncles and my father want to prosecute him, my aunts, on the other hand, have helped him leave the country. This tension has completely divided my family. This hurts me, but my mother has taken me and my sisters to counseling, which I'm going through now for her.

I needed to be taught to become an adult not when I was 18 but when I was 14, 15, or 16. Now that I'm 18 in New York City, I am no longer eligible for the programs I still need. I have nowhere to go. I need to learn to balance a checkbook, maintain an account, pay my bills, and clean my apartment. I needed to start learning these skills more than just 2 months before my 18th birthday. I needed to know about the values and responsibilities of independence and leadership. My mother is the only one now who teaches me. Mother needed and needs help, though. She and I need other people to be helping me in learning some life skills.

JILL'S STORY (TOPEKA, KANSAS)

My problems began when I was 14, but they weren't discovered by my parents until I was 16. I had started to hang around an older group of mostly males. When I was with them, I drank alcohol and did drugs. It was legal for them to drink, so I thought it was okay for me also.

One night, I missed my curfew and stayed out all night. I awoke to the police banging on the door. They took me home to my parents. My parents put me on severe restrictions. They didn't report me as a runaway because this was my first offense. They allowed me no phone calls, no visitors, no nothing. My mother allowed me to talk to only one person, which turned out to be a mistake. When my best friend decided to run away from the shelter where she lived, she asked if I wanted to run with her. I did.

One night my father dropped me off at church. After I watched him leave, I walked away in the rain wearing five sets of clothing in the dead of summer. He didn't even notice.

Four days later, the police found me in a bar and arrested me. They took me to juvenile intake, and then I was transferred to a hospital for an evaluation. The doctors diagnosed me with substance abuse, severe depression, and hypomania.

My parents made a deal with me. They said if I stayed clean, stopped smoking, and behaved, they would buy me a new car. I wanted a new car, so I agreed to the deal. The day the hospital released me, I went and got my new car. I had the car 1 day. I stayed out all night. My parents took me back to the hospital in my new car that I could no longer drive.

I have been to the hospital a total of five times. The first two times, I was assigned a social worker. This social worker had worked for my mother [who has an important position with the state], so her interest in what I wanted was minimal. She wanted to please my mother. The second social worker was trained in youth alcohol and drug abuse counseling. She cared about my opinions first, then those of my parents. She facilitated my first wrap-around plan. It included attendant care every day after school until my parents got off work. That's what my parents wanted. I hated it. Imagine being 16 and having someone come and pick you up every day after school. It was one of the most embarrassing times of my life. After a while, my parents allowed me to drive my car to school twice a week.

Things went smoothly until the end of May. I started skipping school so I wouldn't have to take my finals. My parents put me back in the hospital for another stay. They didn't know what to do. Nobody knew what to tell them. I was released. My parents put me into an outpatient drug rehab center 3 nights a week for the rest of the summer.

Around my 18th birthday, my parents and I got into a fight, so I moved out and landed with a drug dealer. My mom was wild. She talked me into coming home for the holidays. She invited me to Kansas City for a shopping trip. She surprised me when we got home. My whole wraparound team was sitting in my living room. They called this surprise my intervention. They told me I had to go to rehab. I was 18, so of course, I refused. My parents kicked me out.

I found another friend. I lived with her a week. This time I had no car, no money, no family. So I went off again, this time to rehab. I did the program. One night, my mother and father came and got me for dinner.

Instead, they took me to a surprise interview at a halfway house. I was mad but I did the interview. The program accepted me. I moved in. After only 2 months, I was evicted. They were not set up to help transition an 18-year-old female to living on her own. I was evicted for what was labeled as irresponsible and disruptive behavior.

What I need is to learn life skills: how to live on my own, how to run a household, how to survive without having my parents there to bail me out. I need a wraparound plan that fits my needs instead of the needs of my parents. I needed support from the halfway house instead of criticism and blame. I did not receive support from the halfway house, from treatment after my release, from anywhere.

Family therapy with my social worker has improved the relationships between my mother, father, brother, and sister. My wraparound team gave support to my whole family and to the people who try to provide services to us. I am still alone, though.

SEAN'S STORY (ALBUQUERQUE, NEW MEXICO)

I am 18 and was born in Albuquerque, New Mexico. I live with my fifth-grade teacher, who is also my therapeutic foster mother, Judi. She is the person who managed to keep me alive and out of jail.

My parents divorced and I started getting into trouble about the age of 5. I shoplifted and set fires until I turned 13. I set cars and houses on fire. My mom had me shoplift for her. I was in and out of state custody until I came to live with Judi. My mom had many boyfriends, some abusive. One raped my sister when she was in first grade. I still feel guilty that I didn't do anything to protect her. I am now learning that I couldn't do anything because I was just a kid myself.

I started in special education when I was in kindergarten. I was always in the class for the "bad kids." It was easy to see myself as "bad" and feel that I had to live up to that reputation. I was always stealing, fighting, and running away. By the age of 7, I was in and out of a detention center, a hospital, and a group home. I had been on probation for as long as I could remember. Nothing helped until I got in Judi's fifth-grade class. I knew I could trust her and that she would always be there for me. When I was in her class, I stopped running from school and I started running to it. Judi came to court with me, and the judge decided she should be listed as a significant person in my life. He made her a part of my probation plan.

Then I left her class and went to middle school. I got into a lot of trouble again. The teachers didn't care, and I got arrested for assault and battery. I knew Judi would come if I was put in the hospital or the detention center. My family moved 200 miles from Albuquerque when I was in a treatment facility, and things didn't work when I went back to them. I ran away and hitchhiked back to Albuquerque and called Judi. She said I could live with her but it would have to be legally. She got me back in treatment while she got her therapeutic foster care license. She visited me every day, and I have been with her ever since.

I was into drugs. I did marijuana, acid, hashish, nitrous oxide, and peyote since I was 10. I have been diagnosed with multiple illnesses at one point or another. My current diagnosis is bipolar disorder, attention-deficit/hyperactivity disorder, oppositional defiant disorder, conduct disorder, and posttraumatic stress disorder. The bipolar is what gets me in trouble, and it took living with Judi for me to get educated and to take my disorder seriously.

During my 16th summer, I went through a major depression where I would sleep between 16 and 22 hours a day. When school was about to start, I was put on an antidepressant. This put me into a major manic episode. I honestly believed I could do anything, so I robbed a bank with a water gun. It looked real. With Judi's willpower, connections, and determination, I managed to spend only 1 month in jail but then had to serve 8 months in a secure treatment facility.

I have been in Judi's therapeutic foster care since 1994. I am on medication, attend therapy, and see a psychiatrist regularly. I am also on probation until my 21st birthday for the bank robbery. A condition of the probation is that I attend a relapse support group and go in for random drug testing. I have no contact with my biological parents, and they don't want to have contact with me.

I am currently doing very well at working and holding a job and will attend college in the fall. What worked for me is someone believing in me and giving me their unconditional love. For me, the someone was my fifth-grade teacher. I just happened to meet the only person who loves me.

THEMES FROM YOUNG ADULTS' EXPERIENCES

These three autobiographical narratives are characterized by multiple themes. These themes include needing, using, and relying on a parent's or other significant adult's support and guidance, moving beyond that support, needing life skills and confidence to live on one's own, maintaining old and developing new relationships with parents and/or significant adults, wanting to have choices to determine one's own life outcomes, and needing people who care. The stories by Amin, Jill, and Sean and those of the young people attending the Youth in Action Conference are not about case management or therapy helping them; rather, they are about people. Significantly minimal in these stories are descriptions of services. Were these not relevant? The people in their lives were important. When Amin, Jill, and Sean discuss services, they criticize them. Jill talks about being criticized, fined, blamed, and sent away. She talks about providers and service planners who planned programs to meet her parents' needs. Amin talks about going to therapy to please his mother, but he does not talk about the usefulness of the therapy. He talks about his mother, how she always listens. Sean states that nothing helped him until he got unconditional love from his fifth-grade teacher. She cared. What these young people talk about are the trusted people in their lives, their relationships with parents and foster parents and teachers. Emerging from the stories are their profound feelings about relationships: love, appreciation, and need as well as hurt and anger. These feelings, except for the last ones, do not surface in their discussion of services. Schorr pointed out that

> Staff members in successful programs build relationships of trust and respect with children and families. They work in settings that provide them with the time, training, skills, and institutional support

necessary to develop meaningful personal relationships and to provide services respectfully, ungrudgingly, and collaboratively. (1991, p. 2)

Parent/Significant Adult Support

In their stories, the young adults recognize decisions parents made regarding their treatments or their lives. They talk about their own parents' needing support in learning skills for childrearing. They recognize that not all parents have the same capacity to handle a child, adolescent, or young adult who has special needs.

Amin states that his mother was always there to support his decisions. She worked to provide for herself and three children while putting herself through school. Amin recognizes her worry about him. He understands her concerns about his health. She worries about where he will obtain services when he moves out on his own. Amin says his mother is the only person who taught him life skills, who stuck with him. She could not do it alone. She needed help from schools and community programs.

Jill's parents put a support system in place for them after her hospital stay. They engaged a wraparound team to give them advice and support on what to do. According to Jill, her parents would have been overwhelmed if they had not had that support. That support somehow did not reach Jill.

Sean's therapeutic foster mother, Judi, managed to help him in many ways. Judi sought training as a therapeutic foster parent before she had Sean move in. She used the support through the connections she had to get him the treatment he needed. Apparently, she was an effective case manager. If there had been support for Sean's biological parents, they might have understood what was happening to their son and would still have a relationship with him.

Each young person attending the Youth in Action Conference participated in a ceremony that recognized individuals who had "helped them the most" and presented certificates and gifts to their honorees. The young people recognized parents, teachers, case managers, and other adult caregivers as those who had stood by them with unconditional love, trust, and support. The adults who accompanied the young people to the conference expressed frustration with trying to receive support and training to cope with the special needs of these young people as well as anger with a system that ignored or trivialized their concerns.

Moving Away and Learning New Life Skills

These young adults want to move out on their own. But they want to maintain relationships with people they love even as they redefine the relationships from authority to support. Young people in transition who have special needs may feel competent to handle life on their own but soon realize that they have significant needs (e.g., skills for holding a job, medical coverage, a mentor, friends for fun and recreation). In a study of mental health services for young adults in transition, Zebley, Boezio, Carlson, and Chamberlain found that "young adults in need of transition assistance require active outreach, individualization of treatment, normalization within the community, development of a positive social network, and early and intensive focus on coping skills, employment and independent living" (1996, p. i).

Amin talks about how his mother was afraid he would not be able to get the insurance he needed if he moved out on his own. The difficulties involved with having health conditions that require medications include, among others, the expense. It was also difficult for Amin to move out on his own because there was only one person, his mother, who was supportive of him and taught him the skills he needed.

Jill tried to move out of her parents' home several times. One time she moved into a setting that was designed to aid her in getting the skills she needed to live successfully on her own. She was not taught the skills she needed in a positive way. If she made a mistake, she was not told constructively, "You did not do that right. You need to act this way." Instead, she was fined and told, "Do it differently." According to Jill, if the staff had shown her the correct way, she might have learned how to manage a household instead of how to use her parents to buy her way out of trouble. She moved in with friends, which was fun for a while. The atmosphere later turned into a big party, and it was impossible for her to meet her work responsibilities with little sleep. She lacked the skills or the practice to confront or hold her own with peers. Like Angela, she had been too controlled, with no opportunity to voice her needs and to pursue her interests and goals.

The young participants at the Youth in Action Conference also expressed the need for skills and training in living independently and for the opportunity to be heard. These young people say they want choices and the dignity to become independent. Writing about successful programs, Schorr noted that staff members who are responsive represent a major piece of the success:

> No one in these programs says, "This may be what you need, but helping you get it is not part of my job or [is]outside our jurisdiction." While always keeping their primary mission in mind, staff seem to be forever willing, in the words of Harvard University's Kennedy School Professor Mary Jo Bane, to "push the boundaries of their job description" and to take on an "extended role" in the lives of their students (or patients or clients). (1991, p. 3)

Maintaining Old Relationships and Developing New Ones

> Relationships change throughout all of one's life. We have to permit that change to occur to keep deepening our relationship. Our loving experiences reshape us, reshape the way we use ourselves and create the energy that deepens us individually and communally. (Keleman, 1979, p. 69)

Amin recognizes his mother's support and direction. He says she is behind him every step of the way. She did not try to control him but talked with him to find a compromise on every situation. Amin says his mother talked him into family counseling. He says he goes when needed and that his mother taught him many of the life skills he needs to survive. It seems that Amin's relationship with his mother is a positive one.

Jill and her parents had a good relationship. Her parents cared about her and did what they believed was best for her, all at their own expense. When questionable events arose, they turned to members of the wraparound team for guidance. Jill's parents stood by her no matter what the cost.

Sean's biological mother was supportive of the things that got Sean into trouble. Instead of telling him not to steal, she had him steal for her. To fill the void left by his biological mother, Sean discovered a bond with his teacher, Judi. Judi became his therapeutic foster mother and has shown him the unconditional love of a parent. She stands behind him and supports him through all of his ordeals. She visits him daily. Sean calls her Mother.

These three young people condemn the service systems and declare that they did not receive services relevant to them or their families. They believe that they needed to have a service array that respected them as individuals and in which they could have a choice and a voice.

UNISON VOICE OF YOUNG PEOPLE

One of the outcomes of the Youth in Action Conference was the creation of a forum for young people to speak publicly about services that are working or have worked for them. During the activities and small-group work, young people were encouraged to articulate their needs and opinions. Care was taken to establish a safe environment for free expression. The structure of the conference was designed to promote sharing. By the last day of the conference, the following lists of "what worked" and "what is needed now" were distilled from the group meetings.

What worked was having teachers and professionals with a positive, optimistic attitude who cared about young people. Being heard and getting fair treatment also worked. Getting support and understanding from those who surround young people on an everyday basis and knowing that there are other young people in the world who also have the same problems worked. These few personal, familial, and ecological attributes can awaken strengths—enabling young people to make decisions and commitments that increase their confidence and their ability to accomplish goals that lead to better transition outcomes.

What young people need now is to know that there are people who care at home, in school, and within the service system. They also need access to appropriate services for themselves and their families in a timely fashion. They voiced the need to be able to interact with service personnel who know how to listen and are trustworthy and hopeful if the service system is ever going to be of help to them and other young people. They also need personnel who are effective counselors and teachers to help them learn more effective personal and community life competencies (e.g., anger management).

Benard pointed out that "being interested in, actively listening to, and validating the feelings of struggling young people as well as getting to know their strengths and gifts conveys the message, 'You matter'" (1998, p. 32). Instead of focusing on risks and viewing young people with a deficit lens, professionals and all individuals involved with young people need to focus on resiliency. Benard noted that longitudinal studies show how individuals develop successfully despite risk, proving that predicting the future in accordance with risk factors is a mistake: "The personal attitudes and competencies most often associated with these resilient individuals include the broad categories of social competence, metacognition, autonomy, and a sense of purpose and belief in a bright future" (1998, p. 31). These are characteristics that have sustained humans throughout history. As stated by Amin, Jill, Sean, and the young people at the conference, young people going through the transition experience must have guidance, understanding, and love.

Guidance is needed to facilitate good decision making and to teach the skills needed for everyday living. It is critical that guidance and teaching occur in a constructive manner.

Understanding is the second most important need. Understand that mistakes will be made. Youth in transition need a clear understanding of expectations and the goals to be accomplished and to feel that they have a voice in the setting of those goals.

Love is the most important need. Youth need love regardless of the choices they make, right or wrong. Love will show support through the rough times and will ensure happiness during the good times.

Who Will Hear Our Voices?

Who will hear our voices
When we can't find the words;
Who will see we're hurting
If we hide our low self-worth?

Who will see our pain
When all appears so well;
Who will know our feelings
When there's no one we choose to tell?

Who will notice a young girl
Who feels a future without hope;
Who will teach this young girl
That there is room for growth?

Who will see I'm lonely
Even when people are there;
Who will see that I don't feel that
Others have time to care?

Who will hear the hurt
And emptiness that's inside?
If others do not listen,
I'll just keep holding it inside.

Who will encourage me to realize
The opportunities that await me;
Who will take the time to
Encourage my goals and dreams?

Who will notice that my actions
And judgments may be poor,
And not because I want trouble
But because I want so much more?

Who will figure out
The mystery of it all;
Who will realize that
Sometimes "being bad" isn't "being bad" at all?

People express their feelings
In many different ways;
It's important to really listen
And hear what they try to say.

It can be especially hard for young people
To try to find the right words,
To share how they are feeling,
Especially when they're hurt.

The way one acts
Is often a means of expression;
If no one is there to hear,
It can soon become depression.

I am so thankful for those
Who helped see me through,
And even though I felt lonely,
I never stopped loving you.

I know I was a lot of work,
But that wasn't my intention;
I was searching for a feeling of worth
And positive attention.

Please do not give up
Or feel life is a waste of time;
Take it from our life stories—
Yours, others, and mine.

I thank God for His patient, loving Grace.

Margie Thompson

REFERENCES

Benard, B. (1998). How to be a turnaround teacher. *Reaching Today's Youth*, 31–35.

Keleman, S. (1979). *Somatic reality*. Berkeley, CA: Center Press.

Schorr, L. (1991). *Successful programs and the bureaucratic dilemma: Current deliberations*. Speech presented to the National Center for Children in Poverty's Council of Advisors.

Wehmiller, P. (1992). When the walls come tumbling down. *Harvard Educational Review, 62*, 373–383.

Zebley, L., Boezio, C., Carlson, L., & Chamberlain, R. (1996). *A study of mental health services to young adults in transition.* Lawrence: University of Kansas, School of Social Welfare, Office of Public Policy Analysis.

10

Driving the System Through Young Adult Involvement and Leadership

*Thomas E. West, Patrice M. Fetzer,
Candace M. Graham, and Jamiley Keller*

---

*When I walked through the doors, I was so surprised. It was
nothing like I expected. This was a drop-in center where
young adults can come in and hang out. There were video
games, a pool table, arcade games, darts, a television, and so
much more. I guess what really put my mind at ease was seeing that a lot of the people there were my age. This was not
just a stuffy counseling agency where people are so uptight. I
loved it. Even a lot of the workers there were young adults ...
this was so cool.—Jamiley*

PHILOSOPHY AND VISION OF YOUNG ADULT INVOLVEMENT

Engaging youth to participate in services that will benefit them is a
challenging yet essential endeavor. This is the population that inher-
ently avoids most adult involvement and would rather spend time with
peers. This is also the population that listens to the advice of peers
before that of adults (Wodarski, 1989). Many young people are tired of
adults and systems telling them what to do, and often they are mis-
trustful of adults as a result of past experiences (Turiel, 1974).
Consequently, these young adults never get the help they need for
their mental, emotional, or behavioral conditions. Candice, a past

195

participant/peer advocate, experienced the mistrust faced by many young adults: "They are like I was, afraid to trust anyone and reach out for help because of their letdowns in the past." It became obvious that to serve this population, there needed to be some adjustments in traditional service delivery paradigms. Because peer relationships are paramount to the young adult population, it became essential to structure service delivery around this indestructible power. There needed to be an opportunity to use this power as a positive force that could meet the specific needs of each young adult. There needed to be a change in the view of young adults as resources, active participants in society, and competent individuals rather than as victims or problems. This chapter illustrates our journey toward involving young adults at all levels of service delivery and how this philosophy and partnership has enhanced programming and empowered the young adults.

Journey Toward Youth and Young Adult Involvement

The Child and Adolescent Service Center (CASC), a private, nonprofit mental health agency in Canton, Ohio, serves children with serious emotional disturbance and their families through community-based individual, group, and family counseling, psychiatric and psychological services, and service coordination strategies (see Figure 1). Referral sources include mental health, child welfare, and juvenile justice agencies, schools, and families.

CASC recognized the need to fill the gaps that existed in service delivery for the 16–22 age group because Stark County lacked services specific for the unique needs of young adults. In 1994, the Transitional Community Treatment Team (TCTT) began its journey toward developing a model to serve transitional youth with the following resources:

- Funding from a National Children's Mental Health Services Initiative grant through the Center for Mental Health Services at the Substance Abuse and Mental Health Services Administration (This grant was designed to provide a broad array of mental health services that are community based, family centered, and individualized for youth with serious emotional, behavioral, or mental disorders.)
- Direction from Clark's Transition to Independence Process (TIP) model (see Chapter 2)
- Direction from the system of care model (Stroul & Friedman, 1986)
- Consultation from staff at the Kaleidoscope program in Chicago (Clark, Unger, & Stewart, 1993)
- A vision derived from an ancient Chinese proverb: "Tell me, I forget. Show me, I remember. Involve me, I understand."

The time had come to understand, respect, and build on the characteristics and strengths of the young people we served. The first step

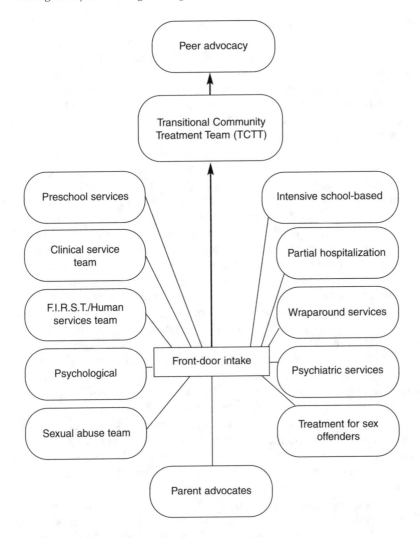

Figure 1. The Child and Adolescent Service Center's program components.

toward effective change was to actually listen to the young people we were trying to serve. This meant that service providers had to stop assuming what was best for them and give young people a chance to tell their stories and what they needed. They had been ignored for too long: "No one was there to listen.... Nobody would hear me talk about my dreams.... I even wrote my state legislator and he didn't respond" (voices of participants Jamiley and Candice).

As a first step in the journey toward young adult involvement, the lead author, as a new coordinator within CASC, hired a young adult to deliver interagency mail. She was a program participant who needed a supportive work environment. Many concerns and stereotypes were expressed by some staff when this young person was hired. However, the future goals for CASC involved developing consumer–professional partnerships in delivery of services. Thus, agency and employee guidelines were developed to address these concerns and set the course for the new partnership goals. Next, a "product of the system" was hired as a secretary. Lesley had recently graduated from high school, had moved out of her foster home, was struggling with homelessness, and desperately needed a job. She needed help with stabilizing her housing situation and dealing with her day-to-day issues so that she could put her energies into her new job. As the issues were resolved, she not only proved to have good secretarial skills, but her advocacy skills soon became apparent. While taking minutes at staff meetings, Lesley would speak up about what the agency and staff were doing right and wrong. She drew on her own past experiences in the system and on her present experiences as a struggling young adult. The teams chose to follow their vision and listen to what she had to say rather than ignore or stifle her ideas. This served to empower her and to improve our services (she was usually right). Her strong and powerful voice was soon put to use at other meetings within the agency and the community, although many adults and professionals still were not ready for this development. Carol Lichtenwalter, Stark County Family Council director, said, "Lesley taught us that kids can speak well for themselves. They don't always need their parents to speak for them."

Young adults at CASC began to look up to Lesley. Soon, she was trained to assist in mentoring other youth and young adults, writing grants, and recruiting young adult volunteers. Lesley was empowered to help herself through a supportive employment opportunity, and other young adults were empowered through her mentoring and advocacy. She was determined to help others while still dealing with her own issues. She never missed an opportunity to reveal her strength, especially when she single-handedly saved a 17-year-old male from drowning while at a conference. Other adults were there, but they hesitated to handle the situation; Lesley, however, acted quickly to pull him out of the pool and use the cardiopulmonary resuscitation technique in which she was trained just 1 week before the trip. Her leadership and ability to help an individual twice her size, with no hesitation, not only overwhelmed and inspired us but also served to strengthen her. The power of young adult involvement began to blossom.

Other young adults who entered services were envious of the opportunity Lesley had. They wanted to know what they had to do to acquire the same opportunity to work. The agency and community also began to witness the strengths of Lesley and the concept of young adult involvement.

Lesley had demonstrated how effective peer advocacy could be, and other young people expressed interest in doing the same. Six peer advocate positions were created. Funding was obtained from the Stark County Family Council (a local council formed to encourage and nurture the development of a unified services system that collaborates with families and pools resources to meet the individual needs of children and their families) and the United Way of Central Stark County. Peer advocates are young adults between the ages of 17 and 23 whose role it is to empower themselves and other youth and young adults within the agency and the community. These are young adults who have overcome different challenges. Many were involved with children's systems but no longer receive these or TCTT services, although they may receive adult services from outside agencies as needed. They motivate and assist young people who are striving to achieve their goals through positive peer role modeling and support. Peer advocates provide many services, such as transporting young people to appointments, supporting them while using public transportation, taking them to apply for jobs, helping them find and move into apartments, and providing support and skills as young adults adjust to living on their own. The peer advocates also benefit from this opportunity:

As a peer advocate, I was given many opportunities that I would not normally have had, such as sitting on boards in the community, traveling across the country to present at conferences, and making sure youth had a voice in many decision-making processes. Most of all, I had the chance to prove that I could handle these responsibilities.—Candice, peer advocate

---

Hiring is based on young people's abilities to relate and provide a sense of hope to the young adults they serve. The best peer advocates are young people who have struggled with issues and conditions common among the population and who have experienced a marked degree of success in overcoming these obstacles. It is assumed that, like many young adults, many peer advocates need a more flexible, accommodating, and supportive work environment that can help them learn professional skills. Thus, prior work experience or the ability to fit in with staff is less important than the ability to relate to and instill hope in other young adults. Otherwise, the hiring process is the same as that for all staff, including interviews, background checks, and confidentiality contracts.

Once the peer advocates were hired, a massive training effort was mounted for them that consisted of in-house training sessions, attendance at national, state, and local conferences, and shadowing of staff within community agencies. New peer advocates were paired with TCTT service coordinators as a way to learn each other's roles and assist each other in providing direct services. Each service coordinator had an area of expertise, including youth with dual diagnoses, the foster care system, the justice system, housing and residential facilities, child and mental health system linkages, and young adult parenting. Peer advocates also worked closely with the TCTT's clinical and medical staff. Before long, peer advocates gained a positive perspective on the roles of staff within the system and could convey this to the participants they served:

> *I always had caseworkers in my life. I hated them. Now I realize that they were only doing their job. It was lonely. It's really different when you don't have parents and the system is portrayed as your parents. CASC became more than my employer. They became my extended family.—Lesley Arnett, TCTT's first peer advocate*

Peer advocates were integrated into all agency functions and many community functions. They represent the young adult voice at agency executive council meetings and within agency and community strategy- and program-planning sessions. On the state level, they have served on school-to-work committees and state legislative committees. On the national level, they have been asked to speak about their experiences in the system as well as about their roles as peer advocates. They have also developed expertise in life domain areas such as vocational training and housing.

YOUNG ADULTS ARE THE ESSENTIAL CORE OF THE TRANSITIONAL COMMUNITY

Peer Involvement

Peer involvement is central to the transitional community (see Figure 2). The transitional community consists of all of the services and supports offered by CASC that young people might use to help them make the transition, in addition to resources available within the community. This means that young adults are an essential part of all services within the center and the community. They are involved in service delivery, staff meetings, janitorial and secretarial services, agency and community planning, and their own advisory board.

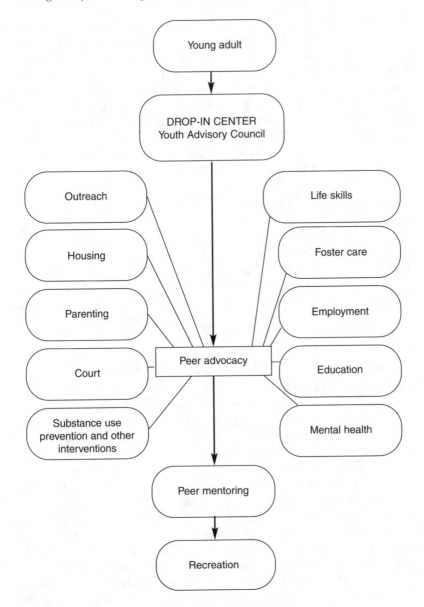

Figure 2.   The Transitional Community Treatment Team (TCTT).

Immediate Peer Involvement

When services are provided to the unique population of young adults, it must be understood that each young adult is different and puts different demands on the program. The function of the transitional community is to provide the very essence of what young adults are looking for in order to form a "bridge over troubled waters." Therefore, the transitional community offers a "one-stop shopping" approach in which young people choose what appeals to them. Peer advocates greet young people as they enter the nonthreatening center, guide them through the intake process, and assist them in obtaining the services they want. Peer-to-peer interactions help motivate youth and young adults to achieve self-determination and self-sufficiency. Peer advocates assist and encourage young people to cross the bridge needed to successfully make the transition into adult services and/or the adult world.

Young Adult–Centered Environment

Young adults who come to CASC are greeted by a young adult receptionist at the front desk and encouraged to enjoy the drop-in center environment, which is staffed by peer advocates. The environment is created to serve young people's interests: pool table, television, video games, jukebox, resource information, free doughnuts (donated by a local doughnut shop), and a store (proceeds benefit activities for the young adults). It is important to note that the drop-in center can be stocked with donations. Young adult staff are able to raise their own funds through fundraisers and grant writing to maintain and expand the drop-in center as needed. This creates a sense of ownership.

Youth Advisory Council

TCTT's first peer advocate founded the Youth Advisory Council, which was launched with the support of the Stark County Mental Health Board and a summertime kids grant from the Stark Community Foundation. The Youth Advisory Council is a group of young adults who are empowered to make changes within systems of which they are or were once "clients." It is made up of young people who have joined together to make positive changes within different social systems and the community. The council gives young adults a vehicle to voice opinions and make positive changes as a team. Some examples of what they have accomplished include sponsoring summertime fun activities for youth, creating a newsletter called *Young Voices*, holding social events (e.g., graduations, holidays, parties), baking and delivering cookies to youth in lockup during Christmas, producing a cookbook for young adults moving out on their own, sponsoring a youth against violence walk, and holding fundraisers such as car washes, flower sales, and concession stands.

Vocational Opportunities Provided On-Site

In addition to the peer advocate positions, young people have been hired to fill janitorial, secretarial, and store attendant positions. These individuals meet the criteria for CASC's Integrating Work into Living Life program, which provides employees with basic employability skills through job coaching and vocational counseling. They are paid at the minimum wage rate and work various part-time hours on-site until they are ready to move on to jobs in the community. This program has created a win–win situation for young people and the agency. Young adults fill positions that the agency was already paying for, CASC job coaches bring additional funds into the agency when they bill the appropriate payment source for services, and young adults are empowered with opportunities. This program also provided the TCTT service providers with easy access to receptionist and janitorial assistance (of which there is never enough at any agency) and easy access to employment for "unemployable" young adults, thus enabling them to address problem behaviors on site, as described below:

Dan, an 18-year-old male, was diagnosed with schizophrenia and was deemed unemployable by his vocational rehabilitation counselor. Dan wanted to work and needed the structured time to fill his day. He began working 1 hour per day delivering mail for the agency. He learned some basic social and employability skills through this experience, and his self-confidence began to increase. He is now successfully working 20 hours per week in a janitorial position. He is no longer unemployable—he has skills and confidence in his abilities.

Jamiley, age 19, struggled with depression, anxiety, and panic attacks that made maintaining a job very difficult. She was hired as a receptionist and began to see improvement in her day-to-day coping skills, assertiveness, and self-confidence. She thrived in this position and is now working full time as a receptionist at another community agency.

Peer Support Services

The peer advocate program is the absolute most wonderful thing I had ever heard of before. The first time I met one of the peer advocates, it turned out I had already known her from school. It was so weird because we went to school together and I always looked up to her and thought she was cool. Never in a million years would I have ever guessed she once had problems like me. I found out she was also a "teenage mom" who lived through the day-to-day struggles of having to be grown up all of a sudden. Maybe I was normal after all. I started to do things with my peer advocate. Sometimes she would take my son and me to the park or fair. Sometimes the whole parenting group would go to the zoo or out for pizza.

> *It made me feel good about myself to be out doing things, having fun with decent people, and not having to worry about getting arrested.—Jamiley*

Peer support services are designed to provide positive peer role modeling, advocacy, support, socialization, and life skills to young people in the community through the use of peer advocates and peer mentors. The peer advocates and mentors in turn are empowered with leadership, advocacy skills, and experiences within their community.

Whereas peer advocates work with TCTT service coordinators and therapists as team members to provide direct services to young adults, peer mentors are young adults hired by CASC to provide direct service to young people on an as-needed basis in various community settings. Outside agencies contract with CASC for peer mentors, and CASC providers may request peer mentors for young people with whom they work. Peer mentors serve individuals who are not necessarily CASC clients. For example, schools hire peer mentors to attend classes with students to maintain their compliance in the classrooms. Families hire peer mentors to spend designated after-school or weekend hours with a child and work on specific goals. Peer mentor services have also been funded by grants that have specified peer mentoring as a service to meet specific needs. Peer mentors are paid on a fee-for-service basis at the hourly rate that is billed to the referral source.

OVERCOMING BARRIERS AND CHALLENGES

Making a change in any agency or community presents challenges and is always accompanied by its evil twin, "problems." Involving a young adult in service delivery was no exception. The first young adult who was hired was confronted with a lack of support from many co-workers, who were uncomfortable with her handling confidential information and hearing office gossip. Unfortunately, she quit after less than 1 month because of the stress of working in an environment that was not ready for this change.

Challenges that Young Adults Face

Young adults struggle with being looked down on because of their age. Age discrimination is prevalent and prevents them from being included on or heard by many decision-making boards that affect the lives of young people. When addressing this challenge, it is important to reinforce young people's self-confidence and professional demeanor and to educate the community about their service.

Young adults are also faced with community agencies and programs that expect them to volunteer their services at a time in their lives when financially supporting themselves is a daily struggle. Tight finances make it difficult for many young adults to afford nice office attire, attend office activities, or obtain child care and reliable transportation. TCTT recognizes the importance of volunteerism but realizes that a decent income and benefits are priorities.

Challenges that Older Employees Face

Employees did not readily accept the idea that young adults with a history of system involvement would be sharing their workplace. They faced an added job responsibility: providing guidance, mentoring, and leniency to young adults who were now going to work in "their" mental health arena. They had numerous concerns and questions. Could young adults practice confidentiality and professionalism? (Yes.) Should young adults be invited to office parties? (Yes.) Should the employees fear thefts from their offices? (This is a reality for any office.) Did they have to stop practicing therapeutic office humor when young adults were around? (Basic respect.) Could or should they maintain boundaries with young adults who were from their same peer group? (Yes.) Could they still be honest and straightforward when presenting case histories in front of young adults? (Yes.)

Peer advocates and mentors are given the same respect and courtesy that would be afforded a new employee out of college or off the street. They are provided with extra supervision and guidance to learn professional guidelines and ethics. Any office humor that could possibly offend any staff member is not tolerated. It is important to the team concept to address openly and quickly any disrespect among team members and to regard each problem as a learning experience. Decisions about personal or relationship boundaries among colleagues should be the same as they would be with any other colleague and should be made on an individual basis. Service coordinators and therapists should be honest and straightforward in presenting case histories, but they must recognize that their views may be altered and enhanced by the perspectives shared by peer advocates. Peer advocates and mentors are a very important part of TCTT and are therefore included in all team activities, including office parties. They often plan these gatherings.

Many service coordinators and therapists held an "us-versus-them" philosophy. They found it difficult to be themselves when young adult mentors and peer advocates were around because they feared offending them or showing them their humanness. Those who supported young adult involvement had to counteract many daily problems and complaints. Problems did occur quite regularly. For example, a few young women invited males into their rooms at out-of-town conferences, which made the staff uncomfortable. One peer advocate made a recommendation at a meeting regarding a young adult participant that was against the committee's wisdom. The powerful psychiatrist had recommended placing the young man in an out-of-county residential treatment facility (at a cost of $150 per day). The peer advocate spoke vigorously about this young man's desire to live on his own and provided a plan for him to stay in his own apartment. She spoke of the services that the TCTT could offer. The committee was stunned by and uncomfortable with her advocacy. Ultimately, this was clearly not a problem and the committee adopted most of her recommendations, but colleagues and other professionals had to become accustomed to and learn to respect such advocacy and energy.

Young adult employees have had difficulties with attendance, dress code, and job responsibilities on a daily basis (typical young adult behaviors). It is important to be prepared to provide clear expectations, guidance, and supervision to young adult employees while staying focused on the philosophy of responding patiently and with accommodations to their needs. Once young adults are empowered and involved, they do not allow the professionals with whom they work to give up on them:

Working side by side with service providers, I was able to learn the treatment plans and encourage and assist young adults to work toward completing their goals. At the same time, I was completing one of my goals—I was giving back to the same agency that once helped me. I really felt good about myself and the work I was doing. I was also able to get help for myself as I started to face issues that most young adults go through (relationships, parents, and immaturity). While working as a peer advocate, I had some downfalls and started to backslide. Instead of firing me, my boss and the entire team believed in me and helped me. The team acted as a trampoline and bounced me back on the right path. My Dad reminds me every day how lucky I am to have my job and such an understanding boss. He says that if I worked for him, I would have been fired a long time ago.—Candice, peer advocate

---

It did not take long to realize that the time it took to teach and prepare young adults for their job responsibilities was far less than the time and energy they gave back. It became obvious that having them as part of "our" workplace was the best therapy and education we could provide for both them and us.

Power of Young Adult Involvement

Young adult involvement clearly improves many aspects of service delivery. Stress and frustration levels decreased as a result of the ability to delegate some of the work to a younger, more energetic work force and to provide services that were previously impossible to accomplish in a traditional work week. Most important, TCTT service coordinators and therapists began to take pride in the noticeable day-to-day accomplishments of their young co-workers. The young workers expressed their gratitude for the opportunities and time given them. The TCTT has been able to see the progress of everyone's efforts, which is vital in this line of work. Young adults have many success stories to share, which is constantly rejuvenating. They have ideas and insight into how best to help other young people. They keep the rest of the staff young and in touch, and they never miss an opportunity to tell us we are old or wrong. They are our "partners," and we definitely do not want to go back to providing services without them.

CONCLUSIONS

Involving young adults in transitional service systems is essential if we expect to break the barriers that exist between youth and service delivery personnel. This philosophy provides a vehicle for communication and empowerment that can be implemented within agencies, schools, community organizations, boards, and planning committees. When searching for the most effective ways to communicate with and empower young people receiving services, consider asking and involving them. They have much to offer. Candice, one of our first peer advocates, who was promoted to a service coordination position at age 21, has been a positive force in the lives of many:

> *I truly believe that because of my life experience I am a stronger person and a better advocate than most people my age. I want to listen and go the extra mile for the young adults I serve. No one was there to listen to me.... The Transitional Community Treatment Team molded me into an adult and a good service provider. They were not afraid to give a "crazy mental health client" a chance to be one of them. The young people I work with hear my story, and it seems to encourage them to break away from the labels like I did and succeed.*

Peer Advocacy

When you're feeling alone, and feeling blue,
You can come to me, I'll listen to you.

At times when you're feeling there's no one on your side,
I am the person in whom you can confide.

I'll help you prepare you for battles you'll face,
And help you to fight with style and grace.

I am not perfect and I'm not always right,
But what I do have is good insight.

I can't make you famous, I can't make you rich,
But I will help pull you out when you're stuck in a "ditch."

I work hard to make good choices for myself everyday,
But occasionally I too get overwhelmed along the way.

This does not mean failure or shame in any way,
It shows our youth I'm human and I too need support day to day.

I role model for youth to follow my lead,
Because I am determined for all to succeed.

I have so much to be thankful for, my life is truly blessed.
And if I can touch one precious life, I know I've done my best.

Margie Thompson, peer advocate

REFERENCES

Clark, H.B., Unger, K., & Stewart, E. (1993). Transition of youth and young adults with emotional/behavioral disorders into employment, education and independent living. *Community Alternatives: International Journal of Family Care, 5,* 19–46.

Stroul, B., & Friedman, R. (1986). *A system of care for severely emotionally disturbed children and youth.* Washington, DC: Georgetown University, Child Development Center, Child and Adolescent Service System Program (CASSP), Technical Assistance Center.

Turiel, E. (1974). Conflict and change in adolescent moral development. *Child Development, 45,* 14–29.

Wodarski, J.S. (1989). *Preventive health services for adolescents.* Springfield, IL: Charles C Thomas.

11

Nurturing and Working in Partnership with Parents During Transition

Renée A. Hatter,
Maxine Williford, and Kevin Dickens

The fruit must have a stem before it grows.—Jabo proverb (Hopson & Hopson, 1998, p. 45)

It was a warm summer morning when Calvin sat down at the table to speak to a group of mental health providers and educators. His purpose was to share his experience as a young adult with emotional or behavioral difficulties who had been involved with public systems and how the systems facilitated the transition process to adulthood. Calvin was stoic as he spoke, almost as if he had removed himself emotionally from the words and experiences he shared:

I was put on medication when I was 6 years old because I would lash out at my teachers. I was suspended from school almost every day, and really my experience with the whole mental health system, I think, was a lot of deception and lies and a lot of threats....

We thank Mr. Kevin Dickens, the young adult who collaborated with the authors on this chapter. To our parent advisors, Mrs. Shawn Williams, Mrs. Diana Levy, Dr. Saundria Jennings, and to those families and young adults who so graciously consented to share their stories, a special thanks. Finally, we thank Lois Jones and Aaron Parker from Parents Helping Parents (a family advocacy agency), who encouraged the writing of this chapter.

Calvin, who is 20, spoke of these events as if they had happened yesterday. Standing at 6 feet, this young African American male should have been excited about embarking on a new life as he embraced adulthood. However, rather than excitement, there was a sense of distrust and anger in the air. It was clear that Calvin's feelings toward systems in general were heavily influenced by his early life experiences. As Calvin continued to speak, the tone of distrust prevailed:

My mom was threatened by a person from the mental health system. I don't know his name, but he wrote a letter to her stating that if I was not put into a facility, I would become a ward of the court. Being my mom wanted to be involved in what happens with me, she had no choice but to put me into a facility.

The deep pain and distrust of systems were obvious in these words. In Calvin's experience, the systems did not serve him or his family well.

The residential facilities and group homes in which Calvin was placed in provided shelter, special education classes, and mental health services that should have enabled him to develop skills for adulthood. However, Calvin feels that he was not prepared to cope with the "real world" and in some ways is inadequately equipped to handle postsecondary school life.

He described feeling frustrated, angry, and distrustful. At no point during the 10 years that Calvin was in residential facilities did he feel that he or his mother had a voice in his placements or programming. Calvin felt that "people" were always making decisions about him without considering his preferences. The professionals neglected to listen to and respect Calvin's preferences. In fact, they failed to facilitate his plans for the future and ignored his desire to have family involvement in his program. Unfortunately, Calvin's experience is all too common.

Family involvement at this early stage in a young person's transition process is important (Hutchins & Renzaglia, 1998). In general, family participation in a young person's life is most desirable. Therefore, one would expect agencies to actively involve families and young people in transition planning. However, the horrible truth is that, more often than not, the service systems have not engaged young people and family members in planning and goal setting (Katsiyannis & Maag, 1998).

The Jabo proverb quoted at the beginning of this chapter—"The fruit must have a stem before it grows"—is symbolic of youth in transition to adulthood. Children are the fruit, and parents are the stems from which they grow. The stem is the source of nurturance, without which fruit cannot flourish and can die. Parents must acknowledge that they are the supporters of youth and that, as parents, they also need to be supported by the natural support network (e.g., family, friends, church, neighbors, teachers) within the community. Stems need to be supported by the trunk. The natural support network in the community becomes the trunk that supports the stems bearing the fruit. Continuing this analogy, when systems overtly or subtly discourage parent involvement, the child's growth into adulthood is stunted.

This chapter focuses on how families of young people in transition are essential to the process of moving successfully into adulthood. We emphasize the importance of viewing transition in the context of systems (family, community, culture, and agencies). The process of facilitating transition occurs across several systems and involves the natural support network of the young person, as described in the Transition to Independence Process (TIP) system in Chapter 2. This chapter addresses transition within the context of school-based transition planning as defined by the Individuals with Disabilities Education Act (IDEA) of 1990 (PL 101-476) and focuses on parents or other individuals fulfilling parental roles. The term *parent* in this chapter refers to the primary caregiver. The goal is to provide readers with practical suggestions and guidelines on how professionals, parents, and young people can interact for successful transitions. Most of the considerations described in this chapter are directly applicable to individuals facilitating transition from noneducation systems.

ORIGINS OF SCHOOL-BASED TRANSITION PLANNING

Historically, there have always been rites of passage that became benchmarks for "children coming of age." However, as society became more industrialized, the once-familiar rituals of our ancestors were replaced by more contemporary benchmarks. When society was legally and morally forced to stop exploiting children in the agricultural and industrial labor forces, school became the primary environment for preparing youth for adult roles. Therefore, the transition from school to postsecondary school life is critical.

In the late 1980s and early 1990s, American employers expressed concern that young people coming out of school were not prepared for work. Longitudinal studies on the transition of students with disabilities confirmed the concern of the work force. Special education students exiting high school were particularly unprepared for the adult world (Wagner, D'Amico, Marder, Newman, & Blackorby, 1992; Wagner et al., 1991). With this knowledge, IDEA was enacted in 1990 and amended in 1991 (the Individuals with Disabilities Education Act

[IDEA] Amendments of 1991 [PL 102-119]) and 1997 (the Individuals with Disabilities Education Act [IDEA] Amendments of 1997 [PL 105-17]). IDEA began to address the issue of young adults' preparedness for transition to adult life. IDEA introduced transition language as a mandatory component of the individualized education programs of all special education students. It was Congress' intent that transition services be designed to promote readiness for work, daily living, self-determination skills, and greater independence.

Many of the activities that schools undertake to prepare special education students for transition are shaped by the dominant culture's view of independence and self-sufficiency. *Dominant culture* refers to individuals in American society who primarily are of European heritage, who are considered the "majority," and who historically have been viewed as empowered and privileged (Helms, 1994; McIntosh, 1989). American society embraces the concept of independence as an indication of one's success and fulfillment. Although some families with special education students fully embrace this value, other families, particularly those made up of people of color, often wish for their young people to be prepared for an adult life that emphasizes group identity (Harrison, Wilson, Pine, Chan, & Buriel, 1995). *People of color* refers to individuals in American society who represent groups previously identified as "minority groups," who are of non-western European heritage, who are often disenfranchised, and who frequently feel a sense of disempowerment (Watts, 1994).

Capra (1994) described the cultural value of interdependence as one in which the individual views him- or herself as connected to others in the community. Similarly, Harry identified the concept of connection as "peoplehood" that provides a protective boundary for African American identity within which members maintain an intimate bond as a result of a "common history of social oppression and ostracism" (1992, p. 52). Thus, individuals planning for transition need to be respectful of different values for young adult "independence."

The ramifications of conflicts between the beliefs and philosophies of independence versus interdependence can be minuscule but multi-faceted. People who belong to the dominant culture tend to have an inherent sense of a "safety net" (an aura of protection, security, and entitlement) for access to the dominant culture's status, power, and other privileges on which people of color cannot count. Thus, sending a young person off into the world is rightfully perceived as more risky by parents of color. This is one reason that families of color encourage connection in the community (Harry, 1992), and this connection needs to be respected by anyone participating in transition planning.

However, part of the difficulty lies within the language of IDEA. For example, schools are mandated to inform young people at age 17, regardless of family wishes, that they have the right to make their own decisions without parental consent or involvement at age 18 (the "age of majority" mandate). Although in the United States individuals legally become their "own person" at the age of 18, for many families this may not be a value that is promoted at this early point in the young person's life.

In the case of a Latino family in which the father owned a small produce stand, his eldest son, Juan, was to assume the role of running the family business after completing high school. When Juan was about to enter his junior year in high school, school personnel began directing him to attend community college after high school. Although it was the father's expectation that Juan would finish high school and work full time in the family business, school personnel and agency representatives believed that Juan could aspire to do other things and therefore encouraged him to make his own decisions contrary to his father's expectations.

This case is an example of a transition nightmare for both professionals and families. In Juan's situation, the conflict between cultural values had serious implications for both him and his family. Although they had good intentions, the professionals neglected to consider the conflict(s) they caused between Juan and his family.

> This concept of the role of the family stands in contrast to that of mainstream U.S. society to the extent that it places the importance of the group above that of the individual, as compared to the American emphasis on the separateness and preeminence of the self (Condon et al., 1979; Ramirez & Casteneda, 1974). To fulfill one's role as a member of a group is to place a higher value on cooperation than on individual competition. Thus, Trueba (1989) referred to the dominant mode of U.S. schools as the "culture of competition," to which students from more cooperatively oriented cultures must adapt. (Harry, 1992, p. 27)

Importance of Empowerment

If young people are going to become self-determined young adults, their empowerment and the empowerment of their natural support system(s) is essential to the transition process. Before the 1990s, specifically within the mental health system, parents were treated as outsiders who were often thought of as the cause of the young person's problems. With the federal legislation of the 1990s (the 1997 IDEA Amendments and accompanying federal regulations), parents are now considered an essential component of the process of healing and growth (Duncan, Burns, & Robertson, 1996). Through the transition mandates of IDEA, parents and young people are required to be actively involved in this process.

For parents and young people to become active participants, it is critical that they become empowered members of the team that may include educators, mental health professionals, and other service providers. *Empowerment* refers to "the degree of control people exercise over their lives" (Prilleltensky & Gonick, 1994, p. 148). To be empowered, a person must be provided with the skills of self-advocacy that enable him to request the information to make informed decisions. Empowering parents and young people is a new, expanded role for all service professionals. Professionals need to take the lead in facilitating a climate in which families and young people are respected for their expertise and knowledge, despite their level of education, language, or sophistication (Kelly, Azelton, Burxette, & Mock, 1994).

In creating a healthy climate that fosters the empowerment of families, professionals should ask themselves the following questions:

- Do I really believe that families are my equal and can provide "expert" information about their young person?
- Do I stop to listen to what parents and young people are saying?
- Do I listen carefully to the parents' point of view?
- Do I speak plainly and avoid intellectual jargon? (Hatter & Harvell, 1998)

IDEA mandates that educational professionals begin to address the transition process of young people with disabilities as early as age 14. For many parents, the thought of their 14-year-old preparing for adulthood is scary and, in some cultures, unthinkable. Unlike the "age of majority" mandate under IDEA, professionals must be sensitive to the reduced flexibility these mandates place on families. Professionals can help parents through this process by maximizing family input during planning. This requires professionals to create an atmosphere of acceptance and respect when asking families what transition planning means to them. By eliciting parental feelings and input, professionals can move parents in the direction of empowerment.

Creation of an empowering climate is dependent on professionals' accepting families and young people as experts and providers of valuable information that enable the young person, with the parents' and the professionals' help, to develop a meaningful plan toward a successful transition. Calvin's story addresses some of the horrors that the transition laws were enacted to prevent. Calvin spoke of residential facilities as places where no one listened to what he had to say. He spoke about wanting to work but believed that he was not taken seriously. It was not until Calvin was 18 years old that he was allowed to have his first work experience. This temporary employment lasted only 3 months, leaving Calvin with minimal experience and no other opportunities to explore other work options before exiting the program. Reflecting on those years, Calvin said that he never had opportunities to develop work readiness skills. In fact, he is still not sure why he was given only a 3-month temporary job when over the years he had repeatedly asked for some employment experiences.

Calvin's attempt to use his voice was met with refusal. If his natural supports had been present in planning, he might have felt more empowered to express his desires. In Calvin's situation, he was never given the power, never given the authority, and never given the guidance to become empowered. Likewise, Calvin's main natural support—his mother—did not feel empowered but instead felt intimidated and disempowered.

Begin Early Partnerships with Parents

Schools or agencies can demystify the process by providing information early in the young person's school life. The transition process should begin early by infusing the concept into the student's special education curriculum throughout the elementary grades and into middle school. Early immersion in the expectations of transition law enables professionals and families to 1) identify goals, 2) examine family expectations for the child within the context of the community, and 3) explore alternatives early to avoid possible conflicting values between the family and the systems.

To accomplish this task, professionals must be sensitive, creative, and flexible in exploring a range of options with the family. Family expectations must be viewed within the context of each family's situation and addressed accordingly. Sensitivity provides the professional an opportunity to determine the family's and the young person's interests and perspectives, thus giving the professional guidance on how to successfully facilitate the transition.

We have found that, traditionally, mother and/or father roles have been those of protector and provider for children. When a child grows up, the parents often have difficulty shifting their perceptions of the child. Parents tend to "hang on" to the familiar roles despite the age or status of the young person, making it difficult for the young person to embrace adulthood.

This shift in roles is often more difficult for parents of young people with significant disabilities. The parent of a child with a disability has an even stronger drive to protect, which is reinforced by the real risks that the vulnerable child will face as a young adult. Consequently, the "letting go" by parents is scary and most difficult.

Involving parents early in the transition-planning process helps them prepare for the new role they encounter as the young person makes the transition to adulthood. Professionals can facilitate this process by listening to parents' fears, exercising patience, and encouraging parents to take small steps toward "letting go." Encouraging parents to seek support systems in their community also facilitates the role-change process. The more parents know about the resources and supports within the community, the more comfortable they will become in their changing role. Harry (1992) spoke to the strengths of African American families and their strong kinship bonds as a major component of African American worldview. Asian and Latino cultures have also been identified as holding similar worldviews (Harry, 1992). Professionals who acknowledge and accept differing worldviews are better prepared to make sense of family expectations in the preparation of the young person's life choices.

Help Families Address Real Concerns

An additional issue that families and young people encounter is whether their child should be labeled as having a disability. Many parents and young people feel compromised and angered by the young person's being labeled with a disability such as "emotionally disturbed." Many families face a dilemma when their child must be labeled to receive services because they know that the label may stigmatize him. Generally, the more severe the diagnosis, the greater the chances of being eligible for services.

After graduating from high school, Jimmy, age 20, did not want anyone to know he had been in special education and labeled as "emotionally disturbed." While in high school, he hated being called stupid or crazy by his peers, and he vowed that once he was out of school he would never let anyone know of his past. The stigma and humiliation he encountered eventually not only affected his self-esteem but prevented him from receiving services as an adult. Because he failed to identify himself as a person with special needs, local service agencies denied him access to needed services.

Professionals familiar with system expectations can provide young people and their families with information and strategies that enable them to advocate for themselves. Part of self-advocacy involves knowing one's strengths and limitations and being able to articulate them to others. Service agencies expect young people to identify their limitations to obtain services.

The art of empowerment and advocating for oneself is not acquired through mystical efforts (Ellis, 1995). Anyone can learn and feel empowered if he has a nurturing environment in which his voice is valued. Professionals can facilitate this process by providing families and young people with a forum in which to be heard.

Facilitating Empowerment

The dynamics of empowerment can be accomplished by professionals' assisting families in

1. Becoming informed by seeking information
2. Knowing their rights
3. Seeking choices and making decisions
4. Asking questions
5. Identifying appropriate coping strategies
6. Learning to speak their voice (i.e., give voice to their needs) (Field, Martin, Miller, Ward, & Wehmeyer, 1998)

Once families feel successfully empowered, they and the professionals with whom they work can model the previous six points of empowerment building for young people.

Linda chose to let people know about her difficulties. Her parents, who over the years had to develop their own sense of empowerment, were able to help Linda see her disability not as a handicap but as a hurdle that she had to work around in her life. Linda's parents taught her to seek information and ask questions about available resources and services within her community. Feeling empowered, Linda was able to inform her postsecondary teachers of her difficulties. Together, she and her teachers were able to create a plan that involved other service agencies that enabled Linda to develop skills for adulthood. Linda's story speaks to the importance of parental empowerment and how it can affect young people. Table 1 provides guidelines for parents and other natural support providers and young people for facilitating successful transitions for youth with emotional or behavioral difficulties.

Barriers to Family Involvement

Families of young people identified as having emotional or behavioral difficulties often feel that they should not intervene in treatment or treatment planning for the young person. Many of these families feel marginalized, which is a sense of feeling deprived of the power to effect change, and therefore there is a concomitant feeling of vulnerability (Prilleltensky & Gonick, 1994). Families of youth with emotional or behavioral difficulties feel marginalized when they perceive that they have no impact on how professionals decide to advise, serve, treat, and educate the young person.

Families of young people of color have to contend with an additional issue regarding empowerment and marginalization. Most people of color are marginalized individuals because of their cultural

Table 1. Role of parents or natural support people and young people in transition

Parents or Natural Support People

Know your rights: Part of family empowerment is becoming informed. Ensure that rights are provided in writing and explained in a language that the parent understands.

Schedule meetings at a convenient time, and attend planning meetings or send a representative.

Be aware of your child's school program and request supports if available.

Be empowered—speak up, request information, and ask professionals to assist in obtaining whichever information or services are necessary.

Before your meeting in a comfortable environment, plan with your child what you wish to be the outcome.

If you feel uncomfortable with and overwhelmed by the process, seek assistance from parent support groups from which advocacy skills can be learned and supported.

Young People

Be open to new learning opportunities, including social skills training if necessary and self-determination skills training, including goal setting and decision making.

See the transition process as yours; be willing to identify areas of interest and preferences, and advocate for those. Know your rights as a young person with emotional or behavioral difficulties.

Take charge of your own transition-planning meetings. That is, run your own meeting, with assistance from adults if you need it.

Feel empowered. This may mean that a professional will have to coach you on what to say, expect, or do in a given situation.

group's historical treatment and their current position in American society (Prilleltensky & Gonick, 1994). Thus, families of color often feel particularly disempowered, which is easily exacerbated by systems' reinforcement of this perception.

First- and second-generation Asian Americans are more likely to see behavioral or emotional difficulties as some form of imbalance between body and mind: "Psychiatric disorders are often interpreted in terms of an imbalance of physiological functions, which creates disharmony among the elements of the body" (Harry, 1992, p. 37). Typically, identification of a disability has a significant negative effect on the image of the family of the young person with the disability. Therefore, there is a strong desire not to be identified or to seek services. This greatly influences the percentage of Asian Americans seeking services through either school or service systems (Harry, 1992).

African Americans have a genuine concern about being misdiagnosed for mental health services and, more specifically, school-based services. Historically, African Americans have been overrepresented in special-needs categories (Wagner et al., 1991). This is seen in numerous legal cases, such as *Mills v. District of Columbia* (1963), in which inappropriate school tracking practices were based on race, and the *Larry P. v. Riles* (N.D. Cal. 1972) ban on IQ testing for African American youth.

Professionals must be sensitive to the many issues that families and young people face. Sensitivity to individual differences, intergenerational conflict, and cultural/ethnic considerations must be addressed by all individuals involved in the transition-planning process (see Table 2). Professionals can help mediate in parents' and young people's conflicts regarding transition goals and can play the "neutral" role of facilitating the transition. Goals and expectations must be clarified with parents and young people to facilitate this problem-solving task.

It is critical that all professionals in service agencies pay close attention to how systems disempower families and young people. The following sections describe barriers to family involvement.

Knowledge Barriers   Barriers occur when minimal information is provided to the family and the young person that would enable them to make sound decisions. Although transition law and the codes of ethics of many systems attempt to guard against the withholding of information, it continues to occur.

Studies have shown that when parents are given limited or no information about the transition process, participation is significantly reduced (Hutchins & Renzaglia, 1998). Parents are inhibited when they are unclear of the purpose of the planning process. Consequently, they are not likely to participate and either 1) present obstacles to the process through lack of cooperation or 2) become overly compliant and accept whatever is recommended.

Communication Barriers   The use of professional jargon erects an instant barrier between family and professional. Typically, when professionals use jargon, it excludes the family and the young person from full and equal participation in the communication. Use of acronyms

Table 2.   Role of professionals and paraprofessionals in transition

Collaborate with all partners equally. This ensures a climate of trust and value among families and youth with emotional or behavioral difficulties.

Encourage the positive dialogue that is critical for successful transition. It is too easy to talk about the nondesired qualities of a young person with emotional or behavioral difficulties. It is critical to emphasize the young person's strengths before exploring her challenges.

Provide a safe environment in which collaborative efforts can grow and be nurtured. For many parents, contact with agencies resurrects stresses based on a history of experiences. "Any collaborative relationship should be marked by a demonstration of respect and compassion for family members; an understanding and an accommodation of different styles of social interaction; the use of straightforward language; creative outreach efforts; respect for families' cultures and experiences" (Bullock & Gable, 1997, p. 7).

Provide flexibility to meet the needs of families and young people with emotional or behavioral difficulties. When working with families of color, systems must respect the family and community hierarchies during transition planning.

such as *ITP* (individualized transition plan) or *ED* (emotionally disturbed) creates an invisible barrier that leaves the outsider "out." Such practice by professionals creates a hierarchy and/or class system, assigning the family and the young person a marginalized role.

Another example is when non–English-speaking families attend meetings at which interpreters are not provided or documents are provided in English only. Even with interpreters available, it is critical to know the credentials of the interpreter. Not everyone who can speak two languages is bicultural. It is important that the interpreter be not only bilingual but also bicultural, because there may be concepts in the family's culture that do not translate into dominant culture concepts, and vice versa. In addition to the bilingual/bicultural issues, it is important that professionals be aware that, in certain languages, there are no direct translations for some mental health terms. Therefore, professionals need to carefully and patiently define terms and phrases for reinterpretation.

Phan, a Vietnamese teenager, was 19 years old with a significant physical disability that interfered with his daily functioning. His family was limited in income yet consistently refused to take advantage of community resources that could assist with Phan's transition. Finally, the bilingual/bicultural interpreter informed the school team that, within the Vietnamese culture, for family members to take anything that they did not pay for would be seen as charity. Consequently, this would devalue the family's status within the community. This example highlights the value of having an interpreter who not only speaks the language but, equally important, understands the culture as well.

Schools and others should use caution when enlisting the children who speak fluent English of parents who do not as interpreters for their parents.

Attitudinal Barriers   Attitudinal barriers can be erected by both parents and professionals. In our experience, professionals often make and act on assumptions about the families and young people they serve. These assumptions are often wrong and insensitive. For example, assuming that all families want their young people to attend college is ethnocentric and insensitive to alternative goals. Being insensitive to the feelings, history, culture, relationships, and roles of young people and their families is a primary barrier to families' feeling empowered and involved in transition planning (Ginavan & Jozwiak, 1993).

Trust, deference, threat, fear, and suspicion are feelings that are commonly found among families in their interactions with schools and other service agencies. These feelings generally stem from previous interactions with systems. Often, trust and deference can seem the same when families interact with agencies such as schools. However, the two attitudes are very different. Trust occurs when the family understands the process, respects the professional, and believes in the integrity of the system, whereas deference occurs when a family adopts an attitude of noninterference and delegation of authority (Harry, 1992). In both situations, professionals are likely to see families and young people agreeing with restraint and without excessive questioning. Similarly, threat, fear, and suspicion could easily present with similar behaviors, such as anger, questioning, excessive distrust, and sometimes posturing. What may seem to be hostile behavior could, in fact, be fear.

It is important for transition facilitators to be respectful and to validate the feelings that parents express. Clearly, some of these feelings need to be addressed and alleviated through open, honest communication.

Ignoring Parental Supports Brian, a high school junior, was identified as having behavioral difficulties. Although assigned to a special education class for his entire day, Brian was eager to find a job. School staff did not consider Brian eligible for work on or off campus because of his extreme behavioral difficulties and skill limitations. Consequently, Brian was not enrolled in a work experience program. Brian's mother, conscious of her son's desires, pursued potential work options within the community. A church provided a job for Brian and helped to shape his behavior into acceptable social skills for the work environment.

Fortunately, Brian's mother was able to advocate for her son. Her familiarity with the community and her desire to seek accommodations for her son enabled her to make use of the family's natural support—the church. Brian's story highlights the importance of professionals' considering the natural supports of the family when preparing young people for adulthood.

Brian's mother and the church were natural supports that the school ignored. When professionals do not consider families' natural support systems, their resource base is undermined and their ability to contribute is compromised. Extended family, close friends, churches, and other individuals and institutions can provide emotional support and guidance to parents as well as opportunities for skill development or other activities identified in the transition plan. If professionals are unaware of natural supports in the parents' and young person's lives, the transition process is handicapped and a source of support for the family and the young person is undermined. Therefore, it is critical that professionals, along with parents and young people, identify the natural supports within the young person's community. To assist professionals with this process, the following questions should act as guidelines:

- What is the focus of community life (for the young person)? (for the family)?
- Where does the young person go to "hang out"? Who are her friends?
- Where do families go? Where do they play?
- Where do families get together?
- With whom do family members spend time? Doing what activities? (Thorp, 1997, p. 266)

It is the natural support system that continues in the young person's life long after the professionals' work has ended.

Reduced Family Resources Families of children with emotional or behavioral difficulties who need services disproportionately have lower incomes and receive little assistance in obtaining mental health services (Cheney & Osher, 1997). The effect of limited resources for these families and young people is devastating emotionally, financially, and socially. Families forced to create their own resources are left to cope with stresses that ultimately affect all members of the family:

> This intensity of effort on the part of families with children with disabilities causes great stress, especially given (a) the prospect of their children's continued dependence (Hanley-Maxwell, Whitney-Thomas, & Pogoloff, 1995) and (b) limited availability of needed community support services (Thorin & Irvin, 1992). Stress also results from the additional responsibilities families shoulder once the public school is completed (Ferguson, Ferguson, & Jones, 1988). (Lehmann, 1998, p. 130)

Lack of Formal Supports Formal supports are those resources specifically designed to aid families and individuals that are not part of the community, such as therapists, agency personnel, managers, and other service providers. Families of young people with disabilities that have insufficient formal supports and services experience enormous daily stressors (Cheney, Hagner, Malloy, Cormier, & Bernstein, 1998). Divorce can become a prominent feature in many homes. In single-parent homes, stress may take on a different profile, as many parents become too busy taking care of the basics of living to devote adequate attention to assisting the young person with emotional or behavioral difficulties in the transition process. Consequently, many young people remain at home after high school with minimal involvement in any postsecondary activities (Wagner et al., 1992). In the absence of sufficient formal supports, many families do not know of or see alternatives to their situation once the young person has made the transition out of high school.

Although this presents a dismal picture for families and young people with emotional or behavioral difficulties, if professionals reach out to assist them they may prevent some of the negative stresses that affect these families. Professionals can encourage and engage in ongoing communication with families and young people with emotional or behavioral difficulties. Educators are the frontline supports for families and often the catalyst to involve other agency professionals. Professionals can empower families by encouraging them to become knowledgeable about resources within their communities. This may require educating some families on how to seek out resources (Cheney & Osher, 1997). Professionals can provide families with alternative means of involvement in young people's planning. Families that live in rural areas or single-parent families may find active participation in young people's transition planning difficult. Alternatives may include professionals' traveling to the families or meeting with families during nontraditional times, such as in the evening. Accommodating families and young people not only reduces some of the family stresses but also ensures parents' involvement and sets a sincere tone of caring.

CONCLUSIONS

There are many issues and challenges that families of young people with emotional or behavioral difficulties face during the transition years. Studies such as the National Longitudinal Transition Study of Special Education (Blackorby & Wagner, 1996) clearly highlight the outcomes for youth who are not prepared adequately for adulthood.

One of the keys to better preparation for adulthood is a partnership with parents in the preparation process. In general, all systems, including but not limited to families, schools, and mental health and other service agencies, must recognize the need to be flexible and must teach families, youth, and professionals to engage in effective collaboration. Inherent in effective collaboration is respect for all individuals involved and sensitivity to the cultural, generational, and gender differences of all participants (Cheney & Osher, 1997).

The story of Calvin that opened this chapter described ineffective collaboration. Effective collaboration for successful transitions involves four basic principles:

1. Collaborating with all partners equally
2. Listening to all "voices"
3. Providing adequate time for planning
4. Being flexible and sensitive to the concerns and needs of diverse families (Hatter & Harvell, 1998)

Tables 1 and 2 provide collaborative guidelines for young people, parents, professionals, and paraprofessionals on promising best practices for effective and successful transitions. If parents, young people, and professionals truly work together on effective collaboration, then studies in the future, similar to the National Longitudinal Transition Study, will reflect that, indeed, working together does have positive outcomes for youth with emotional or behavioral difficulties.

REFERENCES

Blackorby, J., & Wagner, M. (1996). Findings from the National Longitudinal Transition Study. *Exceptional Children, 62,* 399–413.

Bullock, L., & Gable, R. (1997). *Making collaboration work for children, youth, families, schools, and communities.* Reston, VA: Council for Exceptional Children.

Capra, F. (1994, Summer/Fall). From the parts to the whole: Systems thinking in ecology and education. *Elmwood Quarterly, 3,* 31–37.

Cheney, D., & Osher, T. (1997). Collaborate with families. *Journal of Emotional and Behavioral Disorders, 5*(1), 36–44.

Cheney, D., Hagner, D., Malloy, J., Cormier, G., & Bernstein, S. (1998). Transition services for youth and young adults with emotional disturbance: Description of initial results of Project RENEW. *Career Development for Exceptional Individuals, 21,* 17–32.

Duncan, B., Burns, S., & Robertson, M. (1996). Family-centered and family-friendly services. In B. Duncan, S. Burns, & M. Robertson, *Providing quality services to emotionally disturbed students and their families in California* (pp. 13–18). Sacramento: California Department of Education.

Ellis, A. (1995). Rational emotive behavior therapy. In R.J. Corsini & D. Wedding (Eds.), *Current psychotherapies* (5th ed., pp. 162–196). Itasca, IL: F.E. Peacock Publishers.

Field, S., Martin, J., Miller, R., Ward, M., & Wehmeyer, M. (1998). Self-determination for persons with disabilities: A position statement of the division on career development and transition. *Career Development for Exceptional Individuals, 21,* 113–128.

Ginavan, R., & Jozwiak, T. (1993). Self-determination: A critical element in transition planning. In R. Fry & W. Garner (Eds.), *Sixth national forum on issues in vocational assessment, March 4–6, 1993* (pp. 291–299). Menomonie, WI: Stout.

Harrison, A., Wilson, M., Pine, C., Chan, S., & Buriel, R. (1995). Family ecologies of ethnic minority children. In N.R. Goldberger & J. Veroff (Eds.), *The culture and psychology reader* (pp. 292–320). New York: New York University Press.

Harry, B. (1992). *Cultural diversity, families, and the special education system: Communication and empowerment.* New York: Teachers College Press.

Hatter, R., & Harvell, P. (1998, October). The *"what? why? and how?"* of better home/school communication. Formal transition presentation by Diagnostic Center North. Fremont: California State Department of Education.

Helms, J. (1994). The conceptualization of racial identity and other "racial" constructs. In E.J. Trickett, R.J. Watts, & D. Birman (Eds.), *Human diversity: Perspectives on people in context* (pp. 285–311). San Francisco: Jossey-Bass.

Hopson, D.P., & Hopson, D.S. (1998). Listening to soul. In D.P. Hopson & D.S. Hopson, *The power of soul: Pathways to psychological and spiritual growth for African Americans* (pp. 45–67). New York: William Morrow.

Hutchins, M.P., & Renzaglia, A. (1998, March/April). Interviewing families for effective transition to employment. *Teaching Exceptional Children, 64,* 72–78.

Individuals with Disabilities Education Act (IDEA) Amendments of 1991, PL 102-119, 20 U.S.C. §§ 1400 *et seq.*

Individuals with Disabilities Education Act (IDEA) Amendments of 1997, PL 105-17, 20 U.S.C. §§ 1400 *et seq.*

Individuals with Disabilities Education Act (IDEA) of 1990, PL 101-476, 20 U.S.C. §§ 1400 *et seq.*

Katsiyannis, A., & Maag, J. (1998). Challenges facing successful transition for youth with E/BD. *Behavioral Disorders, 23,* 209–221.

Kelly, J., Azelton, S., Burxette, R., & Mock, L. (1994). Creating social settings for diversity: An ecological thesis. In E.J. Trickett, R.J. Watts, & D. Birman (Eds.), *Human diversity: Perspectives on people in context* (pp. 424–451). San Francisco: Jossey-Bass.

Larry P. v. Riles, 343 F. Supp. 1306 (N.D. Cal. 1972).

Lehmann, J. (1998). Mother's roles: A comparison between mothers of adolescents with severe disabilities and mothers of vocational students. *Career Development for Exceptional Individuals, 21*(2), 129–143.

McIntosh, P. (1989). *Feeling like a fraud: Part two.* Wellesley, MA: Wellesley College/Stone Center.

Mills v. District of Columbia, 348 F. Supp. 886 (D.D.C. 1972).

Prilleltensky, I., & Gonick, L.S. (1994). The discourse of oppression in the social sciences: Past, present, and future. In E.J. Trickett, R.J. Watts, & D. Birman (Eds.), *Human diversity: Perspectives on people in context* (pp. 145–177). San Francisco: Jossey-Bass.

Thorp, E.K. (1997). Increasing opportunities for partnership with culturally and linguistically diverse families. *Intervention, 32,* 261–269.

Wagner, M., D'Amico, R., Marder, C., Newman, L., & Blackorby, J. (1992). *What happens next? Trends in post-secondary outcomes of youth with disabilities.* Menlo Park, CA: SRI International.

Wagner, M., Newman, L., D'Amico, R., Jay, E., Butler-Nlin, P., Marder, C., & Cox, R. (1991). *Youth with disabilities: How are they doing?* Menlo Park, CA: SRI International.

Watts, R. (1994). Paradigms of diversity. In E.J. Trickett, R.J. Watts, & D. Birman (Eds.), *Human diversity: Perspectives on people in context* (pp. 49–80). San Francisco: Jossey-Bass.

IV

System, Policy, and Financing Issues

12

Strategies to Finance Transition Services

Cliff Davis, Kristy Fick, and Hewitt B. Clark

Funding for public services on behalf of transition-age youth is a major impediment to successful services for this important group of citizens, both because there is not enough funding and because the resources that are available are likely to carry restrictions or requirements that minimize their effectiveness. This chapter describes funding mechanisms that are used in the delivery of services and supports to assist the transition to adulthood of young people with emotional or behavioral difficulties. Child-oriented services and protections are not relevant or available to older adolescents and young adults, and these young people are virtually invisible to helping systems designed for adults. Information about funding mechanisms is critical in the broader discussion because the need for services for this population greatly exceeds the availability of resources and services.

Unfortunately, the information in this chapter is less definitive than is desirable because there are virtually no dedicated resources for this population; each agency and community attempting to respond to these needs does so with a unique combination and application of multiple resources. Therefore, at best, this chapter describes ways in which individual agencies have been able to secure short-term funding for services and supports, some of which might be applicable to other agencies and communities. At worst, this chapter raises awareness about the inadequacy of resources and the unfortunate but necessary practice of using resources intended for other purposes to meet the comprehensive needs of a population largely unserved by and invisible to community service systems.

So that all readers might better understand the context of service funding for this very specific population, the chapter begins with a brief overview of the structure of funding for public services. Next, key factors that target or restrict the use of public funds are discussed, offering community planners information to aid their selection of fund sources to accomplish desired goals. That list is followed by a listing and short descriptions of many of the fund sources being used to serve this population, with a discussion of multiple strategies for the use of those funds. The basis for these descriptions and the subsequent discussion of funding mechanisms is information gathered in a survey conducted among numerous agencies throughout the United States that actually deliver services for this population (Stimac, Davis, Fick, Clark, & Deschênes, 1999). Finally, recommendations are offered to support resource expansion strategies by agencies and communities attempting to establish or expand the array of services and supports available across the transition domains of employment, education, living situation, and community-life adjustment (see Chapter 2).

STRUCTURE OF FUNDING FOR PUBLIC SERVICES

To better understand funding strategies that might support a specific service or set of services for a particular population, three critical aspects of public fund distribution and management are offered.

First, there is no single or dominant approach to managing the distribution of taxpayer dollars for services. Different federal agencies use different mechanisms to choose who gets what amount of dollars, what limitations are attached to those dollars, and what type and level of accountability must be provided to receive those dollars. In turn, each state uses different mechanisms to perform those functions, and these often vary across separate state agencies (e.g., human services, health and welfare, education, juvenile justice) within a single state. Many states pass at least partial responsibility on to local (county, municipal, township) governments, which in turn manage those funds using different mechanisms and approaches.

Second, when considering a specific group of people, it is possible that the services they most need or use are provided or managed through one primary system or agency (e.g., services for people with mental retardation). In that case, understanding the fund distribution and management mechanisms is relatively simple, limited to understanding the approach of that one primary system, even though other, secondary systems have to be tapped for some needed services. However, when no one agency or system holds or accepts the lead responsibility in serving a particular group, consumers are left to seek help across a variety of agencies and organizations, each with its own application processes, eligibility requirements, and/or performance expectations.

This latter possibility—multiple, disparate funding sources—is the closest description of the funding situation for transition services and supports for youth and young adults with a history of or current emotional or behavioral difficulties. There is no one agency or system mandated in federal or state statutes to fully serve these young people. In most communities, no system at all offers accessible or integrated services for this group of people. Criminal justice system data suggest that these young people, especially males, are more likely to end up in local jails or state prisons than they are to receive any, let alone appropriate, mental health services.

Third, even though government entities use different and unique processes, the basic premise of public service funding is fairly consistent: Finite tax dollars are targeted by elected government bodies or officials toward specific needs and purposes, with limitations (e.g., target population descriptions, eligibility criteria, certification processes), spending rules, and accountability reporting requirements. Restrictions are often added to the end use of public funds (services and supports) in each of these areas. Because each government body is different, especially among states and communities, the type and manner of these restrictions vary widely, creating confusion at best and at worst creating conflicts and restrictions at the service delivery level.

For example, mental health agencies are routinely reimbursed with federal Medicaid funds for delivering mental health services to eligible recipients, and many states have expanded their Medicaid plans to include an array of appropriate mental health services in their reimbursement plans. However, Medicaid policies and/or state agency accountability policies may (and do) limit the reach of those services. For example, when they require that a case number be assigned to the individual recipient for reimbursement purposes, a case number may be assigned only when a full intake form is completed and submitted to the state mental health agency. In this instance, school mental health workers and staff at drop-in shelters may have a difficult time obtaining reimbursement for their services, even though they deliver "reimbursable" services, because the twin issues of confidentiality and parental permission for treatment in the school environment and the transient nature of drop-in services make collecting all of the information needed for an intake form difficult, if not impossible, in those crucial service settings.

The import of these factors is easily summarized: Any person or agency considering how to obtain or provide services for this population must aggressively but patiently identify fund sources for needed services, and generally they must be willing to accept the terms and conditions under which those funds are distributed. However, survey responses (discussed below) indicate that leaders at the agencies that successfully serve this population have pushed the regulatory limits of various funding mechanisms to create and sustain needed services. This day-to-day, year-to-year, grant-to-grant, funding mechanism-to-mechanism approach makes service provision possible, but it also makes accessibility and management of needed services more difficult.

FACTORS THAT DESCRIBE FUNDING SOURCES

Several factors are important to consider as an agency or community seeks funding to support services for young people with mental health needs.

Age Limitations

Very often, funds are marked by Congress and by state legislatures for exclusive application to children or adults from ages 18 to 22. Because the population of concern in this book is young people (approximately ages 14–25), it is inevitable that they will cross one or more of these age thresholds during the transition period. Each line crossed routinely signals an end to one type of support but not necessarily the start of another, and even if it does move the young person into a different age eligibility category, it is highly likely that services and requirements in that new category will be different from those in the previous category.

Priority Population Limitations

Funding for public services is inevitably less than seems necessary to meet all of the needs of all members in broadly defined population groups. Therefore, Congress and state legislatures usually set priorities within broader population groups, targeting finite resources at more narrowly defined groups. An example of a priority population in child mental health is children or adolescents meeting state or federal criteria for having a serious emotional disturbance. In this example, although mental health services may be needed and useful for a wide range of severity levels, policy restrictions focus most available resources on those individuals with the most severe needs. Such restrictions obviously limit the resources available to serve people with less severe needs, and this is a consequence of typical public policy decisions. Furthermore, spread across multiple special focus populations, it is apparent that those policies that directly affect frontline service delivery are set in many different agencies, by decision makers at many levels, with little coherent evidence of integrated or shared policy approaches.

Service Limitation

As with priority populations, resources are routinely targeted by government entities toward specific services or service types. Stated simply, Congress intends mental health resources to be used for what it defines as mental health services, but these services often do not include such supports as housing, transportation, on-site work reimbursement, or job coaching. As a result, many fund sources restrict use by either naming the specific services that can be supported or naming those that cannot, or both. As an example, federal substance abuse and mental health block grant funds cannot be used to purchase residential services (room and board) or to meet capital expenses (building or renovating facilities in which services will take place), even though such services or expenses may be necessary to respond to the needs of individuals seeking services.

Individual versus Family Applicability

The vast majority of, if not all, funds used to support mental health services are directed toward the individual who is manifesting the symptoms that identify the need for services. In mental health jargon, that person is often labeled the "identified client." This individualized focus may severely restrict the type of assistance that might be offered to significant family members in the young adult's life, even though they frequently provide most of the young person's support. This limitation is slowly being addressed in the system of care model of services for children and adolescents with mental health needs, but it is still largely unaddressed in the adult service world. As a result, the families of young adults—parents and others with a commitment to and a lifelong understanding of the needs of their children—are likely to be excluded, because of funding requirements, from service reception at a point in their children's development when their participation is crucial, and possibly critical, to the success of those services and their children. This issue is further complicated by a developmental need in this age group to assert independence from their families as soon as it is legally possible to do so.

Income Eligibility

Many resources are targeted by Congress or state legislatures toward only those individuals who lack the resources to purchase services for themselves privately (through employment income and/or health insurance benefits), although some are targeted toward need categories without regard for income level. Medicaid reimbursement is a well-known example of an income-restricted resource related to the federal poverty level, although states have gained increasing flexibility to set their own thresholds for Medicaid eligibility (e.g., 100% or 150% of the federal poverty level). Implementation of the Child Health Insurance Program (Balanced Budget Act of 1997 [PL 105-33], amended by D.C. Appropriations Act [PL 105-100]) raised that threshold for children in many states. However, individual states may also use less-defined thresholds for eligibility for state resources—such as "most needy"— that have poor or nonexistent operational definitions.

Types of Resources

Funds for services may be allocated or distributed in a variety of ways, as described here across three general categories, each with its own ramifications. *Entitlement resources* (e.g., Title IV-E federal reimbursement for out-of-home care of children; Social Security Act [PL 74-271], as modified by the Adoption Assistance Child Welfare Act of 1980 [PL 96-272] and subsequent legislation) are generally available with minimal limitations, based solely on the number of eligible individuals receiving services and/or the number and type of services received. The number of resources using this open-ended approach has greatly decreased in the 1990s. *Allocated resources* (e.g., federal mental health and substance abuse block grants) are usually made available in set amounts and distributed to states (or counties or agencies) according to a formula and/or based on the number of eligible individuals or the services they receive. Federal resources have shifted significantly to this type of approach. *Grant resources* (e.g., Child Mental Health Services Initiative from the Center for Mental Health Services, private foundations) are made available to selected entities based on competitive or noncompetitive processes, usually for limited periods of time and to accomplish very specific program or system goals. In this approach, local service management is driven by an endless search for start-up and/or replacement grants or for other sources of continued funding. Each of these resource types presents different opportunities and/or restrictions at the service delivery level, which is the level that matters to individuals and families.

Matching Requirements

Federal resources, in particular, are often intended to meet only a portion of the service costs, with state and local funds required to "match" the federal dollars at certain ratios or percentages. States or communities wanting to make use of the federal resources are expected to "pay their share" of the costs to "earn" the federal dollars and to demonstrate commitment to appropriate accountability practices. The amount or proportion of required state/local matching dollars is usually unique to each funding source. It is particularly important to note, however, that most fund sources with matching requirements attach whatever restrictions are applied to the federal or other source dollars to the full amount of matching funds, even though they are state/local tax dollars. In other words, a state or agency that accepts such funds often also must accept additional limitations on funds that it perceives as "its own."

SPECIFIC TRANSITION FUNDING RESOURCES

This section provides brief information about specific fund sources used by a host of agencies and communities working to address the needs of this population. The section that follows analyzes how those agencies and communities report using these funds at their transition service sites.

Each of the categories or funds described in this section is used in some manner to support transition services for young people, demonstrating that these funds can be used to at least partially meet the needs of that population, even though they may or may not have been allocated for that purpose. This listing is not intended to be definitive or exhaustive. Rather, the list may serve as a starting point in the search for resources.

Individuals with Disabilities Education Act

Congress passed and has twice reauthorized the Individuals with Disabilities Education Act (IDEA) of 1990 (PL 101-476) (see also the Individuals with Disabilities Education Act [IDEA] Amendments of 1991 [PL 102-119] and the Individuals with Disabilities Education Act [IDEA] Amendments of 1997 [PL 105-17]), in which service mandates and process requirements are identified to maximize the educational attainment of children and adolescents with disabilities that interfere with the educational process. This is a unique entitlement law in that it requires local schools to use local and state funds to meet those needs— few federal funds are provided—although local planning must meet specific federal legal requirements. Four features of IDEA that are of particular significance to transition efforts are as follows:

1. Annual individualized planning with each classified student must include transition issues for those age 14 or older.
2. School personnel must arrange for participation by other community agencies in transition planning and the provision of services, as necessary, to meet the needs of particular students.
3. IDEA applies to young adults up to their 22nd birthday, if they remain in school.
4. Strong legal protections cover identified youth, with mandatory access to grievance and appeal processes.

The survey process revealed that some transition programs have secured state and federal funds through this mechanism to provide therapeutic services for young people in school-based programming, thus enhancing school participation by those youth. Others have used such funds to bring professional educators into programs primarily clinical in nature and separated from the school environment, further aiding the young adults' preparation for independence and self-support.

Child Welfare (Child Protection and Substitute Care)

The child welfare system uses local, state, and federal funds to care for children and adolescents who are abused, neglected, and/or dependent on the state for their care. Federal funds (Title IV-E) are available to reimburse state costs for youth placed in out-of-home care, with an expectation that the "state-as-parent" will prepare them for a successful transition to adulthood should permanence not be established or maintained until adulthood (in their biological, relatives', or adoptive home). At the local level, many communities use the Independent Living Program (ILP); the Consolidated Omnibus Budget Reconciliation Act [COBRA] of 1985 [PL 99-272]; reauthorized, COBRA 1993; Foster Care Independence Act of 1999 [PL 106-169]) funds to address transition issues for young people in the state's custody. Although such funds generally may be used until an individual's 21st birthday, most state child protection systems relinquish custody of youth when they reach the age of majority (age 18 in most states) to conserve finite funds.

Carl D. Perkins Vocational and Applied Technology Education Act

The Carl D. Perkins Vocational and Applied Technology Education Act (PL 98-524) is a specific program that provides funds to secondary and postsecondary schools for vocational education programs. Each state and local school district receives a formula-driven allocation of funds, accompanied by requirements to serve certain populations, including certain young people whose personal needs may jeopardize their ability to become productive adults. The mission of PL 98-524 states,

> It is the purpose of this Act to make the United States more competitive in the world economy by developing more fully the academic and occupational skills of all segments of the population. This purpose will principally be achieved through concentrating resources on improving the educational programs leading to academic and occupational skills competencies needed to work in a technologically advanced society.

In particular, Title III, Part C (Comprehensive Career Guidance and Counseling Programs) of PL 98-524 enables a state or local school district's funded plan to include career guidance and counseling aimed at mitigating the educational and vocational effects of an identified disability. This funding mechanism is used at many sites to assist students with emotional or behavioral difficulties, reflecting leadership and good partnerships between local school districts and clinical service agencies. Some districts use these funds to pay for youth work experiences with community employers. Funds are also being used to provide job coaches, who can support transition processes more intensively.

Department of Housing and Urban Development
The Department of Housing and Urban Development (HUD) is focused on making housing available for people at lower income levels and on community development in urban areas where there are high concentrations of people in low-income groups (e.g., individuals who are homeless, people with severe functional impairments). As part of its mission, HUD distributes funds directed at services for homeless people (e.g., McKinney homeless grants) and other high-risk target populations (e.g., community development grants) (see also Chapter 5), which may include individuals with serious mental health needs. Interpretation and application of HUD regulations vary significantly among states and communities. HUD also supports a number of initiatives aimed at inner-city youth (e.g., youth on the streets grants) that may be applicable to members of the population addressed in this book. Youth on the streets grants in particular have been used in several communities to support employment placements, direct treatment, and transitional housing for the population of concern.

Social Security
Social Security is best known as a retirement system, but the Social Security Act also addresses the income needs of individuals who are, by virtue of their physical or other disabilities, unable to support themselves (Supplemental Security Income and Social Security Disability Insurance). People whose mental health disabilities interfere with their ability to become self-supporting can become eligible for and receive these benefits, although the eligibility requirements for children (younger than 18) and adults are substantially different. When eligible young people turn 18, they must reestablish their eligibility under adult criteria. It must be understood that this fund source supports individuals, not programs, although the resources received by individuals in a population of concern can then be used by community programs to help collectively address those individuals' needs. Typically, people eligible for this level of support are among those with the most debilitating and complex needs, with significant levels of chronic or recurring acute needs.

Medicaid

Medicaid is the federally managed, state-implemented health care resource for people whose incomes are inadequate to purchase private health insurance and/or medical services. This highly regulated program has been identified as a primary source of support for service array capacity development under the system of care model in state child mental health systems, but its applicability is severely limited by its "medical necessity" requirements, by which any service to be reimbursed must first be demonstrated to be necessary under medical guidelines. This approach is based on models for physical health care services and is generally believed to be less successful in addressing behavioral health needs that may or may not be recognized or understood by physical health care professionals, especially among children and adolescents. Medicaid is a fund stream that carries significant income eligibility requirements, priority population and service type restrictions, and matching requirements. Within those limitations, however, many community agencies cite extensive use of Medicaid to serve eligible transition-age young people.

Juvenile Justice

Several agencies that provide transition services for young adults with mental health needs use both federal and state juvenile justice funds, in recognition of the fact that many adolescents violate the law as a result of or for reasons related to their mental health needs. As with child welfare resources, juvenile justice resources are used to improve the likelihood that a youthful offender will make a successful transition to adulthood, thus reducing the chance of further criminal acts or behaviors, but juvenile justice authorities must simultaneously meet the demands of public safety. The majority of funds in this system are state administered and are used by various local agencies to provide services and supports within the domains of employment, education, independent living, community protection, and community-life adjustment. The population considered in this book seems to benefit most when there are constructive partnerships among the juvenile justice, mental health, substance abuse, education, and health systems.

Vocational Rehabilitation

Many agencies use federal, state, and local vocational rehabilitation resources to help young adults with some type of condition, disability, or injury that interferes with their ability to be self-supporting or make the transition from school to work. Generally, such funds are limited to services that are clearly vocational in nature, thereby only partially addressing the needs of this population. However, they have been used successfully to address concomitant needs, such as psychological treatment to prepare and develop work attitudes and skills.

Job Training and Partnership Act

The Job Training and Partnership Act (JTPA) of 1982 (PL 97-300) channels to the community funds that are used to improve the employability of people, including individuals whose conditions, disabilities, or injuries limit their employability. As with vocational rehabilitation program funds, these resources are focused primarily on services leading directly to improved employability, but community JTPA programs often have much greater flexibility in how they use these funds to achieve that effect.

Grants

Grant funding, whether from federal or state service programs or from private or charitable foundation sources, is the most common means of initiating and supporting transition services for young people with emotional or behavioral difficulties. Such grant funding is often the dominant "first-wave" funding source for newly recognized services or service needs. In addition to limitations on service types and priority populations, grant funding is almost always time limited, forcing communities and agencies to seek alternative or replacement funding long before services are well-enough established to garner more stable or long-term funding support.

SURVEY OF FUNDING MECHANISMS FOR TRANSITION SITES

As part of a larger effort to understand what is being done to address the needs of this population of young people, written and telephone surveys were conducted during 1998 and 1999 with representatives of agencies that provide services targeted to this population. Agencies surveyed were from different disciplines and practices, including educational, treatment, prevention, criminal justice, and child welfare organizations, each with its own restrictions and limitations. They share a commitment to adolescents and young adults, and each was providing one or several services of use to this population. Each representative was asked a variety of questions regarding the type of services and supports provided, the populations targeted, funding sources used, and management of the services (primarily eligibility and accountability requirements). When the information obtained was unclear or additional information was required, follow-up telephone or e-mail conversations were conducted to maximize the understanding of transition site activities and related funding mechanisms. At the time this chapter was in press, 18 agency interviews had been completed partially or completely. This preliminary information, described further in this chapter, provides a unique glimpse at the services provided and funding mechanisms being used to address some of the specific needs of this transition population. The results of the completed survey are available in detail at the following World Wide Web site: http://www.fmhi.usf.edu/cfs/policy/tip/tiphp.htm.

For the population of young people with mental health needs and the people who care about them, there is good news and bad news in the survey results. On the one hand, the survey shows that an agency or group of agencies with a commitment to serving youth and young adults with emotional or behavioral difficulties can find ways to at least partially fund some level of services and/or supports. Each agency uses a different combination of fund sources, drawing from among a host of funds with adequate flexibility to allow use for this population. Each agency offers a different combination of services and supports uniquely tailored to the needs of its clientele and community and to the resources available.

On the other hand, the survey responses describe no obvious, single source or pathway for other agencies and communities interested in establishing such services and supports. Services explicitly responsive to the unique needs of these young people have no single or primary funding source, and most of the surveyed agencies manage a unique, changing portfolio or patchwork of funds with numerous and complex eligibility requirements related to age, type of need, severity, income, and/or educational status.

The first 18 agencies surveyed identified more than 40 discrete funding sources, including the following:

1. Five federal programs (e.g., Medicaid, JTPA) that may each have several subprograms under which funding might be obtained (e.g., subprograms from HUD include McKinney homeless grants, community development grants, and youth on the streets grants)
2. Six state categorical systems (e.g., mental health, child protection, juvenile justice, education) that directly or indirectly support services for portions of this population
3. Dozens of local sources (e.g., community charitable organizations, county-determined grant and allocation programs, local college funds) that can be organized into almost a dozen types of fund sources

At all levels, multiple funding sources and mechanisms were identified.

No more than 6 of the 18 surveyed agencies make use of the same fund source, with most fund sources used by only 2 or 3 agencies. This distribution illustrates the point that every agency and community uses different resources to meet the needs of the young people in this population. The most commonly used source is private funds, such as those obtained through charitable giving (e.g., the United Way agencies) or from private businesses that choose to support efforts on behalf of this population. This is a critical survey finding because it underscores two facts: 1) The major public funding sources are virtually blind to this population, and 2) communities and agencies trying to serve this population rely first on highly variable private sources to fill the void.

A particularly interesting preliminary finding of the survey is that dedicated mental health funding, whether at the federal (grant programs only) or the state level, was named by only 3 of the 18 programs as supporting services for the transition population of people with emotional or behavioral difficulties. Among the other categorical service systems, vocational rehabilitation resources were used by three agencies, child protection resources were used by five agencies, juvenile justice resources were used by two agencies, and state or local education resources were used by eight agencies. Stated more directly, community agencies that attempt to serve this population were more likely to use child protection and/or education funds than they were to use mental health funds. It also must be mentioned that most survey responses describing the use of funds from these two systems indicated serious limitations in the types of services that could be provided using these resources (e.g., education system resources may be used to help a young person with mental health needs obtain a general equivalency diploma but not to treat symptoms that result from a diagnosed mental illness).

Among the 40-plus survey-named funding sources, more than half were identified as time-limited (e.g., grants) rather than sustained (e.g., Medicaid) funding sources. The implication of this finding is that agencies committed to this population are forced into year-by-year (if not day-by-day) management styles and that their services may constantly need to change to reflect the requirements or expectations of ever-evolving funding sources. This constant reshaping to receive funding tends to inhibit individualized and person- or family-centered programming while also limiting the effectiveness of quality management practices.

Another interesting finding is that many of the agency representatives surveyed do not know or understand the sources of funds being used to support services for their transition population. In cases in which support is obtained through partnerships with other systems (e.g., education or child protection systems), respondents were often unfamiliar with where these other local systems got the funds being used, and they were almost completely unaware of the opportunities or restrictions attached to funds from those sources. In other words, the planners and implementers work without the benefit of adequate knowledge of the ways in which these fund sources may be used to address needs within this population.

RECOMMENDATIONS FOR FUNDING

How do agency administrators, community planners, and advocacy groups interested in establishing supports and services for this needy population succeed? Several recommendations are offered to guide the process of system development:

1. *Be creative:* Because there are few, if any, fund sources directed at serving the needs of the transition population, sources that can be flexed or stretched to address those needs must be sought. When a brief fund description lists four major purposes for which it might be used, questions should be asked about "minor" legitimate purposes, especially those needed by the transition-age group. There are flexible mechanisms contained within many major fund streams, but learning about these opportunities requires determination and many specific questions.

2. *Build and strengthen collaborative partnerships:* The survey results described previously make it clear that the mental health system is less likely to support child-to-adult transition services than are some of the other human services systems, such as the education or the child protection system. Planners and advocates must be deliberate about meeting with decision makers in other systems to explore ways in which existing fund streams might be applicable to the needs of this population. Collaborative implementation approaches must then be taken to maximize the use of such funding, as might be accomplished in a community transition consortium.

3. *Build transitional connections between the child and adult mental health systems:* Although these two systems ought to be better aligned with each other than with categorical child-serving partner systems, there are enormous differences in the structure and functioning of the child and adult mental health systems, and it is the young adults making the transition who are most negatively affected by those differences. The child system is often unable to follow a young person into adulthood, because resources to meet child needs are still quite limited and the adult system is designed to meet the needs of mature adults with mental illnesses, particularly those in their late 20s and beyond. Young adults making the transition are simply stranded in the middle. That chasm seems most likely to be addressed when the child and

adult mental health systems work together from both ends. For example, one agency matches child mental health and adult mental health monies to support a transition facilitator, with service coordination authority within both systems.

4.   *Build an array of multiple funding sources:* Of the 18 agencies surveyed, 2 reported use of just one funding source, but those agencies offered very limited or one-dimensional services for the population (e.g., only vocational training). Agencies that pull together treatment resources (e.g., Medicaid) with job training (e.g., JTPA), housing (e.g., McKinney homeless grants from HUD), and private funds are able to offer a more comprehensive array of services and supports to address population needs across all transition domains.

5.   *Seek and explore private resources:* At this stage in the development of care for the transition population, private funds, such as those from charitable foundations, private business, United Way, and other nontax sources committed to specific communities or areas, are more likely to be used to start or support services than any other type of fund. Private funds may offer greater flexibility in addressing the unique needs of specific individuals, but rarely can they be sustained over long periods of time.

6.   *Advocate for the retargeting of existing funds and the establishment of relevant funding streams:* The majority of systems set up to address mental health or other needs seem to be blind to the specific needs of young adults with mental health issues making the transition to adulthood. This will change only when there is an adequate advocacy base to catch the attention of Congress and/or state legislatures and convince them that more permanent and targeted funding sources must be established for this population. Influencing policy makers is often best accomplished by parent and consumer advocacy groups; service system personnel must nurture and support those advocacy groups. (These recommendations were inspired in part by an outline of such provided by Michael Curtis and Phil Wells.)

CONCLUSIONS

The agencies and communities that offer transition services and supports are the pioneers blazing a trail to be followed and improved on in the future. As more communities respond to the needs of this population, funding mechanisms can be expected to shift and evolve to become more like other fund streams used to meet the needs of people with emotional or behavioral difficulties. However, this shift will not occur without a concerted, persistent advocacy effort guided by a clear vision of the required transition system.

REFERENCES

Adoption Assistance Child Welfare Act of 1980, PL 96-272, 42 U.S.C. §§ 5101 *et seq.*

Balanced Budget Act of 1997, PL 105-33, 111 Stat. 251.

Carl D. Perkins Vocational and Applied Technology Education Act, PL 98-524, 98(3) Stat. 2435–2491, 20 U.S.C. §§ 2301 *et seq.*

D.C. Appropriations Act, PL 105-100.

Foster Care Independence Act of 1999, PL 106-169.

Independent Living Initiatives, PL 99-272, 100(1) Stat. 294-297, 42 U.S.C. §§ 31 *et seq.*

Individuals with Disabilities Education Act (IDEA) Amendments of 1991, PL 102-119, 20 U.S.C §§ 1400 *et seq.*

Individuals with Disabilities Education Act (IDEA) Amendments of 1997, PL 105-17, 20 U.S.C. §§ 1400 *et seq.*

Individuals with Disabilities Education Act (IDEA) of 1990, PL 101-476, 20 U.S.C. §§ 1400 *et seq.*

Job Training and Partnership Act (JTPA) of 1982, PL 97-300, 96 Stat. 1322–1399, 29 U.S.C. §§ 1501 *et seq.*

Social Security Act of 1935, PL 74-271, 42 U.S.C. §§ 301 *et seq.*

Stimac, D.J., Davis, C., Fick, K., Clark, H.B., & Deschênes, N. (1999, February). *Filling in the gaps: Funding services to support youth and young adults as they transition into adulthood.* Poster presented at the twelfth annual conference: A System of Care for Children's Mental Health: Expanding the Research Base, University of South Florida, Louis de la Parte Florida Mental Health Institute, Tampa.

13

Policies that Facilitate the Transition Process

Nancy Koroloff, Constance M. Lehman, and Matthew T. Lee

When I was asked to help write this chapter, my first thought was that I just didn't have the time. My life is rich and full. My significant other and I are the proud parents of an 18-month-old named Simon. I am also a full-time college student, and we are about to move into student housing. However, having thought about it, I decided I would work on the chapter, give feedback, and talk about my life experiences.

I have made many transitions. I lived with my mother until age 11. Then I moved in with my father and stepmother. From there I went into foster care, residential treatment, a proctor home, and an independent living apartment. During the process of moving from place to place and program to program, the only people who were there throughout were my father and stepmother. There were people who seemed to care, but they disappeared each time I moved from program to program.

The professionals who helped me had a few things in common. I felt that they put more energy into me than just what

This chapter was supported in part through the Research and Training Center on Family Support and Children's Mental Health by National Institute on Disability and Rehabilitation Research (NIDRR) Grant No. H133B40021-99 from the NIDRR, the U.S. Department of Education, and the U.S. Department of Health and Human Services, Center for Mental Health Services.

was required for the job. They listened to me like I was another person—not a "case." They did not act as if there was a set way to be or lecture me about how they wanted me to be. They showed their human side. They seemed to understand where I was coming from. Jane (a counselor at a residential treatment center) took me out for coffee. That kind of thing helped me think better.

I never actually heard the word "transition" when I was in school. I remember meeting with a school counselor one time and taking a test to find out my career interests and abilities. The results were given to me as a page of numbers that coincided with another page of descriptions. I remember being told that the results showed what I might want to pursue. At that time in my life, I was not interested in the future. I did not have any big plans. I just wanted to have fun and put off any responsibility. I was not asked, nor did I tell, how I felt.
—Matthew T. Lee

INTRODUCTION

Becoming an independent adult is a journey that, hopefully, all of us will get to take. It is an uneasy phase in life, made more difficult for youth who are poor, who have limited opportunities, and who are from disadvantaged communities. Becoming an independent adult is a particularly challenging adjustment for youth with emotional or behavioral difficulties because of the limitations that may arise from their disabilities. There is a consensus that these youth will need special services and opportunities to achieve maximum independence in adulthood and to be able to contribute to society. Given this need for additional support, the transition of these youth into adulthood is further hindered by a complex web of federal and state policies that are well intentioned but incomplete, uncoordinated, and in some cases contradictory. This chapter examines five of the most prominent federal policies that affect the lives of young adults. The policies reviewed here come from three service systems: education/special education, child mental health, and child welfare. A number of federal policies from these arenas could have been included, but we chose to focus on five federal policies that we believe to be good examples of the direction that national policy has taken. The federal policies reviewed are

1. The Individuals with Disabilities Education Act of 1990 (IDEA; PL 101-476) and the Individuals with Disabilities Education Act (IDEA) Amendments of 1997 (PL 105-17)

2. The Comprehensive Community Mental Health Services for Children and Their Families Act (Section 119 [amended] of the ADAMHA Reorganization Act of 1992 [PL 102-321])
3. The John H. Chafee Foster Care Independence Program (FCIP) (formerly known as the Independent Living Program; the Consolidated Omnibus Budget Reconciliation Act [COBRA] of 1985; reauthorized, COBRA 1993; Foster Care Independence Act of 1999 [PL 106-169])
4. Section 504 of the Rehabilitation Act of 1973 and the Rehabilitation Act Amendments of 1992 (PL 102-569)
5. The School-to-Work Opportunities Act of 1994 (PL 103-239)

We chose to include this final piece of legislation as an example of a law that is inclusive of all youth, including youth with disabilities, as opposed to the first four, which focus on specific groups.

FEATURES OF POLICY THAT SUPPORT TRANSITION

To begin this section, it is useful to think of policies as being either substitutive or supportive, a distinction first introduced by Moroney (1976). The social policies in the United States have generally been labeled as *substitutive* (Mallory, 1995), which means that social policy in the United States tends to intervene after families become unable to care for their children (i.e., substituting for the parents) rather than to provide preventative or anticipatory supports. The transition from childhood to adulthood for youth with emotional or behavioral difficulties calls for *supportive* policies, which anticipate the needs of young adults and provide services before they have failed. A review of the literature suggests that some authors (Clark, 1995; Koroloff, 1990; Mallory, 1995) have made an effort to articulate guidelines for the kinds of programs and policies that would be most supportive of this phase of life. These ideas have been used to ground our thinking about the principles that need to be present within policy to support transition. Analysis suggests that supportive policy

1. Requires individualized planning based on the young person's strengths and needs
2. Requires that the young person and her family be involved in transition planning
3. Mandates that transition planning should start at an early age
4. Mandates coordination of planning, funding, and monitoring services across multiple service sectors
5. Requires transition planning for all young people with disabilities

6. Requires that transition planning cover all aspects of independent living
7. Encourages community-based learning and work experience

These features are used as a basis for analyzing the policies described in the next section.

DEFINING THE CONCEPT OF TRANSITION

For the most part, policies that are supportive of transition have been articulated within the categorical service systems established to serve the varying needs of children. For example, the ILP establishes policy only for those children who are or were residing in a foster home at the age of 16. To overcome this emphasis on categorical systems and to conduct useful analysis of policies related to the transition of youth to adult life, we will begin with a discussion of the differences and similarities in the way that transition is defined in the five policy statements reviewed. After consideration of the policy language across the five examples, it was clear that the definition of transition found in special education policy was generally accepted and most often used by the other legislation. To us, this definition most accurately reflects the components that are supportive of transition. Therefore, the definition of *transition* stated in IDEA is the touchstone for this discussion. *Transition* is defined as a

> coordinated set of activities for a student, designed within an outcome-oriented process that promotes movement from school to postschool activities, including postsecondary education, vocational training, integrated employment (including supported employment), continuing and adult education, adult services, independent living, or community participation. (20 U.S.C. § 1401[a][19])

The definition includes a range of life domains that affect an individual's ability to function independently. It implicitly recognizes that educational services for youth with special education needs should lead to their ability to function as independently as possible in their communities after leaving school. The Rehabilitation Act Amendments of 1992 (PL 102-569) and 1998 (PL 105-220) adopted this definition from the special education law. The Children's Mental Health Act of 1992 (PL 102-321) does not provide a specific definition of transition, but it requires that children be provided assistance to make the transition from "services received as a child to services received as an adult." This legislation also uses the special education definition. The child welfare system's FCIP addresses the transition of youth who are or have been living in paid out-of-home placement at age 16 (i.e., foster home, residential care). The development and evolution of these policies is discussed next.

HISTORICAL PERSPECTIVE

Policies that support transition are the result of advocacy from family members, researchers, and providers who demanded social policies that addressed the long-neglected transition needs of youth with a wide range of complex emotional, physical, and environmental issues. The U.S. Office of Special Education and Rehabilitative Services led the way in developing transition policy that first encouraged and later mandated the provision of transition planning and services for youth with disabilities. This section describes the overlapping evolution of the five policies.

Special Education

The U.S. Department of Education, Office of Special Education and Rehabilitative Services, published the transition initiative in 1984 (Will, 1984). The initiative represents a commitment on the part of the federal government to address the needs of youth certified as special education students. The legislation described the types of services needed to facilitate the transition from school to work for students with disabilities. Funding was provided to support model demonstration projects, research and evaluation, and the dissemination of findings.

Two outcome models were widely disseminated during this period. Will's model (1984) emphasized employment as key. Halpern's model (1985) emphasized community adjustment, which consisted of three components: employment, residential adjustment, and the development of social and interpersonal networks. Federal and state policy makers, program developers, and practitioners eventually adopted the philosophy and elements of Halpern's model.

The Education for All Handicapped Children Act of 1975 (PL 94-142) mandated a free appropriate public education designed to meet the individual needs of all children with disabilities. This act has been amended many times. In 1986, the Education of the Handicapped Act Amendments (PL 99-457) authorized the expansion of discretionary programs initiated in 1983. These amendments included specific language to shape 1) state-level transition policy, 2) interagency agreements between special education and vocational rehabilitation, and 3) requirements that states report to the federal government the status of students with disabilities exiting high school. The 1986 amendments had two significant limitations: 1) Transition services were not mandated, and 2) there was no funding mechanism to initiate demonstration projects. These limitations were particularly detrimental for youth with emotional or behavioral difficulties. Because transition services were not mandated, young people with behavioral problems who lacked a strong advocate were unlikely to receive focused transition support. Most recent legislation addresses these important issues.

Mental Health

The Comprehensive Community Mental Health Services for Children and Their Families Act is grounded in the ideas developed through the Child and Adolescent Service System Program (CASSP), which was created in 1984. CASSP provided to states small grants that were to be used to create an infrastructure to support the development of systems of care for children with serious emotional disorders and their families. By 1994, all 50 states and a number of territories had received state CASSP grants. The CASSP principles helped to publicize a number of innovative ideas, including the evolution of family advocacy organizations, the emergence of wraparound technology, and the ongoing emphasis on family-centered and culturally competent services.

The 1992 Children's Mental Health Act advanced the CASSP principles one step further by providing grants to states, communities, or Native American tribes to develop local systems of care for children with serious emotional disorders and their families. This act is administered by the Center for Mental Health Services (within the Substance Abuse and Mental Health Services Administration [SAMHSA]), and more than 60 such grants have been awarded. Local entities are given wide latitude in how they organize their system of care as long as certain basic principles (e.g., community based, family centered, culturally competent) are followed. A clearly articulated component of both CASSP and the Children's Mental Health Act, at least in the written documents, is the focus on early and comprehensive planning for youth who are being served by the children's mental health system and who will need to make the transition to adult mental health services.

Child Welfare

Child welfare refers to publicly or privately funded social services designed to 1) ensure safety for all children, 2) ensure permanent, nurturing homes for children, and 3) enhance the well-being of children and their families. The Administration for Children and Families of the U.S. Department of Health and Human Services is responsible for the implementation of federal child welfare policy. Typically, public child welfare programs serve the nation's most vulnerable children and youth. Abuse and neglect are the main reasons for the placement of children in foster care, although in some cases children are placed in out-of-home care because their difficult behavior makes it impractical to maintain them in the family home.

In a review of research related to independent living for former foster care youth, Mech (1994) examined studies that both preceded and followed the enactment of the Foster Care Independence Act in 1999. Mech suggested that Wiltse (1978) was among the first researchers in the child welfare field to identify the need for transition services for adolescents in foster care, based on the increased numbers in this group. A review of four studies conducted between 1983 and 1991 highlights transition outcomes that indicate the need for additional resources. Educational deficits were reported in three of the four studies. In two of the four studies, employment rates were less than 50% and median income was approximately $10,000. The percentage of youth receiving some form of public assistance (e.g., Temporary Assistance for Needy Families [TANF], food stamps, Medicaid, general assistance) was between 30% and 40% across all four follow-up studies, with females reporting the use of public assistance at nearly three times the rate of males. Rates of pregnancy and parenting ranged from approximately 30% to 60%.

Studies in the 1990s report substantial increases in adolescent foster placement and length of stay (Child Welfare League of America, 1998; Mech, 1994). A national evaluation of FCIPs found that youth with emotional or behavioral difficulties and those with health problems were less likely to receive services than youth without those characteristics (Cook, 1991). In December 1999, the Foster Care Independence Act (PL 106-169) was signed into law by President Clinton. This legislation provides additional resources and a new framework for expanding programs for adolescents and young adults making the transition to independent living.

Vocational Rehabilitation

Enactment of vocational rehabilitation policies that have had an impact on transition services for young adults with emotional or behavioral difficulties originated with Section 504 of the Rehabilitation Act of 1973. The act requires that "no qualified handicapped person shall, on the basis of handicap, be excluded from participation in, be denied the benefits of, or be subjected to discrimination under any program or activity which receives or benefits from federal financial assistance...." Section 504 was the foundation for the Rehabilitation Act Amendments of 1992. These amendments strengthened the policy by including a focus on transition services and adopting the definition of transition used in IDEA. The amendments support the full inclusion of individuals with disabilities in their communities, in employment, and in independent living by providing "reasonable accommodations" and the "tools" to achieve self-sufficiency.

Section 504 and the Rehabilitation Act Amendments of 1992 established policies that expanded the numbers of young adults with emotional or behavioral difficulties who could qualify for transition services. Before this legislation, young adults with mental health disorders had little protection under the law to ensure that they received the appropriate support to assist them in preparing for meaningful employment and independent living. With these two pieces of legislation, individuals who have a physical or mental disability may not be discriminated against in education and employment.

School to Work

The School-to-Work Opportunities Act of 1994 was created as part of a larger national initiative for comprehensive educational reform and emphasizes community partnership. This initiative was developed jointly by the Department of Education and the Department of Labor and proposes to develop systems that will allow "all students to earn credentials, prepare for first jobs with career potential, and increase opportunities for further education." The initiative is not meant to be inclusive of all domains of an individual's life. The intention is "to help students attain high academic and occupational standards"(Section 3). Related legislation that predated the School-to-Work Opportunities Act include the Carl D. Perkins Vocational and Applied Technology Education Act of 1984 (PL 98-524) and its amendment in 1990 (PL 101-392) and its reauthorization in 1998 (PL 105-332). This set of federal policies emphasizes the development of vocational education and technology education.

KEY POLICY PROVISIONS

This section provides a general overview of the provisions of each piece of legislation, with a focus on transition-specific components. The latter are discussed in relation to the features of policy supportive of transition listed in Table 1.

Special Education

IDEA reflects the federal government's response to research findings regarding ineffective services and poor outcomes for young people with emotional or behavioral difficulties (Edgar & Levine, 1987; Neel, Meadows, Levine, & Edgar, 1988; Wagner & Shaver, 1989; Weber, 1987). The legislation appropriated funds to

- Study the state of special education and related services
- Develop methods to improve special education and related services
- Develop strategies to reduce the use of out-of-community residential placement and to increase school district programs
- Develop collaborative demonstration projects with mental health entities, families, and advocates to address the multiple needs of young people with emotional or behavioral difficulties

The allocation of funds to develop collaborative projects encourages interagency and private-sector pooling of resources to improve services. The amendments include four requirements related to transition:

Table 1.   Comparison of policies across features supportive of transition

	Special education	Children's mental health	Child welfare	Vocational rehabilitation (VR)	School-to-work
Group targeted	Students certified eligible for special education services	Young people with serious emotional disorders	Young people who are or were in out-of-home placement at age 16 and are no more than 6 months out of foster care	Young people with a disability who can benefit from VR services	All students
Requires individualized planning based on young person's strengths and needs	Yes	Yes	Yes	Yes	No
Requires that young person and family be involved in transition planning	Yes	Yes	No; encourages young person's involvement	Yes	Young people only
Mandates transition planning to start at an early age	Must state needs by age 14; plan completed by age 16	Requires planning to start at age 14	No	No	Career awareness and exploration programs to begin in seventh grade
Mandates coordination of planning, funding, and monitoring across multiple service sectors	Yes	Yes	No	Must coordinate with education	Yes, at the state agency level, to coordinate planning and development
Requires transition planning for all young people with a disability	Mandates for those eligible	Mandates for those eligible	No	No; individual must be able to benefit in terms of an employment outcome from VR services	Programs are for all students, with some attention to nonstudents
Requires that transition planning cover all aspects of independent living	Yes	No	Yes	Yes	No; secondary education or work only
Encourages community-based learning and work experiences	Yes	Yes, indirectly	No	Yes	Yes, community-based work experience

1. Notification
2. Participation in meetings
3. Content of the individualized education program (IEP)
4. Agency responsibilities

Notification

Notification refers to the requirement that parents be informed in advance that transition issues will be discussed at the IEP meeting. The intent of the notification change is to give parents ample opportunity to prepare for the transition discussion and to invite individuals who may be part of the young person's support network. This change provides parents with greater opportunity to be proactive in the IEP process.

Participation in Meetings

The amendments hold schools responsible for ensuring that youth have a voice in determining their transition preferences and that other agencies be part of the process by mandating the following:

- Students must be included in the IEP meeting beginning no later than age 16. If the student does not attend, the school must ensure that the student's interests are considered.
- Representatives of any agency likely to provide or pay for transition services for the individual must be invited to the IEP meeting. If a representative from the invited agency does not attend, school personnel must inform and include the agency in the process.

Content of the IEP

The IEP must explicitly address each type of transition support that will be provided. In addition, each public agency responsible for providing a specific service must be identified in the IEP. The amendments specify that the IEP team must address the objectives of 1) instruction, 2) community experiences, and 3) development of employment and other postschool adult-living skills.

Agency Responsibilities

The 1990 IDEA legislation mandates that the IEP contain statements of each agency's responsibilities, with instruction to include the financial responsibility associated with each service. Moreover, this amendment provides for the IEP team to reconvene after a student leaves school if the responsible agency (e.g., vocational rehabilitation agency, supported employment program) fails to provide agreed-on services. A student, parent, or professional may request a meeting to determine an alternative strategy to meet the young person's transition needs.

The 1997 IDEA Amendments include three changes relevant to all children identified as having emotional or behavioral difficulties. First, the category "serious emotional disturbance" is now referred to as "emotional disturbance." Second, each IEP must state how parents will be regularly informed of their child's progress toward meeting the annual goals of the IEP. Third, the amendments specify that a child's IEP must address behavioral issues and communication needs, including limited English proficiency.

The definition of *transition services* remains the same. However, there are two new mandates affecting individual young people:

1. Beginning at age 14, and annually thereafter, a student's IEP must contain a statement of transition service needs.
2. Beginning at least 1 year before the student reaches the state's age of majority, the IEP must include a statement that the student has been informed of the transfer of rights as she approaches the age of majority (National Information Center for Children and Youth with Disabilities [NICHCY], 1998).

A review of Table 1 suggests that special education legislation incorporates nearly all of the practices identified as key components of effective transition support. The major limitation of this legislation for youth with emotional or behavioral difficulties is the requirement that the individual be certified as in need of special education services. Many young people with mental health needs object to this label and/or drop out of school before receiving it.

Children's Mental Health Act

The Comprehensive Community Children's Mental Health Act is specifically focused on meeting the needs of children with serious emotional or behavioral difficulties and their families through the development of local systems of care. This act supports the provision of eight specific services in communities that apply for and receive funding. These services include diagnostic, outpatient, and emergency services, intensive home-based and day-treatment services, respite care, and therapeutic foster care. The eighth service specifies "assisting the child in making the transition from the services received as a child to the services to be received as an adult" (PL 102-321, § 119, pt. E, § 562[c][8]). Many of the requirements of a system of care are compatible with the principles of effective transition planning. These include an individualized plan of service, regular review and revision by a multidisciplinary team, and cross-system coordination. As an example, the act requires "collaboration with all public entities that provide human services in the community—including mental health, education, child welfare and juvenile justice" (PL 102-321, § 119, pt. E, § 562[a][3]). Family and youth are included in both planning and implementation of the services through the requirement that "the plan will be developed and carried out with the participation of the family of the child and, unless clinically inappropriate, with the participation of the child" (PL 102-321, § 119, pt. E, § 563[a]). No definition is provided for the term *clinically inappropriate*.

Specific references to the transition process are made in two sections of the act: under the list of required services of the system and under the specifications for the content of the individualized plan. As noted above, systems of care are expected to ensure that children make the transition from the children's services system to the adult services system. As a component of the individualized plan, however, the legislation becomes more specific. The contents of the plan "provide for each of such services that is appropriate to the circumstances of the child, including, except in the case of children who are less than 14 years of age, the provision of appropriate vocational counseling and rehabilitation, and transition services (as defined in section 602[a][19] of the Individuals with Disabilities Education Act)" (PL 102-321, § 119, pt. E, § 563[d]).

Child Welfare Independent Living Program

The FCIP was initially authorized by the Consolidated Omnibus Budget Reconciliation Act of 1985 (PL 99-272) through Section 477 of Title IV-E of the Social Security Act. The purpose of the FCIP policy is to help current or former foster or residential care youth make the transition to independent living. FCIP funding is intended to support intensive, short-term transition services provided by the state. The policy is not a mandate, but it does make money available to states for these activities. Since its enactment, the legislation has been modified in the following ways:

- Continuation of authorization and expansion of eligibility criteria to include those who are likely to remain in foster or residential care until age 18
- Provide money for room and board for those who left foster care at or after their 18th birthday until these individuals reach age 21
- Expand eligibility for those younger than age 18 to those who have been adopted or who have obtained permanency
- Allow funds to be spent on preparation for independent living activities for those younger than age 16
- Permanently reauthorize FCIP as part of the Omnibus Budget Reconciliation Act
- Provide states with more funding and greater flexibility

- Increase the amount of assets allowable for children in foster care
- Provide states the option of Medicaid coverage for adolescents leaving foster care until they reach age 21

All 50 states plus the District of Columbia provide FCIP services through the federal program. Eligibility criteria, expanded in 1999, continue to screen out special populations as runaway youth. In addition, young people who would be eligible after leaving foster care may be unlikely to request FCIP services from their local child welfare office. Because the changes to the FCIP are so recent, it is important to monitor the changes that states make in the first few years of the 21st century.

FCIP legislation provides states with great latitude regarding how transition services are provided. In addition, the types of services and the planning process to some extent parallel those specified in special education and vocational rehabilitation legislation. For example, types of FCIP services include 1) educational support to obtain a high school diploma or general equivalency diploma, 2) life skills training (e.g., career planning, locating housing and other community resources, daily living skills), and 3) counseling. Of particular significance for young people with emotional or behavioral difficulties is their eligibility for extended Medicaid coverage, which opens up the doors for continued treatment. FCIPs may also use funding to pay for staff to assist in coordination of services for participants and to implement outreach programs to bring eligible youth into the programs. It is recommended that each participant have a written transitional independent living plan, based on the assessment of his needs, and that the plan be incorporated into the case plan. The knowledge and experience of leaders in the state regarding the needs of youth in transition are the primary determinants of program design and implementation.

Vocational Rehabilitation
The Rehabilitation Act of 1973 is considered a bill of rights for individuals with disabilities. The act is broadly focused, addressing the rights of all individuals with disabilities regardless of age. Although the definition of disability includes a broad range of physical and mental disabilities, individuals can qualify for services only when they are determined to be able to "benefit in terms of an employment outcome from VR services."

The Rehabilitation Act Amendments of 1992 address the transition needs of youth and young adults by requiring that the written rehabilitation plan document how vocational rehabilitation services for each young person are being coordinated with school services. New assessment recommendations specify the time limit to determine eligibility. Within 60 days of application, a determination must be made. Exceptions can be made for individuals with severe disabilities to ensure that they will benefit from vocational rehabilitation services. This effort to stream-line the assessment process is supported by the recommendation that assessment information from other sources, such as public schools, indi-vidual applicants, and family members, be used to determine eligibility. Additional information is to be collected only when needed. There is a presumption of employability for all individuals, regardless of severity of disability. The legislation calls for a focus on the strengths and prefer-ences of the individual and mandates the active involvement of the con-sumer in the assessment process. It should be noted that services resulting from this act generally are short-term.

Statements in the policy suggest great commonalities between special education and vocational rehabilitation philosophy and values. These policy statements include

- A mandate to coordinate services with other entities (e.g., Social Security Administration, state and federal agencies that provide services under IDEA, the Carl D. Perkins Vocational and Applied Technology Education Act (PL 98-524), and the Wagner-O'Day Act (PL 92-28)
- A mandate to develop a state advisory council whose majority mem-bers are individuals with disabilities who are not state employees
- An emphasis on identifying natural supports (such as co-workers) when individuals require supported employment and/or ongoing services after involvement with vocational rehabilitation ends
- Authorization of "personal assistance services," which must be job related but can take place away from the job (e.g., assistance with personal hygiene)

School-to-Work Opportunities Act
The purpose of the School-to-Work Opportunities Act of 1994 was to establish a national framework within which each state could develop its own statewide school-to-work system. The School-to-Work Opportunities Act uses the workplace as a learning environment, is dependent on local partnerships with employers, and attempts to obtain higher-paying, skilled, and career-oriented employment for youth. The programs funded under this act are for all students, explic-itly including youth with disabilities. The act expires in 2001.

To obtain funds, each state must have developed a plan that includes the following components: 1) a school-based component, 2) a work-based component, and 3) connecting activities. The school-based component must contain career awareness and career exploration activities, academic content that would prepare students for postsecondary education, curriculum that integrates academic and vocational learning, and regularly scheduled evaluations with students and school dropouts. The work-based component includes work experience, job training, workplace mentoring, instruction in workplace competencies, and broad instruction in all aspects of industry. Connecting activities focus on developing systems to support the partnerships with employers by providing technical assistance, encouraging active participation, assisting with job finding, and linking youth with community services. Related funding is available through the Office of Special Education Research Service to provide for Transition Systems Change Projects. These projects focus on improving services and supports to ensure successful outcomes from school to adult life for youth with disabilities.

Although the School-to-Work Opportunities Act does not specifically address the needs of youth with emotional or behavioral difficulties, by its inclusion of all young people, including students with disabilities, it offers an umbrella that could be supportive of young adults in the mental health system.

DISCUSSION

Our common understanding of how to provide comprehensive transition support for youth with emotional or behavioral difficulties has evolved since the 1970s. Although public policies that address education, special education, vocational rehabilitation, mental health, and child welfare reflect collaborative efforts to develop and implement transition legislation, there are a number of discrepancies that contribute to fragmented services and confusion in the field. A review of Table 1 suggests that the special education transition policy most closely conforms to policy features that are supportive of transition. The Children's Mental Health Act incorporates most of the components while focusing on a narrowly defined group of youth and primarily on that group's mental health service needs. The other policies discussed here specify some aspects of supportive transition policies and not others. This variation results in uneven and incomplete services across categorical groups of young people.

It is important to recognize that written policy, no matter how well constructed, cannot by itself change or improve services. The following points are intended to advance the discussion of the interplay between policy and practice.

1. Written policy, although influencing practice, does not create state and community systems designed to implement all that is mandated or recommended. The difference between policy and practice

may be most obvious when a policy includes a series of mandates that are inconsistently and incompletely implemented.

2.   Policy that looks good on paper may be relatively unrelated to what is delivered on a day-to-day basis as transition services. States are under no obligation to demonstrate that students receive the services outlined in the transition plan. Furthermore, there is no organized effort to evaluate the effectiveness of transition services that emanate from these policies to determine whether they should be continued or replaced with other approaches.

3.   Under most of these policies, the youth must be formally diagnosed as emotionally disturbed to receive needed support. Eligibility criteria, certification, or diagnosis are barriers to access within almost all of the federal policies discussed and remain the most prominent factor in the exclusion of many young adults from services. For example, youth exhibiting antisocial behavior may become involved with the juvenile justice system, where, because of their perceived "conduct disorder," they are denied any consideration of their potential mental health problems. Once incarcerated in the juvenile corrections system, these individuals are not eligible for independent living programs administered by the state's child welfare system, and they do not often receive special education services. Furthermore, youth who are homeless and/or have left the educational system rarely receive the assessment required to make them eligible for the services provided under federal legislation.

4.   With the exception of child welfare policies, the policies discussed include a requirement to coordinate planning and monitoring of services and to share resources across service systems. However, the mechanisms and resources to ensure that funds are shared and services are coordinated are absent. Thus, with funding remaining categorical across service systems, the provision of services remains, in large part, categorical (see Chapter 12).

5.   The short-term nature of transition support is especially present in child welfare policy. The legislation makes no suggestion of the need for longer-term follow-up services after the initial few months of support. The lack of program mandates and funding contribute to poor monitoring and supervision of young people who are living in semi-independent settings.

6.   Issues related to family life and single parenting are real concerns for many young people. Tied to these roles are economic factors such as unemployment, underemployment, and the need for housing and continued education. Transition policies do not explicitly address these substantial components of family life. The implicit assumption made by most federal policies is that these youth will remain children rather than assume the usual roles of adulthood, including parenthood.

Analysis of the education, mental health, and child welfare policies suggests that positive efforts have been made to recognize the need for individual transition planning for young people with disabilities and to accept the state role in providing some of these services. In addition, there is evidence of some collaboration among policy makers at the national level. Since the late 1980s, the Office of Special Education and Rehabilitative Services within the U.S. Department of Education has reflected a proactive commitment to developing and strengthening transition policy. In the 1990s, children's mental health legislation acknowledged the need for transition support for youth as they make the transition to the adult mental health services system. The passage of the Foster Care Independence Act of 1999 demonstrates a revitalized effort to address the transition needs of youth in the child welfare system. These efforts by policy makers are reflected more in the features of legislation and regulations that encourage collaborative, supportive transition planning and services than in the associated funding mechanisms, which remain highly exclusionary and categorical (see Chapter 12).

Parent advocacy organizations and supportive practitioners, educators, administrators, researchers, and policy makers at the local, state, and federal levels have improved policy significantly. Yet much work is still needed to ensure that these supportive features for facilitating transition are incorporated into legislation, regulations, and funding to support effective practice at the community level. With continued attention to issues of accountability and effectiveness, these beginnings can serve as the ground for providing the kinds of support that young people need.

EPILOGUE

After getting into lots of trouble, doing poorly in school, and running away, I was moved out of my home. The "treatment" I got was mostly group therapy and, later on, group classes. I did not do well—I am not a "group" person. I figured out what I was supposed to say or do, whatever it took to get through the loopholes. When I think about what could have been done differently, I go back to my elementary school years. If I had gotten some help—if somebody could have talked with me in school—maybe a mentor, some kind of role model. I don't remember anyone talking with me. I think all through my life I needed one person who I could rely on, to talk to about anything. Later on, my father became that person.

Transition seems to be what life is about. As a young adult who made it through many challenging years, it seems that the system failed to act in my interests until very late.

Moreover, I don't recall any professional asking me what I wanted for my life until long after I was in out-of-home placement. I feel that I have been very lucky, and some people say I am resilient; in spite of the system, I am succeeding. Today I am learning about how to maintain a fulfilling relationship with my partner in life. We talk with my father and stepmother a great deal and find time to spend quality time with each other. I am learning more about myself each day by caring for Simon. I am focusing on my education, and I feel that my life is full of possibility.—Matthew T. Lee

REFERENCES

ADAMHA Reorganization Act, PL 102-321, 42 U.S.C. §§ 290ff *et seq.*

Carl D. Perkins Vocational and Applied Technology Education Act Amendments of 1990, PL 101-392, 104 Stat. 753-804, 806-834.

Carl D. Perkins Vocational and Applied Technology Education Act Amendments of 1998, PL 105-332, 20 U.S.C. §§ 2301 *et seq.*

Carl D. Perkins Vocational and Applied Technology Education Act of 1984, PL 98-524, 20 US.C. §§ 2301 *et seq.*

Child Welfare League of America. (1998). *State agency survey.* Washington, DC: Author.

Children's Mental Health Act of 1992, PL 102-321, 42 U.S.C. §§ 290ff *et seq.*

Clark, H.B. (1995). *Transition to Independence Process: TIP operations manual.* Tampa: University of South Florida, Louis de la Parte Florida Mental Health Institute.

Comprehensive Community Mental Health Services for Children and Their Families Act (Section 119 [amended] of the ADAMHA Reorganization Act of 1992), PL 102-321, 42 U.S.C. §§ 290ff *et seq.*

Cook, R. (1991). *A national evaluation of Title IV-E foster care independent living programs for youth, phase 2* (Final rep.). Rockville, MD: WESTAT.

Edgar, E., & Levine, P. (1987). *Special education students in transition: Washington state data, 1976–1986.* Seattle: University of Washington, Experimental Education Unit.

Education for All Handicapped Children Act of 1975, PL 94-142, 89 Stat. 773, 20 U.S.C. §§ 1400 *et seq.*

Education of the Handicapped Act Amendments of 1986, PL 99-457, 20 U.S.C. §§ 1400 *et seq.*

Foster Care Independence Act of 1999, PL 106-169, 42 U.S.C. §§ 677 *et seq.*

Halpern, A. (1985). Transition: A look at the foundations. *Exceptional Children, 51,* 479–486.

Independent Living Program (ILP), COBRA 1985, PL 99-272, 42 U.S.C. §§ 677 *et seq.;* reauthorized COBRA 1993, PL 103-66, 42 U.S.C. §§ 677 *et seq.*

Individuals with Disabilities Education Act (IDEA) Amendments of 1997, PL 105-17, 20 U.S.C. §§ 1400 *et seq.*

Individuals with Disabilities Education Act (IDEA) of 1990, PL 101-476, 20 U.S.C. §§ 1400 *et seq.*

Koroloff, N.M. (1990). Moving out: Transition policies for youth with serious emotional disabilities. *Journal of Mental Health Administration, 17*(1), 78–86.

Mallory, B.L. (1995). The role of social policy in life-cycle transitions. *Exceptional Children, 62(3)*, 213–223.

Mech, E.V. (1994). Foster youths in transition: Research perspectives on preparation for independent living. *Child Welfare, 78(5)*, 603–623.

Moroney, R.M. (1976). *The family and the state: Considerations for social policy.* London: Addison Wesley Longman.

National Information Center for Children and Youth with Disabilities (NICHCY). (1998). The IDEA Amendments of 1997. *News Digest, 26.*

Neel, R., Meadows, N., Levine, P., & Edgar, E. (1988). What happens after special education: A statewide follow-up study of secondary students who have behavioral disorders. *Behavioral Disorders, 13*, 209–216.

Rehabilitation Act Amendments of 1992, PL 102-569, 29 U.S.C. §§ 701 *et seq.*

Rehabilitation Act Amendments of 1998, PL 105-220, 29 U.S.C. §§ 403 *et seq.*

Rehabilitation Act of 1973, § 504, PL 93-112, 29 U.S.C. §§ 701 *et seq.*

School-to-Work Opportunities Act of 1994, PL 103-239, 20 U.S.C. §§ 6101 *et seq.*

Social Security Act of 1935, PL 74-271, 42 U.S.C. §§ 301 *et seq.*

Wagner-O'Day Act of 1938, PL 92-28, 41 U.S.C. §§ 46 *et seq.*

Wagner, M., & Shaver, D. (1989). *Educational programs and achievements of secondary special education students: Findings from the National Longitudinal Transition Study.* Menlo Park, CA: SRI International.

Weber, J. (1987). *Strengthening vocational education's role in decreasing the school dropout rate.* Columbus: Ohio State University, Center for Research in Vocational Education.

Will, M. (1984). *OSERS program for the transition of youth with disabilities: Bridges from school to working life.* Washington, DC: U.S. Department of Education, Office of Special Education and Rehabilitative Services.

Wiltse, K. (1978). Current issues and new directions in foster care. In A. Kadushin (Ed.), *Child welfare strategy in the coming years* (pp 51–89). Washington, DC: U.S. Department of Health, Education, and Welfare.

V

Conclusion

14

Transition

Current Issues and Recommendations for the Future

Maryann Davis and Hewitt B. Clark

In this book we have heard loud and clear, from young people themselves and from numerous studies, that the transition from adolescence to adulthood is an arduous one for young people with emotional or behavioral difficulties. There are many exciting opportunities for young people at this point in their lives, such as obtaining their first job, car, or apartment, finding loving romantic relationships, discovering music that speaks to them, and meeting friends with whom they can share the highs and lows of their lives. The path to these exciting possibilities is fraught with obstacles for youth and young adults with emotional or behavioral difficulties.

DIFFICULT TRANSITIONS

For many young people, emotional or behavioral difficulties have gotten in the way of forming solid friendships or finding romantic partners. Emotional or behavioral difficulties can interfere with the persistence needed to finish school, to get and maintain a job, or to establish one's own household. The families of these young people often face a variety of challenges, such as having marginal financial resources with no insurance, being headed by a single parent, residing in neighborhood war zones, or having insufficient social or professional support. These challenges can limit the support that these families can provide their children during the transition period.

267

There is ample evidence that we have a long way to go in helping these young people develop into adults who are content with their lives and doing well by society's standards. The studies presented in Chapter 1 highlight how treacherous the transition is for these young folks and the shortcomings of the current "helping" systems. The young adults' stories in Chapter 9 clearly describe the many ways in which even well-intentioned professionals can interfere with their developing the skills and relationships that are necessary for successful entry into adulthood. The authors and editors of this book have provided guidance for many of the changes that are needed to improve the well-being and future success of these vulnerable young people.

INCLUDE YOUNG PEOPLE'S VOICES

There is no doubt that we have much to learn about providing the assistance that young people need in moving toward adulthood. Fortunately, the authors whose work is presented here have already made tremendous progress on the learning curve. Foremost, in every chapter young people themselves have communicated the utter necessity of their central involvement in every aspect of policy, service, and treatment development at the system, agency, and individual levels. The system implicitly communicates a developmentally inappropriate message when young people are left out of the equation. We cannot expect young people to take responsibility for themselves when we communicate that they are not capable of making decisions about their own treatment or services. Most important, no one knows better than young people themselves what appeals to them. Policies, practices, and treatments that are implemented without their input are doomed.

GUIDING VALUES AND PRACTICES

In Chapter 2, Clark, Deschênes, and Jones provide a comprehensive framework for the development of programs and services that fully embraces the central involvement of youth and young adults. Each program and approach described in this book embraces the values, practices, and guidelines of the Transition to Independence Process (TIP) system put forth in this chapter. Consistent with what has been learned from young people, the TIP system emphasizes that their interests, strengths, and values must drive transition planning, services, supports, and treatment. Young people's goals and dreams provide the direction, and young people are empowered to pursue them. Perhaps the most explicit and innovative example of this principle is the systematic involvement of young people in responsible roles in the Transitional Community Treatment Team that West, Fetzer, Graham, and Keller describe in Chapter 10.

The other TIP system guidelines follow naturally from what is needed to centrally involve and effectively serve young people. Services, supports, and treatment must be individualized and comprehensive if they are to be responsive to youth. The system should emphasize young people's natural support systems because these are the individuals who know the young people, with whom they have established relationships, and with whom they will share their lives long after system involvement ends. The involvement of parents and others in young people's natural support systems and the related cultural considerations have been sensitively and thoughtfully described by Hatter, Williford, and Dickens in Chapter 11.

TIP system supports and services are coordinated and outcome oriented so that they are comprehensive, not redundant, and continue as long as the young person needs assistance to achieve her goals. The TIP system emphasizes the building of young people's competencies and describes practices that promote the development of community-relevant skills. It is important to note that the TIP system provides a framework, which can be locally tailored, for the development and operation of a transition system at the practice, program, and community level, with implications for aligning related systems and funding mechanisms at the state level. Thus, state or local agencies, such as public mental health, foster care, juvenile justice, and special education systems, can base the expansion of their systems to assist young people in transition on the framework provided by the TIP system.

Each of the chapters in Section II provides a wealth of practical knowledge about the operation of a major component of the TIP system. The chapters are primarily organized by the major domains of life that are the focus of young people in transition—school, employment, living situation, and community-life adjustment—and the coordination of these services. One of the recurrent themes in each chapter is that functioning in one transition domain is inevitably related to functioning in other domains. For example, a young woman whose depressive symptoms flare up loses her job because she has been unable to rouse herself from bed for a week. Her roommates ask her to leave because this is the fourth job she has lost and she is constantly unable to pay her rent. A young man gets into a shoving match with his girlfriend, who had appeared with a hickey on her neck from someone else. The police come. He reports feeling suicidal and is sent to a hospital. In all the drama, he fails to notify his boss that he will not be in, and he loses his job. As the chapters in Section II describe, programs that focus on one transition domain, such as employment, are more successful when they also address young people's lives comprehensively.

Out of necessity, many transition programs attempt to take a comprehensive approach. Even in 2000, when a single program obtains funding it is often the only service agency available to transition-age young people in that area. As a result, program personnel typically struggle to address needs that go beyond the particular funding mechanisms secured. This is considerably different from the child or adult systems, in which a service coordinator helps consumers choose from an array of services that are paid for by the system to address comprehensive needs. In these systems, individual programs tend to focus on a particular domain, such as vocational preparation, supported living, or mental health treatment. Ideally, as the system for young people in transition expands, individual programs will continue to address the diversity of transition needs and the system will provide a coordinated, comprehensive array of services and supports (see Chapters 2 and 8).

LOOKING TOWARD THE FUTURE

Several mechanisms could be used to promote rapid changes in transition support. Informed changes in policies, laws, and funding would have the most rapid impact on youth in transition. The following subsections summarize how future efforts can make a difference.

Current Status of Funding and Transition Policies

Although there have been tremendous gains in our understanding of how to assist youth and young adults with emotional or behavioral difficulties, several substantial hurdles remain along the path to full realization of TIP system goals. Perhaps the most difficult hurdle is funding.

As Davis, Fick, and Clark describe with great clarity in Chapter 12, current funding for transition programs and services is piecemeal. Programs wanting to offer transition services usually have difficulty securing consistent funding streams. Funding is often tied to strict eligibility definitions or provision of narrowly defined services. As a result, agencies either put together a funding mosaic to serve those in need and provide the array of needed services and supports or offer only limited services to a small part of the population. Both of these options are difficult for agencies. For families and young people, particularly those who have been involved with child welfare, juvenile justice, public mental health, or special education, the funding hurdles result in a tremendous reduction in available, appropriate formal supports at a time when specialized assistance is often needed.

Funding is strongly shaped by policy, which, in turn, shapes the manner in which money is spent. Koroloff, Lehman, and Lee describe with great lucidity the interrelatedness of funding and policy in

Chapter 13. Perhaps more than any other chapter, this chapter describes both the progress and the limitations affecting this field. As reported there, the Individuals with Disabilities Education Act (IDEA) of 1990 (PL 101-476) comes close to being an ideal policy regarding the design of services and supports for youth in transition. The authors describe the many strengths of other federal policies that affect this population in transition, and they have developed a policy framework to guide advocacy in the formulation of future transition policies.

The authors also describe how good policy can fall considerably short of ensuring good practice. One of the major reasons that IDEA transition activities are insufficiently implemented is the lack of funds with which to do so. IDEA provides no appropriations for educational or human services agencies to implement the services described in student transition plans. In the absence of federal funding, adult agencies generally do not implement the transition plans of the many students who do not meet their adult system eligibility criteria. Furthermore, few "adult" services are tailored for young adult needs, and they are often inappropriate for them (Unger, Anthony, Sciarappa, & Rogers, 1991). Thus, mandating existing services to support the transition to adulthood does not ensure delivery of appropriate services.

Recommendations for Future Funding and Transition Policies

As long as funding remains difficult and policies have no real power to enforce transition services, progress in transition supports and services will be slow and many young people will continue to fall through system cracks into blighted adulthood. Chapter 12 outlines specific actions that agencies, advocates, administrators, and policy makers can take to enhance fund availability for transition support services. Three of these actions can make a difference at the local or state level:

1. Build and strengthen collaborative partnerships between systems that have some funds available for transition services
2. Build transitional connections between child and adult mental health systems (e.g., extending child mental health services through age 22 years for youth who have been served previously)
3. Advocate for the retargeting of existing funds and the establishment of relevant funding streams

Clearly, changes at the federal level could have far-reaching implications for these young people, but determined practitioners, advocates, and administrators at the community, regional, and state levels can make significant progress as well.

Filling the holes in federal policy and providing budgetary support would go a long way toward meeting the needs of young people in transition. As Koroloff and colleagues (Chapter 13) clearly describe, extending the rights and processes in IDEA to students with emotional or behavioral difficulties who are not served in special education or who have left school prematurely would help cover more young people who would benefit from transition planning through age 21. A coordinating mechanism that has the power and funding to ensure the cooperation of all involved agencies targeted in transition plans is also needed to enact and monitor transition plans and services.

In 1983, the Child and Adolescent Service System Program (CASSP) was initiated by the National Institute of Mental Health. CASSP was designed to improve the system serving children and adolescents with serious emotional disturbance. CASSP, and subsequently the Child, Adolescent, and Family Branch of the Center for Mental Health Services, has provided grants to states to

1. Require interagency collaboration among child-serving agencies
2. Increase the capacity to provide child mental health services at the community level, emphasizing less restrictive, more coordinated care
3. Strengthen the role of families in the care of their children and in the development of service systems
4. Make the system more responsive to the needs of children and families with varied cultural traditions and roots

CASSP developed and promoted the framework of an ideal system of care (Stroul & Friedman, 1986). CASSP and its subsequent embodiment as the Child, Adolescent, and Family Branch have provided technical assistance, research demonstration grants, policy guidelines, and grants to build system capacity for children and adolescents. This type of federal leadership is needed for the population in transition.

The Need for Research
The best policies and the mere presence of funds do not guarantee that treatment and services for young people with emotional or behavioral difficulties will be efficacious. Research on this population and the services they receive still has many questions to answer if practices and policies are to be well informed.

Longitudinal research findings have made it clear that adolescents with emotional or behavioral difficulties have great trouble in young adulthood and provide some indication of who, within this population, is at greatest risk (Davis & Vander Stoep, 1997; see also Chapter 1). However, we do not know the patterns of unemployment, living arrangements, criminal activity, or service use over time or the process by which changes occur in these domains. We have some understanding of risk factors for some outcomes within the population of young people with emotional or behavioral difficulties, but more information is needed to help identify those at risk. More to the point, we have few objective evaluative data on the service practices described in this book and elsewhere. Several groups have gathered evaluation data on their programs but have not been able to compare these outcomes with those of other services, no services, or a well-matched comparison group without emotional or behavioral difficulties (e.g., Bullis et al., 1994; Cook & Rosenberg, 1994; Cook, Solomon, Farrell, Koziel, & Jonikas, 1997; Hagner, Cheney, & Malloy, 1999; Malloy, Cheney, & Cormier, 1998; see also Chapter 8). Although the reported outcomes are encouraging, we do not know whether similar results would have been achieved simply with time or maturation or how one approach might compare with another. Knowing how well a matched comparison group of individuals without disabilities does would help determine what outcomes can be reasonably expected.

One of the reasons that studies are limited is that research has some of the same funding gaps that services do. Federal granting programs also tend to be organized by developmental stage: adults or children/adolescents. Grant programs focused on adults with mental illness are less interested in research on the population in transition, and those focused on children and adolescents give priority to research on child and adolescent populations or programs and not to young adults. In addition, random assignment of participants to treatment conditions is strongly emphasized in federal research grants, but it is anathema to local service providers. In particular, providers who embrace the values of the TIP system (e.g., providing services that uniquely address each person's strengths and needs) may find random assignment to any other type of service difficult to embrace. Federal grant initiatives that target or emphasize the population in transition, such as those from the U.S. Department of Education, Office of Special Education and Rehabilitative Services, would encourage much needed research in this area.

There are several areas of systematic data collection that would add greatly to our knowledge base and improve the effectiveness of practice and system initiatives for transition-age individuals with emotional or behavioral difficulties. These include the following:

1. Documentation of the typical progression of experiences and service use across transition domains for young people with and without emotional or behavioral difficulties
2. Development and implementation of a community TIP system
3. Characteristics of the individuals being served
4. Progress on the goals of these young people
5. Types and amounts of services and supports used across the different transition domains

6. Funding mechanisms used to provide these services
7. Follow-up of individuals to assess their progress in the domains of employment, educational opportunities, living situation, and community-life adjustment after transition services end

Creative researchers can work together with service personnel and advocates to design ways in which these data can be collected and analyzed. As Clark and colleagues describe in Chapter 2, these data are relatively easy for a community system to collect, particularly if reasonable funding is designated for evaluation. These data are invaluable to stakeholders for assessing the strengths and weaknesses of their evolving system and for targeting ways to continue to improve the service system. The findings from these descriptive and efficacy-type studies, in combination with other appropriate federal research funding initiatives, would enable researchers, advocates, and administrators to design and conduct larger-scale, multicommunity, longitudinal-type studies to evaluate the feasibility and, ultimately, through random assignment, the effectiveness of the TIP system in improving outcomes for individuals in early adulthood (Burns, Hoagwood, & Maultsby, 1998; Friedman, 1997; Hernandez, Hodges, & Cascardi, 1998; Rosenblatt, 1996).

Facilitating System Change
Changes in funding, policy, research, and practice will be accelerated through increased awareness and advocacy. Systems need education about this group of young people. Extensive system change has occurred in the child system of care since the mid-1980s (Stroul, 1996), and much can be learned from and built on these efforts.

Davis and Vander Stoep (1996) recommended steps to be taken to build a collaborative effort to address needed system reform based on Bruner's (1991) recommendations for change in the children's system. Bruner described it as a top-down strategy for bottom-up collaboration. The following are highlights of this approach.

Build on the state-level interagency planning councils or boards, as required by the State Comprehensive Mental Health Care Act of 1986 (PL 99-660), that already exist in each state. Interagency councils should include not only those agencies that provide needed services for transitional youth but also those agencies that receive this population as a default when they slip through the cracks (e.g., corrections, substance abuse). These councils need to bring their resources to bear on specific planning for transitional youth. Community system needs assessments should be done to establish which services are available for transitional youth, where there are redundancies, and what professionals, consumers, and their families want in terms of preparation for adulthood. Many state and local agencies have interagency case review processes for development of individualized treatment plans for children and adolescents. These procedures should be expanded for the particular needs of transitional youth. Specifically, representatives from "adult" agencies need to be involved symbolically, physically, and financially. Much of what has been learned from the interagency case review process with child and adolescent services can be directly translated to this kind of process for transitional youth. In states where there are minimal or no interagency case review processes, formal and informal linkages between relevant agencies should be established to promote communication, exchange of expertise, and agreements to provide services for this population. For example, in-service training by vocational specialists can help mental health treatment programs gear their services to the pressing vocational needs of this population. Also, some mental health systems have hired transition facilitators half-time in the children's arena and half-time in the adult arena so that they have authority within both systems.

As Clark and colleagues illustrate in Chapter 2, many aspects of the community TIP system can be accomplished without significant additional funds. Adolescent programs and services can reevaluate and change their efforts to prepare adolescents for entry into adulthood. Programs that serve young people who do or will eventually fall into the gaps in IDEA can implement their own transition planning processes. Parent advocacy organizations can offer support groups for parents of young people in transition. Programs can also identify available funding to build or enhance transition supports (e.g., independent living and extended care funding for foster care youth). However, there are clear limitations to what can be accomplished without significant system change.

It is the hope of the editors of this book that reading it serves as a springboard for advocacy efforts at the individual, local, state, and federal levels and for the development and expansion of community TIP systems. These efforts will allow people and systems to better assist young people with emotional or behavioral difficulties to become interdependent, self-sufficient adults who earn reasonable incomes, live in places of their choosing, believe that they are members of a community, have rich resources of friends and family, and can pursue their dreams.

REFERENCES

Bruner, C. (1991). *Thinking collaboratively: Ten questions and answers to help policy makers improve children's services.* Washington, DC: Education and Human Services Consortium.

Bullis, M., Fredericks, H.D.B., Lehman, C., Paris, K., Corbitt, J., & Johnson, B. (1994). Description and evaluation of the Job Designs program for adolescents and young adults with emotional or behavioral disorders. *Behavioral Disorders, 19*(4), 254–268.

Burns, B.J., Hoagwood, K., & Maultsby, L.T. (1998). Improving outcomes for children and adolescents with serious emotional and behavioral disorders: Current and future directions. In M.H. Epstein, K. Kutash, & A. Duchnowski (Eds.), *Outcomes for children and youth with emotional and behavioral disorders and their families: Programs and evaluation best practices* (pp. 685–707). Austin, TX: PRO-ED.

Cook, J.A., & Rosenberg, H. (1994). Predicting community employment among persons with psychiatric disability: A logistic regression analysis. *Journal of Rehabilitation Administration, 18*(1), 6–22.

Cook, J.A., Solomon, M.L., Farrell, D., Koziel, M., & Jonikas, J. (1997). Vocational initiatives for transition-age youths with severe mental illness. In S.W. Henggeler & A.B. Santos (Eds.), *Innovative approaches for difficult-to-treat populations* (pp. 139–163). Washington, DC: American Psychiatric Press.

Davis, M., & Vander Stoep, A. (1996). *The transition to adulthood among adolescents who have serious emotional disturbances: At risk for homelessness.* Delmar, NY: National Resource Center on Homelessness and Mental Illness.

Friedman, R.M. (1997). Services and service delivery systems for children with serious emotional disorders: Issues in assessing effectiveness. C.T. Nixon & D.A. Northup (Eds.), *Evaluation mental health services: How do programs for children "work" in the real world? Children's mental health services* (Vol. 3, pp. 16–44). Thousand Oaks, CA: Sage Publications.

Hagner, D., Cheney, D., & Malloy, J. (1999). Career-related outcomes of a model transition demonstration for young adults with emotional disturbance. *Rehabilitation Counseling Bulletin, 42*(3), 228–242.

Hernandez, M., Hodges, S., & Cascardi, M. (1998). The ecology of outcomes: System accountability in children's mental health. *Journal of Behavioral Health Services and Research, 25*(2), 136–150.

Individuals with Disabilities Education Act (IDEA) of 1990, PL 101-476, 20 U.S.C. §§ 1400 *et seq.*

Malloy, J., Cheney, D., & Cormier, G.M. (1998). Interagency collaboration and the transition to adulthood for students with emotional or behavioral disabilities. *Education and Treatment of Children, 21*(3), 303–320.

Rosenblatt, A. (1996). Bows and ribbons, tape and wine: Wrapping the wraparound process for children with multi-system needs. *Journal of Child and Family Studies, 5*(1), 101–116.

State Comprehensive Mental Health Plan Act of 1986, PL 99-660, 42 U.S.C. §§ 300x-3 *et seq.*

Stroul, B.A. (Ed.). (1996). *Children's mental health: Creating systems of care in a changing society.* Baltimore: Paul H. Brookes Publishing Co.

Stroul, B.A., & Friedman, R.M. (1986). *A system of care for severely emotionally disturbed children and youth.* Washington, DC: Georgetown University, Child Development Center, Child and Adolescent Service System Program (CASSP), Technical Assistance Center.

Unger, K.V., Anthony, W.A., Sciarappa, K., & Rogers, S. (1991). A supported education program for young adults with mental illness. *Hospital and Community Psychiatry, 42*(8), 838–842.

Index

Page numbers followed by "f" or "t" indicate figures or tables, respectively.